KU-634-647

Greenhill Books

The Story of
Aviation

A CONCISE HISTORY OF FLIGHT

The Story of
Aviation

A CONCISE HISTORY OF FLIGHT

Edited by Ray Bonds

GREENHILL BOOKS, LONDON

Greenhill Books

The Story of Aviation
first published 1997 by Greenhill Books,
Lionel Leventhal Limited, Park House, 1 Russell Gardens,
London NW11 9NN

© Elephant Editions Limited, 1997

The moral rights of the authors have been asserted.

All rights reserved. No part of this publication may be
reproduced stored in a retrieval system or transmitted in any
form or by any means, electronic, mechanical or otherwise
without the prior permission of Elephant Editions Limited.

British Library Cataloguing in Publication Data
Bonds, Ray
The story of aviation : a concise history of flight
1. Aeronautics - History
I. Title
629.1'3'09

ISBN 1-85367-296-3

Credits

Editor: Ray Bonds
Design: Bob Mathias / Helen Mathias, Publishing Workshop
Photo research: Tony Moore
Typesetting and colour reproduction: SX Composing DTP
Printed and bound in Spain by Book Print, S.L.

611630
MORAY COUNCIL
Department Technical
& Leisure Services
629.1309

The Authors

Bill Gunston, O.B.E., is a former RAF pilot and flying instructor, and has acted as an advisor to several aviation companies. With scores of books to his credit, he has become one of the most internationally respected authors and broadcasters on aviation and scientific subjects. An assistant compiler of *Jane's All the World's Aircraft*, he was formerly technical editor of *Flight International* and technology editor of *Science Journal*.

Sue Bushell has been a freelance aviation journalist since 1985, having spent several years on the editorial staff of two leading aviation magazines. She has edited *Air World International*, *Scale Aviation Modeller* and *Aviation News* magazines, and is currently a member of the *Jane's All the World's Aircraft* compiling team. Recent work includes articles in the *USAF Yearbook* and *RAF Yearbook*.

Mike Spick is a leading commentator on military aviation, with almost 40 books to his credit, many of which have been translated into several languages. For many years a consultant to the Swiss-based helicopter program Project Atlas, he is currently a consultant to *AirForces Monthly*, and occasional contributor to *Air International*, *Air Enthusiast*, and the Malaysian-based *Asia Pacific Defense Review*.

Frank Mason served with the Royal Air Force and Hawker Aircraft Ltd., and has been a prolific author of books on aviation and aircraft, with 88 published to date. He has broadcast on television and radio on the subject, was formerly Editor of *Flying Review International*, Editorial Manager of Guinness Superlatives, and Managing Director of Profile Publications Ltd.

Robin Kerrod has chronicled the assault on the space frontier since Apollo days in a string of best-selling titles, including *Illustrated History of NASA*, *Apollo*, *The Journeys of Voyager*, *Space Shuttle* and *Man In Space*. He has recently authored a multimedia *Space Encyclopedia* on CD-Rom.

Editor's acknowledgements

A great many people have provided valuable assistance in the preparation of this book, most notably by providing photographs, and the Editor extends his gratitude to all of them. A list of photo credits is given on page 144. Particular thanks are due to Bruce Robertson, who scoured his archive and loaned very many rare and interesting photographs, and to Jeremy Flack and Phillip Jarrett who similarly gave up precious time in this way.

Jacket and front matter photos:

Jacket front: Fondly remembered, a Trans World Airlines Lockheed Constellation heads out from New York Harbor.

Jacket back:
Main pic: Concorde, arguably the most graceful airliner ever.

Bottom left: A Douglas SBD-3 Dauntless divebomber lands on USS *Ranger* in October 1942.

Bottom right: Charles A. Lindbergh in his Ryan NYP (New York-Paris) Spirit of St. Louis.

Front matter pics:
Page 1: A strange sight in the sky: the USAF F-117A 'stealth' fighter/attack/recce airplane.

Page 3: A Gates Learjet 31 scuds across the clouds.

Pages 4-5: The most famous aviation photo: Wilbur Wright runs alongside his brother Orville during the first powered, controlled flight of a heavier-than-air aircraft, December 17 1903.

Pages 6-7: F-16s of USAF 31st Fighter Wing, Aviano, Italy, in support of ground forces in Bosnia.

CONTENTS

INTRODUCTION **Page 8**

CHAPTER ONE: INTO THE SKY by Bill Gunston **Page 10**

CHAPTER TWO: CIVIL AVIATION   by Sue Bushell **Page 30**

CHAPTER THREE: AERIAL WARFARE   by Mike Spick **Page 68**

CHAPTER FOUR: THE AVIATORS   by Frank Mason **Page 106**

CHAPTER FIVE: SPACEFLIGHT   by Robin Kerrod **Page 122**

INDEX **Page 142**

PICTURE CREDITS **Page 144**

Introduction

'…they cannot say indeed they have yet made an Eagle's flight, or that it doth not cost now and then a Leg or an Arm to one of these new birds; but they may serve to represent the first Plank that were launched on the Water … The Art of Flying is but newly invented, it will improve by degrees, and in time grow perfect; then we may fly as far as the Moon.'

John Glanville: A Plurality of Worlds, 1688

The two photographs shown here, together with those on the previous pages, perhaps symbolize better than any other way the fantastic development of what was a completely new form of transportation less than a hundred years ago. When Claude Grahame-White flew down East Executive Drive between the White House and the Executive Offices, Washington D.C., on October 14 1910, what a spectacle it must have been to those people standing well back on each side of the Drive, some of them even on the rooftops! How many of them could have fore-

seen that each year millions of people in later generations would travel the world in fabulous intercontinental jet airliners such as the Boeing 777 seen here on one of the hundreds of thousands of miles of purpose-built runways all around the globe? Or that millions more people would be employed in an incredible new industry established to build, fly, load and unload, service and clean these fabulous flying machines? Or that other substantial industries would grow just to make component parts, from washers to wiring, just to ensure these aircraft get off the ground in one place, fly safely to another, where they disgorge their human and inanimate cargoes, load up and fly back?

Or, more sinister, that millions more people would be involved in arming and flying what would prove to be the most lethal weapon platforms the world has ever known?

Even more fantastic, how many of those people holding their breath in Washington almost a century ago would have believed that descendants of their contemporaries would be carried aloft in rocket-powered flying contraptions, be thrust out of the Earth's gravitational pull and land on the Moon?

Very few of the Washington observers would have dreamed any of this would be possible. After all, as Frank Mason points out in his chapter on The Aviators later in this book, it was not much more than a decade before this flight that fewer than a dozen people had been airborne in a heavier-than-air craft, and it was still less than seven years since Orville Wright had remained airborne for just 12 seconds when he made the world's first sustained, powered and manned flight by a heavier-than-air machine, The Flyer, on December 17 1903.

It is as well that there were such dreamers and visionaries such as Glanville, the Wright brothers and Grahame-White (and thousands more), since the history of aviation is littered with feet-on-the-ground disbelievers, who have said 'It will never work.' Well, it has worked, and aviation now touches all our lives. Whether we are traveling short or long journeys for business or pleasure, sending produce or products from one place to another, transporting or receiving life-saving supplies and medicines, rescuing or being rescued, being spied upon by miles-high strategic camera carriers or having our traffic transgressions reported by airborne law officers, flying to make war or keep the peace, or just plain watching fantastic aerial performances at air shows throughout the world, we are all affected in some way by aviation. Its history is short by the standards of other forms of transport, but it is the most fascinating and thrilling of all.

Ray Bonds

CHAPTER ONE
Into the Sky

BELOW: The first aerial passengers were a sheep, a cock and a duck, taken aloft on September 19 1783. They were inside a basket slung under this Montgolfier hot-air balloon, seen lifting off from Versailles, near Paris. The 37,500cu ft [1,062m^3] balloon was 57ft [17.4m] high.

People must have dreamed of flying through the sky for thousands of years. For most of that time the only way they could imagine of doing this was to flap wings like a bird. History records many would-be aviators who tried to do this. Even today nobody has succeeded.

Utterly unexpectedly, the first way people rose off the Earth was with a completely different kind of vehicle, a balloon. The brothers Joseph and Etienne Montgolfier, papermakers at Annonay, near Lyons in France, wondered why pieces of charred paper rose into the sky above a bonfire. The reason, of course, is that hot air is less dense than cold air, so it is displaced upwards, but they thought some special gas was produced.

They made little balloons to try to catch some of this gas. In the autumn of 1783 they made a huge balloon out of linen lined with paper. On October 15 a wire-mesh fire basket was put underneath. After a while it rose off the ground carrying an adventurer, Pilâtre de Rozier, though it was tethered, so it could not rise far. On November 21 1783, in front of a vast crowd, an even bigger Montgolfier balloon made a free flight across Paris carrying de Rozier and the Marquis d'Arlandes.

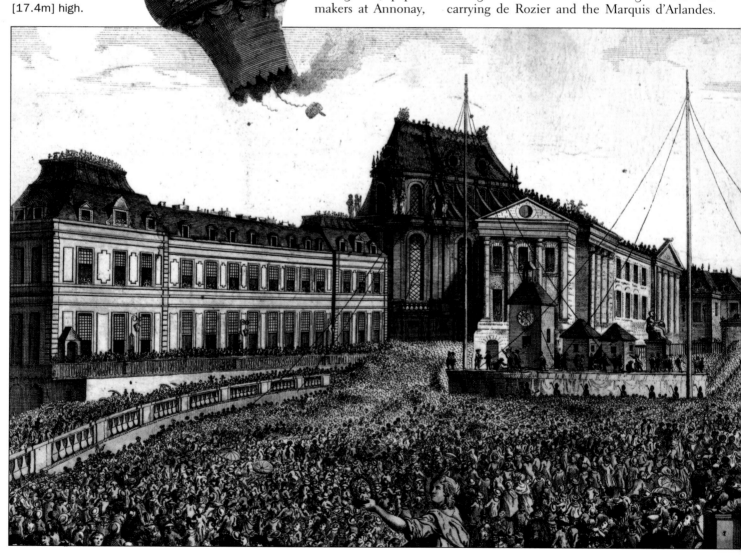

They were the first humans to fly.

Less than two weeks later a balloon filled with hydrogen gas carried two other "aeronauts" across Paris. Over the next 200-odd years thousands of gas-filled balloons have carried passengers, soldiers, letters and other loads. More recently the hot-air balloon has come back into popularity, but mainly for fun. Because they are at the mercy of the winds, balloons are not very useful as a means of transport.

Meanwhile, inventors kept trying to build "aerodynes", heavier-than-air flying machines that fly with the aid of wings. While the Montgolfiers were building their first balloons an Englishman, Sir George Cayley, had the first of a succession of brilliant ideas. Instead of trying to build an ornithopter (flapping-wing machine), he decided to separate the lift and propulsion. In 1799 he engraved a silver disk with a picture of the first aeroplane, with a propeller on the nose for propulsion, a fixed wing in the middle for lift and a tail at the back for control. This was perhaps the greatest single breakthrough in the history of aviation.

In 1804 Cayley flew a model glider, and as an old man in 1853 he built a big glider which his coachman flew across a valley (and promptly gave notice, saying "I was hired to drive, not fly!"). Amazingly, hardly anyone took much notice of

LEFT: A strange representation of the first flight of the Marquis d'Arlandes and Pilâtre de Rozier. It is strange because the balloon used on this occasion, on November 15 1783, actually looked totally different. At least the artist has shown the two men balancing each other on opposite sides of the bonfire.

Cayley's work until a century later, and in any case he could not make a powered aeroplane because no engine was light enough.

On the other hand, in 1852 Henri Giffard flew the first airship in Paris. This was a long balloon with pointed ends under which was hung a small steam engine which could drive the airship at 5mph (8km/h). Successive airships grew larger, and in 1884 two captains in the French army made the first controlled circular flight at about 14mph (22km/h), arriving back at their starting point. Their airship, called *La France*, was one of the few flying machines to have been powered by an electric motor.

In July 1900 a German, Count von Zeppelin, flew the first airship of a new type. It differed not only in being very large – 420ft (128m) long – but in having a rigid framework of aluminium. Inside this were 17 gasbags full of hydrogen. Underneath were two cars each with a large propeller driven by

ABOVE: A technically accurate drawing of the airship of Henri Giffard, first tested in 1852. This was the first man-made vehicle able to navigate in the air, with propulsion from a steam-driven propeller, and steering from a cloth-covered rudder at the back.

ABOVE: The first of over 130 Zeppelin rigid airships. LZ 1 is seen here moving slowly above the Bodensee (Lake Constance) on July 2 1900. With a length of 420ft [128m], it really needed much more power than the two 15-hp Daimler engines, one in each passenger car.

a 15hp Daimler gasoline (petrol) engine. Zeppelin's airships grew bigger and bigger, and in 1909 the world's first airline, DELAG, was formed. It carried passengers high over Germany, and soon to Denmark and Sweden, some of them enjoying a gourmet dinner with china plates and silver cutlery. But, following accidents to giant airships in the 1930s, they faded from the scene.

By the end of the 19th Century the development of the internal-combustion engine at last made it possible to consider building a practical aeroplane. Some designers just put such an engine into a flying machine and imagined that they could climb in like a chauffeur and rise into the sky. One of the most famous was yet another Parisien, Clément Ader. On October 9 1890 his bat-like machine rose just off the ground and then sank back. It is fortunate that it rose no higher, because he had no means of controlling it.

One of the few pioneer aviators who recognized the vital importance of providing some means of flight control was a German, Otto Lilienthal. Having no engine, he made a succession of gliders, some biplanes with a pair of superimposed wings but mostly monoplanes. They were made of peeled willow stems over which was stretched waxed cloth, very like a bat in appearance. Lilienthal then lifted the glider over his head and took off down a hill, controlling the glide by shifting his body weight. He made over 2,000 glides before being tragically killed by losing control in a sudden gust of wind in August 1896.

He can fairly be called the first pilot. He was followed by an Englishman, Percy Pilcher. When he too was killed on October 2 1899 he had almost completed a powered aeroplane. This was the first to be constructed on a basis of knowledge, by a man who already knew how to control a flying machine. With Pilcher's death it was left to two bicycle makers in Ohio to succeed where so many had failed.

In 1903 the wealthy Samuel P. Langley completed a flying machine fitted with two sets of monoplane wings in tandem. Though it was powered by a superb 52hp engine, it crashed on each of its two attempted takeoffs. In contrast the humble Ohio brothers, Orville and Wilbur Wright, attacked the problem in a methodical manner. They read all they could. They made a wind tunnel and tested models. They got their mechanic, Charlie Taylor, to build a simple four-cylinder engine. They spent three years learning how to fly gliders, at the same time developing a control system. Finally, on December 17 1903, Orville made the first flight of a fully controllable aeroplane.

It was a simple biplane. The pilot lay face-down on the lower wing. His weight balanced the engine on the other side of the centerline, and the motive power was geared down by bicycle chains to two slow-turning pusher propellers. His controls comprised biplane foreplanes in front for control in pitch, twin rudders at the back and (something overlooked by almost all previous would-be aviators) a means of lateral control. Previous aeroplanes had no lateral control, so if they had succeeded in flying they might well have rolled upside-down. The Wrights made their wings deliberately flexible in torsion so that they could be "warped", twisting them to lift more on one side and less on the other. Later this idea was replaced by fitting ailerons, separate hinged surfaces near the wingtips.

In 1906 a tiny Brazilian, Alberto Santos-Dumont, made the first aeroplane flight in Europe. Already the toast of Paris for flying an airship round the Eiffel Tower, he designed what at first glance looked like a modern monoplane. On closer inspection it could be seen that the tail was at the front and the engine and propeller at the back. By 1907 Paris was full of aircraft designers. Most built biplanes, but Louis Blériot built monoplanes, and in 1909 he was one of the first to fit the new Gnome engine.

Beautifully made out of steel, it had its cylinders arranged radially like spokes of a wheel. More

LEFT: Tiny Brazilian Alberto Santos-Dumont was the toast of Paris. Not least of his many escapades was to fly this small airship (his No 6) round the Eiffel Tower on October 19 1906. This won him 100,000 gold francs; he gave 25,000 to the men who built his airship and the other 75,000 to the poor people of Paris.

BELOW: Perhaps the most famous photograph in the history of aviation, this shows Orville Wright just after takeoff on December 17 1903, with brother Wilbur running alongside. Into the teeth of a cold wind, the Flyer could not cover the ground much faster than Wilbur could run.

RIGHT: Louis Blériot, whose real business was car headlamps, sitting in the cockpit of the first of his Type XI monoplanes. A slightly improved version was the first aeroplane to make an international or overwater flight when, on July 25 1909, Blériot flew from France to England.

BELOW: S.E.5a fighters in production by Wolseley Motors at Adderley Park, Birmingham, in late 1917. This batch are fitted with the same company's Viper engine, a direct-drive (ie, not geared) version of the 200-hp Hispano-Suiza V-8. These were among the best fighters of the war.

strangely, the crankshaft was fixed to the aircraft and the engine rotated with the propeller, to help cool the cylinders. Though expensive, it was lighter than any rival engine. Until the end of World War I in 1918 this and related rotary engines powered many thousands of aircraft. The factories of both Gnome and Blériot were deluged with work after the Blériot XI monoplane flew from France to England on July 25 1909. From this time onwards the public's perception of aviation gradually changed from being a pastime of idiots to being something that might be important, in peace and in war.

Aeroplanes began to carry tiny bombs, and even machine guns, from 1910. At that time the fastest aeroplanes were monoplanes made of beautiful thin veneers of tulip wood to give a streamlined shape. Most aircraft were biplanes, made

either of wood, such as spruce, or of welded steel tubing, and covered with fabric stretched in place, sewn and then made taut with dope (cellulose paint). Virtually all aircraft needed struts and carefully tightened bracing wires to give them structural strength.

In World War I aeroplanes and airships developed rapidly. In 1914 the most powerful engines gave about 100hp, and were unreliable. By 1918 engines were giving 400hp, with far better reliability. The gem-like rotaries could not be developed beyond 230hp, and the most powerful engines were massive inline types with (typically) two rows each of six water-cooled cylinders arranged in a V seen from the front, both banks of cylinders driving the same crankshaft.

The vast majority of 1914-18 aircraft were biplanes, though a few small fighters were tri-

LEFT: Launching Royal Naval Air Service No 8677, a Curtiss H-12 flying boat rebuilt with a Porte hull. Operating with War Flight from Felixstowe, No 8677 shot down Zeppelin L 43 on June 14 1917, off Vlieland. On April 25 1918 No 8677 was itself shot down, by Oberlt. Christiansen.

planes because some designers thought this made for the best agility. A significant proportion of the warplanes operated from water, either with two or three carefully shaped floats or with a planing bottom to the fuselage (the body), which in such machines was called the hull. In the USA all were called seaplanes, while in Britain the aircraft with floating hulls were called flying boats.

In the 20 years between the World Wars flying boats were very important, both as civil airliners and as long-range oceanic patrol and bombing aircraft. After World War II Britain and France persisted with giant civil flying boats, but they could not compete with the faster and more economic landplanes which were made possible by the long paved runways which had been constructed all over the world.

These runways made it possible to be much bolder in aircraft design. The biplane bombers or airliners of the late 1920s had a wing loading (weight supported by unit area of wing) of about 8lb/sq ft ($39kg/m^2$). By 1940 a typical figure was 40lb/sq ft ($195kg/m^2$), and by the end of World War II this had doubled again to 86lb/sq ft ($420kg/m^2$). This utterly transformed aircraft speed, range and carrying capacity. It was made possible only by a series of other parallel developments.

One of the most important was how the airframe (the structure of the aeroplane) was made. Even today a high proportion of light aircraft are still made in very much the same way as in World War II, but by the end of that conflict designers were cautiously trying new methods. These methods were based on the use of light alloys (aluminium mixed with copper and traces of other metals) in which the metal made not only the underlying structure but also the skin that covered the aircraft.

This became known as stressed-skin construction, because the thin covering of the airframe now contributed a significant part of its strength. This opened the way to a revolution in the way aircraft were designed. Until the 1920s it was very

LEFT: The crowded deck of US Navy carrier CV-3, USS *Saratoga*, in 1929. The fighters in the foreground are Boeing F3B-1s, while in the rear are larger Martin T4M-1 torpedo bombers. Every aircraft in the photograph has its Pratt & Whitney aircooled radial engine running.

difficult to design a monoplane, but it was easy to build biplanes, because their superimposed wings could be braced by struts and wires to form a structure that was both strong and torsionally stiff to resist twisting, and also light. The drawback was that such aircraft had high drag, and hardly ever exceeded 155mph (250km/h).

With stressed-skin construction it was possible to make a monoplane wing that was quite thin and completely without any struts or wires, and yet

RIGHT: Modern all-metal stressed-skin construction was the key to eliminating external struts and wires, and making aircraft streamlined. One of the first of this new species was the Martin Bomber of 1932, which led three years later to this B-10B of the US Army Air Corps.

strong and stiff enough to resist the severe bending and twisting loads of pulling out from dives or making combat maneuvers. Thus, a new species of all-metal aircraft became possible which could be made streamlined. Of course, designers had achieved some success in making streamlined wooden aircraft, such as the Lockheed Vega of 1927. The all-metal stressed-skin aircraft could have a thinner wing, and go even faster.

To show the dramatic change in design this

be streamlined, and fly faster, it was better to design the landing gears to retract, folding away into the fuselage, wings or engine nacelles. It was worth paying more attention to the engine installation. Aircooled radial engines were encased in specially designed cowlings shaped like circular wings which could almost help to pull the aircraft along. Adjustable shutters were added round the back of the cowl to control the cooling airflow. Liquid-cooled engines were enclosed in stream-

structural revolution made possible, compare the bombers of the US Army Air Corps in the early 1930s. The chief type was the Keystone B-6A, weighing 13,374lb (6,066kg) loaded, with a maximum speed of 121mph (195km/h) and range of 363 miles (584km). In March 1932 the Army received the first Martin 123, later called the B-10. This stressed-skin monoplane weighed 12,560lb (5,697kg) when carrying the same bombload as the B-6A, but it could fly at 207mph (333km/h) and had a range of 640 miles (1,030km).

This revolution in aircraft design brought new developments in its train. Because aircraft could

lined cowlings, with the necessary cooling radiator inside an adjustable duct which, by 1940, could even be designed to give negative drag, in other words to help propel the aircraft.

Compared with the fabric-covered biplanes, the metal monoplanes had wings of much smaller total area. As we have seen, wing-loading rose alarmingly. Thus, they took off and landed much faster. Accordingly, designers began fitting wings with flaps. These were hinged surfaces added under the trailing edge, at the back of the wing. Some flaps were flat plates hinged down under a fixed trailing edge, known as split flaps. Some,

RIGHT: One of the most significant aircraft of all time was the Douglas DC-1, first flown on July 1 1933. Though it cost $306,778 to develop, it was sold to the airline TWA for $125,000, because Douglas knew more would follow. In fact there were no more DC-1s, but hundreds of DC-2s and nearly 11,000 DC-3s.

LEFT: The 840-hp Bristol Mercury engines of the Blenheim bomber drove Hamilton variable-pitch propellers made in England under licence be de Havilland. The ring round the front of the cowling collected the exhaust from the nine radial cylinders. Round the back of the cowling were controllable gills to adjust the cooling airflow.

called plain flaps, just hinged the whole trailing edge.

Slotted flaps hinged the trailing edge but with a carefully designed gap through which air could flow. The most effective was the Fowler, in which a surface like a miniature wing could be run out on tracks behind the wing. Extended a little way, for takeoff, the Fowler increased the wing's area and lift. Fully extended, the flap also rotated downwards to increase drag as well, for landing.

Thus, whereas the old biplanes, might have taken off at 56mph (90km/h) and cruised at 100mph (160km/h), the new monoplanes might take off at 65mph (105km/h) and cruise at 200mph (322km/h). With such a large difference between takeoff and cruising speed, it paid designers to use variable-pitch propellers. The propeller blades would be set to fine pitch for takeoff, to allow the engine(s) to develop maximum power at low airspeed, like first gear in a car. In cruising flight the blades could be set to coarse pitch, for economical slow engine speed despite the high speed of the aircraft, like a car in overdrive. Soon propellers had constant-speed units, making pitch changes automatic.

In the search for higher flight performance, engine designers sought ways to make engines give more power at high altitude, where the air is thin. Engine power is proportional to air density, so at a height of 22,000ft (6,700m), where the air density is half that at sea level, a 1,000hp engine will give only 500hp. The answer was to make the engine drive an air compressor called a supercharger. In most engines this was a high-speed blower driven by gearwheels, but some engines were fitted with a turbosupercharger driven by a turbine spun by the white-hot exhaust gas.

ABOVE: The famous Supermarine Spitfire was one of the first fighters with a modern stressed-skin structure. This example, X4942, was a rare high-altitude MkVI, with a pressurized cockpit and extended and pointed wingtips. It was photographed on test from Boscombe Down on September 12 1941.

RIGHT: Most of the 11,461 Wellington bombers had radial engines, but the MkII was powered by Rolls-Royce Merlin engines. It set a fashion among RAF bombers by having a power-operated gun turret at nose and tail. An unusual feature was its 'geodetic' structure resembling metal basketwork, some of which can be seen through the windows.

Large military aircraft had been defended by gunners in open cockpits who aimed machine guns by hand. With the new fast monoplanes the gunners had to be inside transparent turrets driven by power to aim the guns accurately despite the surrounding high-speed airflow. Heavy bombloads could no longer be hung outside, but were put inside bomb bays fitted with large hinged bomb doors. Flying boats were fitted with stabilizing floats which could be retracted up into or beyond the wingtips, while airliners began to appear with power-operated doors and hinged staircases.

Thus, aircraft became much more complicated, with different kinds of functioning systems. The engines needed reliable cooling systems, controllable automatically and also by the pilot. They had to be fed by fuel systems capable of drawing fuel from numerous tanks in the correct sequence, so that the aircraft never became unbalanced, with filters

ABOVE: Britain's first high-speed bomber was the Bristol Blenheim of 1936. A feature was a power-driven B.1 turret in the top of the fuselage. Early marks had a single Lewis or Vickers machine gun, but this later B.1 Mk IV had twin Brownings.

CENTER: Did this German pilot have toothache? He was photographed flying a Heinkel He 111H bomber, with totally glazed-over nose.

for ice crystals or solid matter. Fire-protection systems were needed, as well as oxygen for the crew. Hydraulic systems filled with oil at perhaps 3,000lb/sq in (210kg/cm²), driven by pumps on the engine(s), were needed to work the flaps, retractable landing gears, turrets, bomb doors and other items. Electric motors were sometimes used instead, and in any case electricity was needed for lighting, radio and many other purposes. Compressed air was sometimes used for the wheel brakes and, as an alternative to electric heaters, to protect the wings and tail against any build-up of ice by fitting pulsating inflatable rubber tubing.

As aircraft became ever larger and heavier, so did the sheer physical piloting task get tougher. They also flew higher and higher, airliners to get above the bumpy clouds and bad weather and military aircraft to try to avoid enemy anti-aircraft fire and fighters. This made aircraft even more complex. By World War 2 the biggest aircraft were being fitted with powered flight controls, in which the cables or rods from the cockpit were connected to hydraulic actuators which operated the ailerons, elevators and rudder. At first the pilot's

efforts were merely assisted, but by the 1950s many aircraft had fully powered controls. Special systems were added to give the pilot an indication of "feel", which he previously knew from how difficult the controls were to move, so that the signals he sent to the surface power units could never overstress the aircraft.

The quest for height led to cockpits and eventually even the entire fuselages of giant passenger airliners being pressurized. Instead of being a convenient square box shape the cabin had to be a circular tube, with every door and window specially designed. The floor would be put in at just below the widest part, and the large space under the floor would be used for baggage, cargo, landing gear, systems and fuel. The pressurization system had to be reliable, and carefully controlled so that, with-

BELOW: The spacious interior of this cabin, one of four in a Pan American Boeing 314A flying boat of 1939, contrasts sharply with airline accommodation of only a few years previously, when a typical cabin contained just a few loose wicker chairs. On each side of the ceiling are sleeping bunks, here folded away in the daytime.

out making occupants' eardrums pop, the pressure would fall away from takeoff more slowly than the true atmospheric pressure outside. Thus, at 30,000ft (9,144m), the pressure in the cabin would be equivalent to flight at only 6,000ft (1,830m), which would not cause distress to anyone. Of course, it would also be heated to a comfortable temperature (the outside being colder than the Antarctic) and prevented from becoming too dry.

At all times, safety was of paramount importance. In the earliest days of flying many pilots were killed by apparently making a spiral dive into the ground. It took great courage for pilots to try to find out what was happening. It was discovered that a wing gives lift as long as the air is accelerated across the arched upper surface, but that trying to fly too slowly causes the flow suddenly to break down. The flow no longer gives lift but separates from the upper surface in turbulent eddies. This is called the stall.

Stalling is not dangerous if the aircraft is high enough. The pilot then pushes the controls forward, dives to pick up speed and then pulls out to level flight, taking care never to let the speed

ABOVE: One of the ironies of aviation is that Juan de la Cierva, who devoted his life to making flying machines lifted by rotors, which he thought safer than wings, should have been killed in the crash of a fixed-wing aeroplane. Here a C.4, one of his first autogiros, is seen at Cuatro Vientos in his native Spain on January 9 1923.

RIGHT: It is generally considered that the first wholly successful helicopter was Igor Sikorsky's VS-300. Here Sikorsky talks by telephone to a passenger in the VS-300's eventual production version, the R-4 of January 1942. This was one of the first machines to have one main rotor and a small anti-torque rotor pushing sideways at the tail.

nothing is done a crash is inevitable. Early pilots in spins furiously tried to pull the stick back, making things worse. The cure is to stamp on full opposite rudder, to arrest the rotation. This converts the spin into a dive, from which a pull-out is possible.

In 1919 Handley Page in England patented the idea of the slat, small auxiliary wings along the leading edge. As the wing gets near the stall the slats open, forming a slot through which air flows to delay the stall. This helped a bit, and designers also found that small details could improve stall quality and either avoid spins or make recovery easier. Of course, the objective is never to lose control in the first place. With some aircraft the drill on getting into a spin is: get out fast. As speeds got higher in the jet age this demanded the use of ever more complex ejection seats blown out by cartridges or rockets.

Spaniard Juan de la Cierva tried to overcome

bleed off again. But if the aeroplane stalls in a turn, with the rudder deflected, it enters a regime called a spin. It "autorotates", to left or right, with the fuselage usually inclined downwards, but sometimes even in an almost level attitude. If

the problem by making his wings spin round like a horizontal propeller. Between the World Wars he perfected the autogyro, in which the aircraft is pulled or pushed by a propeller while the air flowing obliquely up past the blades makes them spin round to give lift. Most autogyros are small, and need only a short run for takeoff and landing.

Other inventors tried to make a practical helicopter. This is quite different in that the lifting rotor is driven by the engine. To stop the fuselage from spinning round in the opposite direction a separate rotor has to be added at the tail, blowing sideways to give an exactly equal torque reaction. Alternatively, some helicopters have two main rotors turning in opposite directions, either at the nose and tail or coaxial, one above the other. The mechanical design and aerodynamics of helicopters are complex. Unlike the autogyro, the air flows through the main rotor in a diagonally

downwards direction (vertically when the machine hovers).

In forward flight, one side of the rotor is "advancing", rotating forwards against the oncoming air, while the other half is "retreating", traveling backwards. At some point the retreating blade is stationary with respect to the surrounding air, and in any case the retreating blade finds it difficult to generate lift. The powerful lift from the advancing blade would then roll the machine over. To avoid this, the lift from the left and right halves of the rotor must be made equal, by cyclic pitch change. The angle of the blades is reduced round the advancing side of the rotor, and greatly increased round the retreating half.

In most helicopters the blades are attached to the hub by various pivoted links. The pitch bearings allow the cyclic pitch to oscillate continuously as each blade rotates. The pilot also has a control called the collective-pitch lever, which varies the pitch of all blades together. Whilst simultaneously adjusting engine power, the collective makes the machine take off, hover or sink to the ground. The flapping hinges allow the blades to rise and fall, balancing the lift force against centrifugal force. The drag hinges allow blades to pivot slightly fore and aft within the plane of rotation. Many modern helicopters have so-called rigid rotors, but of course still have cyclic and collective pitch variation.

A few helicopters flew uncertainly in the 1930s, but it was the Russian emigré Igor Sikorsky who really achieved success and started the world helicopter industry. Early machines, like the first aeroplanes, were difficult to fly and were slow and very limited in capability. Gradually they became larger and more capable, and then from the mid-1950s helicopters were transformed by the development of gas-turbine engines.

Such engines had been patented from the

CENTER LEFT: Chief designer of the original Bell Model 30 helicopter was Arthur Young, here seen flying the prototype NX41867 in mid-1943. It had first flown in December 1942, and been repeatedly modified. Today more than 33,000 Bell helicopters have followed it.

BELOW: First flown as a Navy prototype in December 1953, the Sikorsky S-56 was one of the last and most powerful helicopters to be powered by piston engines. The two Pratt & Whitney Double Wasps each developed 2,100 hp, driving through two sets of shafts to the main gearbox under the five-blade main rotor. An unusual feature was the retractable main landing gears, though maximum speed was only 130mph (209km/h).

ABOVE: If Frank Whittle had been able to find anyone who believed in his engine Britain could have flown a simple jet prototype in 1931 and had squadrons of jet fighters by 1936. As it was, Germany flew the first jet aircraft, the Heinkel He 178, in August 1939. It accomplished very little, and was soon put in a museum.

beginning of the century, but achieved nothing until in 1929 an RAF test pilot, Frank Whittle, proposed making a gas turbine not to drive a shaft but purely in order to generate a high-speed propulsive jet of hot gas. His patent was published in January 1930, and caused great interest in many places, except in Whittle's own country. The British Air Ministry had Whittle interviewed by an expert, who basically said the young officer's ideas were flawed and of no importance. Approaches to the British aero-engine industry, and to firms concerned with fuel combustion or high-temperature metals, were rebuffed.

In January 1935 Whittle's patent ran out, and he could not afford to pay the £5 to renew it. Unknown to the British Air Ministry – who said they had no intention of paying the £5 fee themselves – inventors in Germany were now working on precisely the same idea, and it was a German Heinkel He 178 which opened the jet age on August 27 1939. Had Whittle been taken

seriously, by this time the RAF could have been a jet air force!

Whittle saw from the start that the combination of piston engines and propellers could never achieve flight speeds greater than about 800km/h (500mph). Even to achieve this needed huge and complicated engines driving propellers which, at such speeds, were very inefficient. A barrier was imposed by the fact that sound waves travel through air at about 760mph (1,220km/h), a value which in the cold air at high altitude falls to about 660mph (1,060km/h). At or above the speed of sound the moving aircraft cannot signal its presence ahead. Shockwaves are created, at first like a sheet in front of the aircraft, and fold back like a cone as the speed increases. At Mach 2 (twice the speed of sound in the surrounding air) the shockwaves lean back at 60 degrees.

At the speed of sound several basic rules of aerodynamics are reversed. For example, at subsonic speed (below the speed of sound, or M1.0) airflow through a contracting duct speeds up but reduces in pressure, just the opposite to what might be expected. At over M1.0, supersonic flow does this in an *expanding* duct. Thus, to propel a supersonic aircraft, by a turbojet or rocket, the engine nozzle has to begin with a convergent shape, to reach supersonic speed in the narrowest place called the throat, and then continue expanding and accelerating in a final divergent section.

At subsonic speeds an air inlet facing forwards does not compress the air very much, though of course such inlets do face forwards to take advantage of what "ram effect" there is. At M1.0, the speed of sound, this effect becomes quite important, and at Mach 2 it compresses the air to 10 times that in the surrounding atmosphere. Thus, if only a way could be found to start from rest, the simplest supersonic engine is the ramjet, which is nothing but a carefully shaped duct, with fuel burned in the slow-flowing combustion chamber in the middle. To start from rest we have to use what Whittle invented, a turbojet. This first compresses the air in a compressor, then mixes it with burning fuel and then lets it escape past the blades of a rapidly revolving turbine which drives the compressor.

The turbojet puts out a high-velocity jet of hot gas. This is good for a very fast aircraft, but it is extremely noisy and not very fuel-efficient. In 1936 Whittle suggested making an engine called a turbofan, in which the compressor is made larger. This needs extra rows of turbine blades to drive it. Only part of the airflow goes through the combustion chamber and turbine. The rest forms a propulsive jet of cooler air. The much bigger jet is more efficient than before, and also quieter. Today the bypass ratio of the latest airline engines is as high as 9 or 10; of every 11 units of air sucked into the engine, 10 form the cool jet from the fan and 1 comes out as a central hot jet of gas.

It took a long time for designers to realize that such engines made sense. They were much

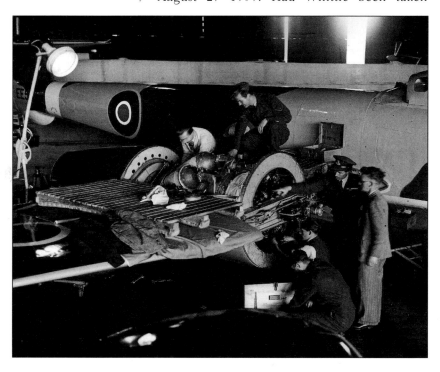

LEFT: The engineer inspecting the fan blades of this Pratt & Whitney PW4000 is dwarfed by the 93.6in [2.38m] diameter fan, but later PW4000 engines have a fan with even larger blades, with a diameter of 112in [2.845m]. This engine is being tested on a pivoting outdoor rig to measure noise and check inlet behavior in crosswinds.

FAR LEFT: Having set a world speed record in November 1945, the Gloster Meteor improved on its own record on September 7 1946. Here the record aircraft, EE549, is having its Rolls-Royce Derwent V engines inspected at Tangmere shortly before the record runs. Note the special metal cockpit canopy.

quicker in adopting turboprops, in which "core engines" like turbojets with extra stages of turbine blades drove a gearbox which reduced the turbine speed (anything from 5,000 to 50,000rpm) to the 900 to 1,200rpm of an ordinary propeller. A third kind of gas turbine is the turboshaft. This is just like a turboprop core engine, without the gearbox. Its high-speed shaft drives the big gearbox of a helicopter from which come relatively very slow-turning shafts to drive the helicopter's rotors.

Modern helicopters are almost all turbine-engined. Military and naval machines have special inlets which keep out salt spray, mud and dust, and special jetpipes which mix the hot gas with cool air and make it difficult for heat-seeking missiles to find a target. To show the difference such engines made, in 1960 the most powerful US helicopter was the Sikorsky S-56, with two large piston engines. Together, these engines developed 4,200hp. With cooling fans they weighed over 6,000lb (2,720kg), and they overheated in hovering flight. Since 1977 the most powerful helicopter, the Mi-26, has two turbine engines. Together they weigh 4,630lb (2,100kg), develop 23,000hp and need no cooling fans.

RIGHT: This F-86D
Saber is a radar-
equipped version of
the first fighter to fly
with sweptback
wings (the
Germans
pioneered the
idea, but never
got a swept-wing
fighter into the
sky). Whereas the
straight-wing Meteor
set records at up to
616mph [991km/h],
an F-86D set a
record at over
715mph
[1,150km/h].

Jet engines became common after World War II, which ended in 1945. At that time few designers knew how to shape aeroplanes to fly at the much higher speeds which the new engines made possible. It was almost universally agreed that, to postpone the tremendous increase in drag near the speed of sound, the wings and tail should be inclined backwards. Such surfaces, called "swept", became almost universal for fighters and jet airliners. At first the commonest angle of sweep was 35 degrees, and this was seen in such aircraft as the F-86 Saber, MiG-15 and Boeing 707.

With greater engine power, designers thrust ahead with sweep angles around 60 degrees, seen in the MiG-19 and Lightning. Other designers simply made their wings very thin, without sweepback, but they had to be strong and heavy; an example was the Lockheed F-104. The crucial factor is the ratio of thickness to chord (distance from

BELOW: The Harrier in
the foreground has
an ordinary swept
wing, but the
Lightning peeeling
away behind it has
an unusual wing, with
both the leading and
trailing edges sharply
swept at 60 degrees
and with the ailerons
mounted across the
tips. The power-
controlled tailplanes
echoed the same
shape.

leading edge to trailing edge across the wing). Thus, instead of making the wing thinner, high speeds can be achieved by increasing the chord.

Accordingly, a popular answer was to extend the wing to the back of the aircraft, fitting it with elevons (surfaces able to operate as either elevators or ailerons), doing away with the horizontal tail. With a swept leading edge, such a wing became triangular, known as a delta wing from the Greek letter of that name D . The Concorde supersonic airliner has a delta wing with a graceful curved leading edge which at takeoff and landing generates a strong swirling vortex to increase lift. Many delta aircraft now have a canard or foreplane added at the front to give better combat agility and to enable high-lift flaps to be fitted, which is difficult with a plain delta wing.

Highly swept and delta wings are inefficient at low speeds, and this tends to mean a long takeoff run. One answer is to use variable sweep, by pivoting the wings and setting them to different angles by powerful irreversible actuators. Such aircraft as the F-111, F-14, Su-24 and Tornado take off with wings outstretched at a sweep angle of about 16 degrees and with high-lift slats and flaps extended. For supersonic flight they retract the high-lift surfaces and pivot the wings back to a sweep angle of some 72 degrees. Today such wings have gone out of fashion, and designers prefer a fixed wing with high-lift devices on the leading and trailing edges. Modern airliners and fighters have wings that look almost unswept.

From the earliest days of aeroplanes some designers thought it would be a good idea if they could make an all-wing aircraft, doing away with the drag of the fuselage and tail. The designer who tried hardest was John K. Northrop, whose all-wing aircraft led by 1945 to huge bombers with

MAIN PICTURE: De Havilland originally planned the Comet jetliner with 40 degrees of sweep, but perhaps short-sightedly reduced the figure to a pointless 20 degrees. Thus, the Comet could not compete with the speed of the Boeing 707, shown here, with 35 degrees of seep. The American jetliner was also much bigger and longer-ranged.

LEFT: At first glance these US Navy fighters appear to be tailless deltas. In fact they are Grumman F-14 Tomcats, with pivoted "swing wings". In the 68 degree maximum-sweep position, seen here, they essentially merge into the horizontal tails. Surprisingly, variable sweep has gone out of fashion.

RIGHT: The rocket-engined X-15 flew faster and higher than any other aeroplane. Here one of the three built is seen on November 9 1961 just after being released from the NB-52 which carried it up to about 40,000ft [18,140m]. On this occasion Maj Bob White took it to Mach 6.04, 4,093mph [6,587km/h].

a span of 172ft (52.4m). These had four piston engines, later replaced by eight jets. By sheer chance the last Northrop aircraft, the B-2A Spirit, is again an all-wing bomber with a span of 172ft (52.4m). Powered by four special turbofans, this has a shape dictated not by aerodynamic reasons but in order to achieve "stealth", invisibility to enemy radars.

Today stealth design is essential for aircraft designed to encounter the enemy. In the 1950s it was thought that the answer was to fly faster and higher. The ultimate aircraft of this type were the huge B-70 Valkyrie bomber and the Lockheed SR-71 "Blackbird" reconnaissance aircraft, which could cross enemy territory at over 2,000mph (3,200km/h) at up to 100,000ft (30,000m). Today, in contrast, heavily defended airspace is penetrat-

ed as close to the Earth's surface as possible, to try to avoid detection by radars. This means flying much slower, and that is why stealth design is so important.

A very small number of extremely fast aircraft have had rocket engines. The big advantage of the rocket is that, instead of its power falling away as the aircraft climbs into the stratosphere, it actually increases, because the atmospheric pressure downstream of the nozzle is reduced. One of the classic aircraft of history was the Bell X-1 (originally called the XS-1), which on October 14 1947 made the first flight faster than sound. It was basically a "brute force and ignorance" design. The fuselage was based on the shape of a 0.5in bullet. The wings and tail were just made thin and extremely strong. The engine was a rocket with four thrust chambers so that the pilot could select four levels of thrust from 1,500lb

RIGHT: After years fighting against political opponents the Bell Boeing V-22 Osprey is at last in production. This tilt-rotor aircraft can hover like a helicopter, as seen here, but can then turn into an aeroplane and fly twice as fast as the latest helicopters, and also roughly twice as far.

(680kg) to 6,000lb (2,720kg).

Later rocket engines were made that could have their thrust varied by the pilot moving a throttle lever, like other engines. The fastest aeroplane ever built, the North American X-15, was at first fitted with two four-chamber engines developed from those of the X-1, but in November 1960 it began flying with a new single-chamber controllable rocket engine with a thrust of 57,000lb (25,855kg) at sea level and about 70,000lb (31,751kg) at high altitude. Later it was fitted with huge external tanks to carry extra rocket propellants, and it achieved an altitude of 354,200ft (107,960m) and speed of 4,534mph (7,297km/h), or M6.72.

Such aircraft are basically projectiles, carried to high altitude under a parent aircraft such as a B-52 bomber. Other fast jets need smooth paved runways, if possible over 12,000ft (3.5km) long. This is fine for airliners but nonsensical for warplanes, because such runways cannot be hidden. By 1960 air forces were looking for ways to make effective combat aircraft operate from village streets and small clearings in jungles and forests. The British Aerospace Harrier achieved this, as well as operating from small platforms on any type of ship. It did so by having a unique turbofan engine with vectored (aimed) nozzles, which could be pointed down to lift the aircraft off the ground and then swivelled to the rear for transonic flight.

Today Boeing and Lockheed Martin are working on a successor to the Harrier, the Joint Strike Fighter, while the Bell/Boeing team are in production with the V-22 Osprey. This is a totally different kind of VTOL (vertical take-off and landing) aircraft. It has a multirole transport type fuselage, with a twin-finned tail. Above the fuselage is a wing carrying on its tips two 6,150hp turbine engines driving giant propellers, each with three blades with a diameter of 38ft (11.58m). For VTO the engines are pivoted up so that the propellers become rotors. After takeoff the landing gear is retracted and the engines gradually rotate into the forward position, turning the rotors into propellers to cruise at 316mph (509km/h), twice as fast as a helicopter.

Such tilt-rotor aircraft are certain to take over from helicopters for a vast range of military and civil tasks, including passenger and cargo transport, SAR (search and rescue), amphibious

BELOW: Here seen with its "drag rudders" open to enable it to hold formation with the photographic aircraft, the Northrop Grumman B-2A Spirit strategic bomber looks like something from another planet. Despite its incredible complexity, this "stealth" aircraft is flown by a crew of two.

LEFT: In 1997 the JSF (Joint Strike fighter) was the subject of what in monetary terms may be the most expensive aircraft program in history. This artist's impression shows a bomb being released from the Boeing proposal, two prototypes of which (in slightly different versions) will be evaluated against rivals by Lockheed Martin.

assault, offshore support, fisheries protection and coastguard surveillance, medical evacuation and disaster relief. As they can fly twice as fast as a helicopter, they can go twice as far on a given quantity of fuel and for an operating cost (however measured, such as per tonne/km or per seat-mile) half as expensive as the best helicopters.

Of course, such aircraft would be impossible without steady progress in supporting systems, especially avionics (aviation electronics). Following earlier experiments, aircraft began using radio during World War I. Gradually airborne radio became lighter, more compact and

thermionic valves by transistors transformed what could be done. New radios operating at much shorter wavelength gave clarity of speech and far better reliability, while the biggest revolution of all was the switch from analog avionics to digital. Except for simple lightplanes, aircraft began to carry computers, and not just one but several.

Today military aircraft and airliners are computerized from nose to tail. When the pilot opens the throttles for takeoff, computers decide how much power is needed and establish the required level (invariably, less than the maximum, to reduce costs and prolong engine life). After rotat-

ABOVE: Maintenance engineers check over the APQ-120 forward-looking radar of a McDonnell Douglas F-4G "Wild Weasel" Phantom at the USAF 37th (later the 35th) Tactical Fighter Wing. The F-4G's role was to destroy hostile anti-aircraft missile systems. The large canoe fairing under the hinged radome houses the APR-38 radar/missile detector.

more reliable. Between the wars, instruments became far more precise, enabling skilled pilots to fly "blind", without reference to the ground, while autopilots were developed which could automatically maintain a set course and altitude. Ground radio stations were developed which could enable suitably equipped aircraft to navigate from one station to another, while systems of radio beams and beacons were devized to help aircraft to land in bad weather.

By 1937 work had begun to produce radars small and light enough to be fitted into aircraft. Different types of radar enabled crews to see pictures of the ground, find ships at sea or, most difficult of all, intercept and destroy enemy aircraft at night or in bad weather. In the 1950s airliners were equipped with radar in the nose to enable them to avoid turbulent clouds, thunderstorms and other aircraft. By the 1960s replacement of

ing into the climb attitude at a precisely predetermined airspeed, the aircraft climbs at the most efficient angle of attack to reach the greatest safe height before cutting back the power to reduce noise on leaving the airfield boundary. Engine failure today is almost unheard-of, but if it did occur the response of the aircraft would be automatic, to re-trim, increase power on the remaining engine(s) and continue straight ahead.

Today's flight deck is almost devoid of circular dial instruments. In their place each pilot has two large displays like color TV screens. One, the primary flight display, gives the information needed about the aircraft's attitude, altitude, speed (and desired "target speed"), and the information needed to make a blind landing using the airport's instrument landing system. The other display, called the navigation display, shows the pilot a detailed map of where he is, together with the

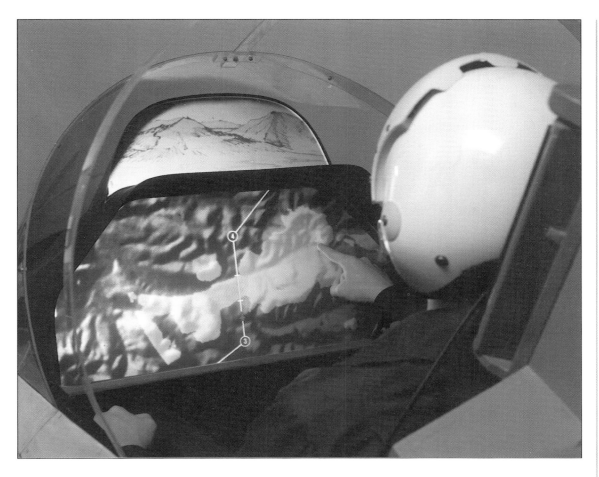

LEFT: As far back as 1984 McDonnell Douglas was testing this "big screen" fighter cockpit to try to make life easier for the overworked pilot. The pilot is pointing to an enemy missile site, and is asking the electronics to tell him not only his flight path but also his vulnerability at each point along it.

future desired track, information on speeds and winds, and every detail needed of the future waypoints (places to be flown over).

Almost the only aircraft that might be found without avionics are hot-air balloons and microlights, but even these are the subject of continuous improvement with new technologies and improved materials. It has never been easy to defy gravity, but today's aircraft can do it efficiently, environmentally benignly and with almost perfect reliability. The future holds almost limitless technological advances to further the art.

LEFT: Europe's Airbus Industrie has from its inception been the world leader in airline cockpits. Typical of those in current production is the cockpit of this A340. Immediately obvious are the things that are not there. There are no ordinary dial instruments and no big flight control yoke, just a small sidestick.

CHAPTER TWO
Civil Aviation

RIGHT: One of Santos-Dumont's airships – a familiar sight above Paris early this century. On October 19 1901 he flew from the headquarters of the Aéro-Club de France at St Cloud to the Eiffel Tower and back in under one hour.

BELOW: Santos-Dumont in the basket of his 1903 steerable balloon. A sensitive man, he was much saddened by the use of aircraft for military purposes.

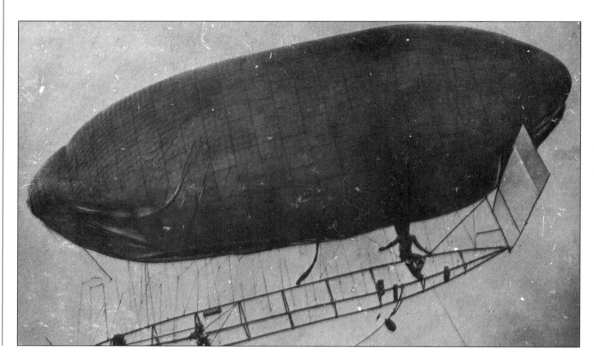

TODAY, TRAVEL BY AIR is a mundane event in many people's lives. Taking the plane for that holiday in the sun is as easy as boarding a train or a bus. Ninety years ago, the story was different. Air travel – and even a long holiday – was an unrealized dream for most of the population, who regarded it to be as likely as man traveling to the Moon. But civil aviation's path has been far from straightforward.

Throughout the 19th Century, the balloon's popularity as a means of transport had been growing. As well as for military service, where balloons were used for observation in the American Civil War, the Franco-Prussian War and the Boer War, they were used by the wealthy for pleasure flying. Unfortunately, they were at the mercy of the elements – a balloon flight was (and to some extent today remains) a mystery tour. Nevertheless, some extremely long distance flights were made, with Count Henri de La Vaulx setting a new non-stop distance record of 1,200 miles (1,931km) on October 8–9 1900. Altitude records were also set as man explored his surroundings. By the turn of the century, balloons had reached altitudes of 30,000 feet (9,144m) and the world altitude record was claimed by Herr Berson and Professor SŸring of Germany on June 30 1901 when –

assisted by oxygen – they reached 35,435 feet (10,800m) in the gas balloon *Preussen*. But without any method of steering, balloons did not have commercial application.

Naturally, a method of steering was sought and the outcome was the airship or dirigible ("that can be steered"), a tube-shaped gas-filled balloon to which steering fins could be attached. In Europe, one of the first pioneers to prove that air travel had real possibility was Alberto Santos-Dumont, a Brazilian who took up residence in Paris during the last decade of the 19th Century. A wealthy man, he devoted much time and energy to creating a series of airships and his first, the imaginatively named No.1, made its first flight from Paris on September 20 1898. But it was back to the drawing board the next day after the flight ended in a crash landing.

Santos-Dumont was not deterred and during the following years he and his dirigibles became a regular sight in the Parisian skies; by 1900 he was flying No.4 over the Tuileries palace. Much encouraged by the potential of airships and keen to foster France's place at the forefront of aviation development, financier Henri Deutsch de la Meurthe announced the establishment of a prize of FF100,000 to be awarded to the first person to fly from the Aéro-Club de France's headquarters at Saint-Cloud to the Eiffel Tower, a distance of around 7 miles (11km). Among the eager aspirants were Santos-Dumont and Count von Zeppelin (of whom more later).

Santos-Dumont was the eventual winner, on his third attempt. His first ended in a tree and on his second attempt on August 8 1901 his airship No.5 began to lose gas as it rounded the Eiffel Tower and came down on a hotel in the center of Paris. A third and final attempt on November 4 1901 was successful when he flew a round trip from Saint-Cloud to the Eiffel Tower in less than 30 minutes, but he was informed on landing that his guide rope was not secured until past the one-hour time limit. After a two-week campaign in which he was backed by the Parisiens themselves, Santos-Dumont was awarded the prize and immediately endeared himself further by giving it away – FF75,000 to charity and the remainder to his airship construction crew.

While Santos-Dumont was hugging the limelight, in Germany Count von Zeppelin was working towards the same goal. A wealthy Prussian aristocrat and veteran of the American Civil War, he was able to finance his development and construction program himself when the German War Ministry refused official backing. Zeppelin's first creation, LZ1, made its first flight on July 2 1900 and remained airborne for 20 minutes, during which time it covered 9¼ miles (14.8km). Zeppelin continued developing his ideas and by the outbreak of the First World War was the world's leading airship producer.

The Wright Flyer

In parallel with balloon and airship development, work continued on perfecting heavier-than-air craft around the world. In France, Germany, the UK and the USA, experiments were underway with gliders and aeroplanes. Pioneers such as Chanute, Lilienthal, Pilcher and Langley all brought an element of science to the hitherto "enthusiastic amateur" approach, meticulously recording their experiments. Some – such as Lilienthal and Pilcher – paid the ultimate price for their places at the forefront of technology, while others progressed towards fitting their gliders with engines.

Octave Chanute, French-born but resident in the USA, was the first to put pen to paper and produce a comprehensive history of aviation up to that time. He attracted the attention of a pair of bicycle manufacturers based at Dayton, Ohio – Wilbur and Orville Wright. Correspondence

BOTTOM: Zeppelin launched his airships from floating hangars moored on Lake Constance near Friedrichshafen. By rotating the hangars into the wind, he was able to take advantage of weather conditions to launch the Zeppelins.

BELOW: Count Ferdinand von Zeppelin (1838–1917) was responsible for much of the early development in the airship field. Germany used the Count's airships to mount bombing raids on London in the First World War.

RIGHT: The first official world record holder: Santos-Dumont's No.14 bis first flew on September 13 1906, covering a magnificent 20 feet (6.1m). during trials, the "back-to-front" pusher made a flight of 722ft (220m) on November 12 1906, the first official sustained flight in Europe.

BELOW: Orville and Wilbur Wright spent three years experimenting with wind tunnels and gliders before eventually constructing their first powered biplane. Their second 1902 glider, seen here in trials, had a single rear rudder. Once they had wrung as much experience as possible from the gliders in over 1,000 flights, they moved on to the Wright Flyer.

reveals that Chanute's advice was to first build a glider before launching into a full-scale aeroplane, and above all to be methodical. History shows that the Wright brothers, after three years of experimenting with gliders and their own wing-warping method of control, made the world's first heavier-than-air powered flight on the sands of Kitty Hawk, North Carolina, on December 17 1903. That first hop lasted just 12 seconds and covered 120 feet (36.6m), but by the end of that day's testing (brought to a premature halt by a gust of wind that flipped the Wright Flyer over) Wilbur Wright had covered 852 feet (260m) in a single flight lasting 59 seconds. The Wright brothers had set the world on fire – everyone was talking about their achievement, but the French, who believed themselves to be world leaders in aviation, refused to believe it!

European competition

Although the important breakthrough had been made, powered flight was still in its infancy. Not until 1906 was the first flight made in Europe – the indefatigable Santos-Dumont getting No.14bis aloft in Paris on October 23 to win a FF3,000 prize for the first aircraft to fly further than 82 feet (25m), having already achieved a 20-foot (6m) hop on September 13. Santos-Dumont was back again on November 12 1906 to fly 722 feet (220m) and capture another FF1,500 for the first to fly further than 328 feet (100m).

Frantic efforts to put France back "on top" brought many other early aviators to the forefront of public perception, among them Louis Blériot, Charles Voisin, Henri Farman and Robert Esnault-Pelterie, who was the first to use a control stick to steer his aircraft. Although the Wright brothers had flown a circular flight in September 1904, Europe was again behind and not until January 13 1908 could Henri Farman claim the FF50,000 Deutsch-Archdeacon prize as the first European to fly a 1-kilometre circular course.

Civil aviation really got going in 1909, when the competition to be first across the English Channel in a powered aeroplane (as opposed to a balloon or airship) saw entrants from both sides of the channel race to claim the £1,000 Britiish *Daily Mail* newspaper prize. The ultimate winner was Louis Blériot, who crossed from Les Barraques to Dover in 37 minutes on the morning of July 25 1909. Meanwhile, the first all-British aircraft, Alliott Verdon Roe's Avroplane, had made its first flight just two days previously. Air exhibitions were held all over Europe – Reims Grand Flying Week, covering August 22–29, offered FF200,000 in prize money and attracted 500,000 visitors, and a two-day exhibition the following month was viewed by more than 100,000 people. At Frankfurt, the first International Airship Show

ABOVE: First man to fly across the English Channel was Louis Blériot (far left) on July 25 1909 in his Blériot XI, seen here at the landing site on Northfall Meadow near Dover.

LEFT: The first British aerial postman prepares to take off from Hendon on September 9 1911, his mail sack slung under the seat. Destination: Windsor, to deliver mail for King George V.

was dominated by Zeppelin. That autumn, other flying meetings were held at Doncaster and Blackpool in England, Brescia in Italy and Johannistal in Germany. America's first aviation meet was held at Los Angeles on January 10–20 1910.

A further milestone was reached on November 10 1909, when the world's first commercial airline was established – Deutsche Luftschiffahrt AG (DELAG) was formed to fly Zeppelin airships. Early operations were by no means successful and DELAG's first airship, LZ7 *Deutschland,* came to grief soon after it entered service; its replacement lasted little longer. However, when services finally got underway they were successful, even though no timetable was published due to the unpredictability of the weather and serviceability of the airships. DELAG began the world's first international passenger service on September 19 1912 when its LZ13 *Hansa* flew to Copenhagen in Denmark and Malmπ in Sweden. Between June 1910 and July 1914 DELAG carried over 34,000 passengers on 1,588 flights without serious incident. The outbreak of the First World War put

paid to DELAG's operations and its Zeppelins were pressed into military service.

The world's mail services were quick to see the merit in transporting letters by air, particularly in the more outflung posts of the British Empire, and began low-key experiments. The world's first official air mail service was flown on February 18 1911, when Frenchman Henri Piquet flew from Allahabad to Naini Junction in India on behalf of the British Army, carrying 6,500 letters. In the UK, the first British service was operated over the period September 9-26 from Hendon and Windsor and flown by Gustav Hamel in a Blériot. Among his deliveries were letters for the British Royal Family in the nearby castle.

The first American postal service started on September 23 1911 with Earle Ovington's flight from Nassau, New York, to Mineola, Long Island, using a Blériot monoplane. Aircraft were also used for freight deliveries – the first recorded journey being undertaken by Horatio Barber using a Valkyrie monoplane, flying from Shoreham to Hove on July 4 1911, carrying a box of Osram lightbulbs. On November 7 1911 the first

RIGHT: January 1 1914 heralded the start of the world's first scheduled airline service, in a Benoist flying boat from St Petersburg to Tampa, USA, a distance of 19 miles (30km).

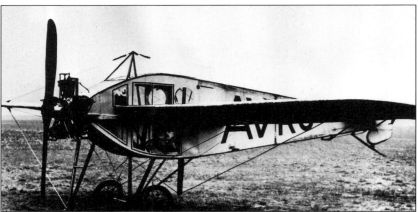

ABOVE: The Avro Type F, first flown on May 1 1912, the world's first aircraft to feature an enclosed cabin for its pilot. Sceptics believed that the cabin windows would end up covered in oil, a fate that befell pilots at a time when they were offered only rudimentary protection from the elements.

recorded American freight flight saw Philip Parmalee transport silk from Dayton to Columbus, Ohio. The first regular (as opposed to chartered) freight service in the US began on January 13 1913 with flights from Boston to New York, with a cargo of baked beans.

On November 5 1911 the first trans-American flight was eventually completed, a protracted affair lasting 49 days. Pilot Calbraith Rodgers had left New York on September 17 and when he finally arrived at Long Beach, California, he had made 69 stops during the 4,321 mile (6,954km) journey and suffered 16 crash landings. By the time he reached his destination, very little of his original aircraft remained! Sadly, Rodgers did not live long to enjoy his triumph as he was killed on April 3 1912 during an air show at Long Beach.

The privilege of operating the first scheduled service using heavier-than-aircraft fell to an American company, the St Petersburg-Tampa Airboat Line, which began services on January 1 1914, using a Benoist flying boat to cover the short 19-mile (30km) hop between the two cities. Costing $5 for a one-way ticket, the four-times daily service immediately proved popular, so much so that a second flying boat was pressed into service by the end of the month. Activities came to a halt during April, due to a combination of the end of the lucrative tourist season and renewed fighting in the Mexican War. Britain's first recorded scheduled passenger service was flown between Leeds and Bradford using a Blackburn monoplane – the inaugural flight being made on July 22 1914.

In parallel with land-based aircraft, seaplanes were also developed, although it was not until 1912 that the world's first seaplane competition was held. This took place at Monaco at the end of

March 1913; the overall winner was the Belgian Jules Fischer, flying a Henri Farman which had been converted by removing the wheeled undercarriage and replacing it with floats. The following year saw the inauguration of the Schneider Trophy for seaplanes, won by Maurice Prévost; the series eventually culminated in an outright win for Great Britain in the twelfth competition held in 1931.

Developments in pilot and passenger comfort were also given serious consideration – Roe's Type F made its first flight on May 1 1912 to become the world's first aircraft with an enclosed cockpit. In Russia, Igor Sikorsky had been working on large-scale aircraft for commercial passenger operations. His first, the Bolshoi Baltiskii, was the world's largest aircraft when it was first flown on May 10 1913. Carrying eight passengers plus its pilot, it was later superseded by the Ilya Muromets I (first flown February 12 1914) and Ilya Muromets II (first flown July 11 1914), probably the world's first aircraft to feature a lavatory!

Although all these early record-breaking flights were of small commercial value at the time, they did much to prove that air transportation, be it of passengers, mail or freight, was feasible, in the near future. Evolution was indeed to come, but in a circuitous route as all civilian activities in Europe ceased at the outbreak of the First World War, and although they continued in the USA and Canada they took second place to advances in military aviation.

Even before the end of the First World War, thoughts were turning to the use of aircraft during peacetime. Aircraft design had progressed dramatically during the conflict, and problems such as stability and reliability had been tackled with the official enthusiasm only seen under wartime conditions. Although the Zeppelins of DELAG had inaugurated international services before the War, international air transport was in its infancy and its legal ramifications under constant evolution.

George Holt Thomas, owner of Airco, which had been responsible for the construction of a whole series of de Havilland designs during the conflict, wanted to get in early on what he saw as a lucrative line of business. So too did Handley Page. Both adapted their wartime aircraft to commercial duties – DH.16 versions of the DH.9A bomber for the former and O/400 conversions for the latter. Due to the restrictions of the Defence of the Realm Act which precluded civil flying until Air Navigation Regulations were in place, neither was destined to be the first post-war European civil airline, and the Germans began the world's first daily scheduled service on February 5 1919,

Deutsche Luft Reederei (DLR) flying from Berlin to Weimar. February 8 saw the Farman company begin operations on the Paris-London route, using F.60 Goliaths. It was not until August 25 that British airlines flew internationally: Holt Thomas's Aircraft Transport & Travel Company started services from London-Hounslow to Paris while Handley Page Transport Ltd operated from London-Cricklewood to the French capital, although the inaugural flight left from Hounslow, which was the first British airport to offer customs

ABOVE: The magnificent Sikorsky Ilya Muromets was fitted with a passenger promenade deck on top of the rear fuselage and could carry up to 16 passengers.

LEFT: Aircraft Transport and Travel Ltd, began services on August 25 1919 between London and Paris. This DH.16 was an early member of AT&T's fleet, carrying four passengers – who entered via the upward hinging cabin roof – on the two-and-a-half-hour flight.

RIGHT: Ground crew prepare to start the 450hp (335kW) Napier Lion engine of a de Havilland DH.17. G-EAWO was delivered to Ihstone Air Line on May 21 1921 but was destroyed in the world's first mid-air crash on April 7 1922.

RIGHT: The Handley Page W.8 airliner of 1919 carried 16 passengers in its (relatively) spacious cabin. The prototype's borrowed 450 horsepower (335kW) engines meant that it could not enter the revenue-earning service until October 21 1921.

BELOW: The first prototype Vickers Vimy Commercial, carrying the early British registration K-107, made its first flight on April 19 1919.

facilities. Nine DH.16s were built and served with both AT&T and the Dutch airline KLM. They seated four passengers in an enclosed cabin and cruised at 100mph (160km/h), a creditable speed for the day. Handley Page's O/400 could carry up to 16 passengers in its comfortable cabin, but was slightly slower. It proved more popular as an airliner and saw service in such far-flung outposts as India and South America.

The first post-war airliner produced by Airco to be designed specifically as such was the DH.18. Of typical de Havilland layout, the DH.18 could carry eight passengers in an enclosed cabin. Although only six were built, they remained in service until 1923, a relatively long life by the standards of the day. De Havilland's other successful post-First World War airliner was the DH.34, of which 11 were built for service with Daimler, Instone and the Soviet Dobrolet airline. The DH.34 incorporated several new innovations for civil aircraft, including an inertia starter which negated the need to hand-swing the propellers, and hinged access panels on the engine cowlings, providing mechanics with ideally placed working platforms. The Napier Lion engines were also installed in detachable units complete with their cooling systems, so engine changes were less fraught.

Handley Page's first true commercial design was the W.8, which marked an important forward step in cabin design. Handley Page's earlier conversions had, of necessity, retained the internal bracing designed into the aircraft structure. The

VICKERS VIMY COMMERCIAL

Wingspan	68ft 0in (20.73m)
Length	42ft 8in (13.00m)
Powerplants	2 Rolls-Royce Eagle VIII rated at 360hp (268kW)
Passenger capacity	10
Maximum speed	103mph (166km/h)
Range	450 miles (714km)
Date of entry into service	1920
Number built	44

new W.8 cabin eliminated these by using braced vertical struts, enabling the internal cabin width of 4ft 6in (1.37m) to be used to its fullest extent. A retired O/400 acted as an interim prototype for the new design, and received a new single-fin tail unit, new undercarriage and equal span wings. It first flew on August 22 1919. The true prototype W.8, meanwhile, was nearing completion at Handley Page's Cricklewood factory. Rather than the 400hp (298kW) Cosmos Jupiter engines that the company had proposed to install into the W.8, the Air Ministry lent a pair of 450hp (336kW) Napier Lion engines. Registered G-EAPJ, the W.8

first flew on December 2 1919 but could not enter commercial service at this time due to its loaned engines, and so in the interim it was demonstrated around Europe. Lack of government subsidisation meant that all British air transport ceased on February 28 1921 as the airlines could not compete with the subsidised French airlines, and the government was forced to step in with handouts to enable services to Paris to restart on March 19, with fares set at the same rate as the French airlines. Eventually, G-EAPJ flew its first service on October 21 1921, a flight from Croydon – now the customs terminal for Handley Page Transport Ltd – to Paris. In all, 22 W.8s (including the prototype) were built and remained in service until the early 1930s; they also equipped the Belgian airline SABENA.

The third major British manufacturer to show

HANDLEY PAGE W.8c

Wingspan	75ft 0in (22.86m)
Length	60ft 1in (18.31m)
Powerplants	2 Rolls-Royce Eagle IX rated at 390hp (291kW)
Passenger capacity	16
Maximum speed	104mph (167km/h)
Range	500 miles (805km)
Date of entry into service	1921
Number built	22 of all models of W.8

an interest in commercial aviation was Vickers, whose first efforts were conversions of the Vimy bomber which had entered service at the close of the First World War. Unlike the efforts of Airco/de Havilland and Handley Page, Vickers chose to build an entirely new fuselage for its Vimy Commercial. Work on the project began in January 1919 and the prototype made its first flight on April 13 1919 from Joyce Green. In production terms, the design could be counted a success as 40 were sold to China at the end of the year as part of a large package designed to start civil aviation in that country. It was not popular in the West and including the prototype only four were built. The first British-registered production aircraft went into service with Instone & Co later that year. Others went to the Soviet Union and France, and five were sold to the Royal Air Force for use as air ambulances. Later, the design was developed further for the military as the Vernon.

To the Vickers Vimy also fell the glory of pioneering true long-range flying. In 1913, the *Daily Mail* newspaper had offered a prize of £10,000 for the first to fly the Atlantic non-stop. The war had intervened, and when peace returned competition for the money was fierce. One of the first to take up the challenge was Harry Hawker who, along with Lieutenant-Commander K Mackenzie-Grieve, took off from St John's, Newfoundland, on May 18 1919. Their Sopwith Atlantic was around half-way across when its engine cooling system failed and they were forced to ditch alongside a ship. Nine days later on May 27 a US Navy Curtiss flying boat made the trip from St John's to Lisbon, Portugal, to become the first aeroplane to make the trip, but it stopped off at the Azores and was therefore not eligible for the prize.

Record-breaking Vimy

It fell to two Britons to claim the prize: pilot Captain John Alcock and navigator Lieutenant Arthur Whitten Brown took off from St John's at 4.13 pm GMT on June 14, 1919 en route for the UK. The momentous 1,890-mile (3,042km) flight lasted for 16 hours and 27 minutes and ended in a

ABOVE: Post-War, the next major flying milestone was crossing the Atlantic. The US Navy was first to complete the feat. Three Curtiss flying boats left Rockaway Naval Air Station in New York on May 9 1919 on the first leg. Two aircraft dropped out en route and only NC-4 made it to Lisbon following stops at Halifax, Trepassey and the Azores.

ABOVE: Vickers
Aircraft staff refuel
Vimy G-UAAV Silver
Queen before she
sets off from
Brooklands on
February 4 1920,
bound for Cape
Town, flown by Lt Col
Pierre Van Ryneveld
and Major C.J.
Quintin Brand. The
intrepid South
Africans eventually
reached their
destination in a
borrowed DH.9.

bog at Derrygimla, County Galway, where the aircraft tipped onto its nose. To enable the Vimy to make the flight, Vickers had extensively modified the aircraft, removing all its military equipment and installing extra fuel tanks, increasing capacity from 516 to 865 gallons (2,346 to 3,932 litres) and thus range to 2,440 miles (3,927km). The two Rolls Royce Eagle VIII engines each produced 360hp (268kW) and performed reliably throughout the flight, even though they iced up on occasion due to the weather conditions. Following its record-breaking flight, the Vimy was rescued from the bog and returned to Vickers' Weybridge factory before being rebuilt and placed on display in the Science Museum. King George V knighted the two airmen upon their return to the UK; sadly Sir John Alcock was killed in a flying accident on December 18 1919.

The Vimy became the aircraft of choice for other record-breakers. Next to make a major flight were the Australian Smith brothers, in response to an Australian Government offer of £A10,000 for the first flight by Australians from Britain to Australia – completed by the end of the year and within 30 days of departure. Captain Ross Smith and Lieutenant Keith Smith were accompanied by two mechanics – Sergeants Shiers and Bennett. They flew an almost-standard Vimy straight from the production line, the main difference being the provision of additional stores for use in tropical

conditions, rather than the normal military equipment, and extra fuel tanks. The Smith brothers took off from Hounslow on November 12 1919 and followed a route that had been carefully planned and provisioned. They made it through to arrive at Darwin on December 10 1919 after a flight of 11,130 miles (17,912km) undertaken in 135 hours and 55 minutes of flying time.

Long-distance flight number three for the Vimy was actually undertaken by two aircraft! On February 4 1920 Lt-Col Pierre Van Ryneveld and Major C J Quintin Brand of the newly-established South African Air Force left Brooklands in a Vimy, bound for Cape Town. All went well on the flight across Europe, but between Cairo and Khartoum disaster struck when a radiator sprang a leak. The Egyptian Air Force loaned the pair a second Vimy to complete the task, and this got as far as Bulawayo in Southern Rhodesia, where it was damaged after failing to get airborne during take-off. Undaunted, Van Ryneveld and Quintin Brand borrowed a DH.9 to complete their flight and claim £5,000 each from the South African Government. The prototype Vimy Commercial had also left Brooklands on an attempted Cape Town flight on January 24, but came down in Tanganyika on February 27 as a result of contaminated water in a radiator.

The first non-stop crossing of the USA, a distance of some 2,650 miles (4,265km), had to wait until 1923 when it was finally conquered by Oakley Kelly and John MacReady in a Fokker T-2. They landed at Rockwell Field, San Diego, on

May 3 1923 after a 26 hour 50 minute flight from Long Island, New York. The following year, an even more ambitious American long-distance flight was started. Using four Douglas World Cruisers that had been specially purchased for the record attempt, a team of US Army Air Service pilots set out from Seattle in April 1924 en route for Alaska and Japan on the first part of a round-the-world flight that would take until September 28 to complete. During the 26,345 mile (42,398km) flight, which took 175 days to complete, two aircraft were damaged beyond repair, without injury to their crew.

Next into the limelight was Alan Cobham, who made a series of long-distance flights using light aircraft. During the winter of 1924-25 he had flown Sir Sefton Brancker, the inspirational Director of Civil Aviation, on a tour of the Far East to survey air routes, and on May 29 1925 he took the prototype DH.60 Moth from Croydon to Zurich and back in a day – a distance of 1,000 miles (1,609km).

Cobham went on to set long-distance records and make many pioneering flights. In November 1925 he left England for South Africa in a de Havilland DH.50J to undertake a route-proving journey which laid the foundations for Imperial Airways' later services. He returned to the UK on March 13 1926 as a national hero, having checked out 27 possible landing sites in Africa between Cairo and Cape Town, a distance of over 8,000 miles (12,875km). Three months later, on June 30 he was off again in the same aircraft, this time bound for Australia via the Middle East, India and Singapore, arriving at Melbourne on August 15. Returning the same way, he alighted on the Thames outside the Houses of Parliament on October 1 1926 following a flight of 26,703 miles (42,974km). Shortly afterwards, he was knighted for his services to aviation and exploration, which continued the following winter with a round-Africa flight in a Short Singapore flying boat. From 1932 Cobham embarked on a series of round-Britain summer tours under the banner

ABOVE: Vimy G-EAOU set off from Hounslow, England, on November 12 1919 en route for Australia. Piloted by Ross and Keith Smith with two mechanics, G-EAOU reached Darwin on December 10 after a flight of 11,130 miles (17,912km), the first aircraft to complete the journey.

BACKGROUND PIC: Alan Cobham alights on the Thames on October 1 1926 at the end of his epic England–Australia–England flight. His companion, Arthur Elliott, died of a gunshot wound sustained when he was fired upon by a Bedouin tribesman over the Persian desert.

ABOVE: Australian-born Bert Hinckler with the prototype Avro 581 Avian. When he landed at Darwin on February 22 1928 he became the first pilot to fly solo from England to Australia, having left Croydon on February 7.

'National Aviation Day', working on the principle of taking aviation to rural British towns. Many owed their first taste of flying to Cobham's tours. He was also responsible for a great deal of the early work on air-to-air refueling, culminating in the setting up of his company Flight Refuelling.

Cobham had been accompanied on his record-breaking flights; the kudos of being the first man to fly solo to the Cape went to Lieutenant Dick Bentley of the South African Air Force, flying a de Havilland DH.60X Moth. The flight took most of September 1927 to complete – Bentley left the UK on the 1st of the month and arrived at Cape Town on the 28th. February 1928 saw another Empire record-breaking flight. Bert Hinckler left Croydon on February 7 to return to his homeland, landing in Darwin on the 22nd to set five new records and become the first man to fly solo to Australia. Another of Hinckler's attempts on the Australia record ended in the Italian Dolomites. Leaving Feltham on January 8 1933, he was never seen alive again; his body was found four months later – he'd flown into a mountain in appalling weather conditions.

German commercial services

Commercial airlines grew fastest in Germany, where the Versailles Treaty prevented military aircraft development, and by the end of November 1919 most major German cities were served by airlines, including Hamburg, Frankfurt, Hannover, Leipzig and Munich, although they were not allowed to make international aircraft flights until January 1 1923. German companies threw their efforts into producing modern airliners. Junkers unveiled its new F 13 to the public in June 1919, the first airliner to be constructed entirely out of metal. Originally conceived in 1910, the F 13 was descended from a line of successful designs pro-

duced for the German war effort. Its trademark corrugated all-metal construction meant that it stood up to the rigors of airline operation from grass airfields very well, and its nine wing spars automatically reduced damage from fatigue. Over 450 were eventually built and remained in service for more than a decade – as late as 1931 Deutsche Lufthansa was operating a fleet of 43 of these attractive little monoplanes. The Junkers F 13 was also radical in offering an enclosed cabin for its flight crew – something that had been eschewed by British pilots who "liked to be out in the open".

Junkers' main competitor in Europe during the

LEFT: One of the 50 single-engined Fokker F VIIs. after 15 years of service with the Dutch national airline KLM, it was destroyed at Schiphol by advancing German troops in May 1940.

early part of the 1920s was the Dutch company Fokker whose head, Anthony Fokker, was an outstanding aircraft designer. He had produced numerous monoplane, biplane and triplane designs for the Germans during the First World War, and his first airliner, the Fokker F II, was designed before he returned to his home country. Unlike the low-wing, all-metal Junkers F 13, the Fokker F II featured a steel tube fuselage and wooden high wing. The prototype F II took to the air in October 1919 and was followed by a whole series of airliners to the same basic layout – the five-passenger Fokker F III was a relative success, although the F IV and F V were commercial failures. Fokker hit the big time with the F VII. The eight single-engined early F VIIs were all operated by KLM, but were superseded by the improved F VIIA of which Fokker built 42 and licensed its production in other countries. Both were outshone by the three-engined F VIIA-3m, which first appeared in 1925, and the improved F VIIB-3m, most popular of all the Fokker airliners. The

FOKKER F.VIIB-3m

Wingspan	71ft 2in (21.69m)
Length	47ft 7in (14.50m)
Powerplants	3 Wright Whirlwinds rated at 300hp (224kW); other engines could be fitted
Passenger capacity	8
Maximum speed	130mph (209km/h)
Range	600 miles (966km)
Date of entry into service	1928
Number built	116 including earlier F.VIIA-3m

company eventually built 116 of these rugged trimotors, which found favor on both sides of the Atlantic.

Across in the USA, the Post Office had been pioneering mail flights around the country since 1918, although its long-distance flights were initially unsuccessful. It extended these to international services on March 3 1919 when Hubbard Air Service made an experimental test flight from Seattle to Vancouver. Accompanying pilot Eddie Hubbard was a passenger who was to have a huge impact on commercial aviation – one William E. Boeing. The US Post Office eventually got its mail airborne in May 1919, starting with trips from Chicago to Cleveland. By the beginning of 1921, it had completed its cross-country network – at a price. During the year nearly 45,000,000 letters were carried by air, but nine post office employees (eight pilots and one mechanic) were killed in the process.

The Post Office persevered, and in August 1923 began operating a night service between Chicago and Cheyenne, using high-powered searchlights to illuminate airfields on the route. The nighttime service was eventually expanded, using more searchlights as waypoint beacons, and by 1925 the transcontinental flight time had been reduced to around 35 hours, using a team of six pilots and aircraft. Dangerous or not, there was no shortage of pilots prepared to take on mail flying. Base pay was around double the average wage, with mileage payments on top taking some of the more experienced pilots up to around $8,000 – a considerable sum in the depression-hit mid-1920s.

LEFT: The Junkers F 13, which first flew on June 25 1919, was developed from a range of duralumin aircraft designed and flown in Germany during the First World War. The cabin carried four passengers – note the built-in stairs to assist with entry.

RIGHT: Airliners from France and Germany join those of Imperial Airways on the apron in front of Croydon's modern (1926) control tower and terminal, the world's first purpose-built international airport.

ABOVE: Robertson Aircraft Corporation was one of five American companies awarded mail contracts under the Kelly Act of 1925. In the cockpit the airline's chief pilot, Charles A. Lindbergh, waits to get started for the flight from St. Louis to Chicago.

Improvements in radio and weather forecasting enabled further advances in the service. Eventually, on February 2 1925 the Kelly Bill was passed, allowing the US Post Office to contract out its air mail services to private companies.

Though private companies carried the mail for nearly a decade, the US Army Air Corps had to be called in to take over the routes in February 1934 after allegations of collusion and favoritism resulted in a Senate committee being appointed. Heavy loss of life among US Army pilots resulted in the service being returned to private contract under stringent conditions by June.

In the early days of commercial transportation, little control was needed at airports. Things rapidly changed, however, and it fell to Tempelhof airport in Berlin to introduce the first form of air traffic control, which consisted of keeping arriving and departing aircraft on separate areas on the airfield. The main hazard to flying was still the weather, and the first British civil airline disaster was caused by fog when a Handley Page O/400 taking off from Cricklewood on December 14 1920 crashed into a tree and burst into flames.

By the end of 1920 air transport had taken off in a big way: Le Bourget was believed to be the busiest airport in the world, handling 7,000 passengers that year. Croydon, which had started life as a collection of huts and canvas hangars, now boasted a superb permanent terminal with the most modern facilities and was officially opened on March 31 1921. Hounslow, still essentially a collection of wartime buildings, eventually fell into disuse.

Air transport safety

Tragedy struck on April 7 1922 when the first air-to-air collision between two airliners occurred north of Paris – a DH.18 operated by new airline Daimler Airways collided in mist with a Farman Goliath belonging to Grands Express Aériens. All seven occupants of both aircraft were killed in the head-on collision. After the tragedy, new air corridors between the two cities were defined to keep the conflicting traffic well apart.

Another improvement came with the formation of the International Commission for Air Navigation (ICAN). In June 1924 ICAN inaugurated the first international meteorological service, enabling pilots to receive reports of weather conditions at their destination airfield as well as en route. The following year, a wireless station was opened near Orly to direct aircraft in flight on the 900-metre wave band. By 1929, direction finding using radio transmissions had been introduced, allowing navigators to plot their aircraft's position more accurately. In the USA, work resulted in research scientists being able to track aircraft in flight by wireless detection in 1930.

On the ground, airports sprang up everywhere. Newark airport was opened for commercial traffic on October 1 1928 and rapidly became the world's busiest airport, handling 28,000 flights a year by 1930. It was one of the first airports to use

runway lighting to assist pilots flying at night and boasted a 1,600 foot (488m) long tarmac runway. Development of North Beach Airport in New York, just eight miles (13km) from Manhattan, began in the mid-1930s; it was renamed La

Guardia after the city's forward-thinking aviation-minded mayor. In Europe, improvements were made to Le Bourget, Berlin and Croydon airports, and Gatwick aerodrome, handily situated next to the London-Brighton railway line, opened for airline business in 1936.

The Q-code system was introduced in April 1932 – a series of three-letter codes to enable pilots to receive and impart flight information quickly, even if they did not speak each other's language. Radio stations were installed all over the world, enabling pilots to navigate their way around. Radar detection was honed throughout the 1930s but was at the time seen to have only military application; early tests were carried out in utmost secrecy.

Flying for all was believed to be a distinct possibility after the First World War. Thousands of men had trained as pilots during the war and they would surely take up flying as a hobby when in "civvie street". Sadly, the economic situation that

prevailed post-War was to crush this dream. Dozens of aircraft companies had been placed in jeopardy at the end of the conflict, as the protagonists cancelled orders for aircraft wholesale. Light aviation in Europe was brought to its knees, again seen as the hobby of the better off.

Despite this rather gloomy outlook, there were some glimmers of hope. The *Daily Mail* newspaper, which prided itself in being at the forefront of aviation endeavor, encouraged light aircraft designers to build aircraft and compete for prizes. The Kings Cup was inaugurated in 1922, encouraging pilots to race against each other. There were prizes there, just for the taking. Aviators were encouraged to get together at meetings, and the first Aéro-Club de France rally was at Tillières on June 18 1922; 34 aircraft attended. The 1923 Lympne trials, held in October, attracted 27 entries in a series of competitions designed to find the best ultralight aircraft. Eventually, the British aircraft industry emerged from the doldrums and

ABOVE: Star of the 1925 Lympne light aircraft trials and a shape destined to become very familiar – the de Havilland DH.60 Moth.

TOP: French airliner design was typified by the Farman Goliath, such as F-MMY seen here at Croydon.

companies like Avro, Blackburn and de Havilland produced light aircraft for civil use. Perhaps most evocative of this era was the de Havilland Moth family; Moths of various marques were used by Amy Johnson, Alan Cobham and Lady Mary Bailey to set endurance records around the world. Best-known of the family was the DH.82A Tiger Moth, destined to be used in vast quantities for pilot training during the Second World War.

In the United States, with the depression just around the corner, barnstorming became the

RIGHT: Joe Campi attempts to extract himself from a straightjacket while suspended beneath a Curtiss Jenny. Always a tenuous occupation, during the early 1920s dozens of barnstormers were killed attempting spectacular stunt flying.

BELOW: Over 6,000 Curtiss Jennies were built during the First World War. Many found their way on to the second-hand market and were much in demand with flying schools and barnstorming outfits throughout North America.

order of the day for many who had served in the US Army Air Forces. Itinerant pilots would travel the country, putting on impromptu displays of stunt flying, in the hope of raising a few dollars to keep body, soul and aircraft together. It was a dangerous profession, however, for in the year 1923 alone 85 were killed and another 162 injured. Stunt flying was also in demand in the movie industry, which saw the benefit of educating the public about aviation, and many aviation-orientated films were produced. Some, like *Hell's Angels* and *Dawn Patrol*, have gone on

to become timeless classics.

The American public, however, was quick to see the benefits of air travel as a means of crossing the country, and flying was regarded as an occupation that all could participate in. As well as the many Curtiss Jenny trainers declared surplus at the end of the First World War and released for civilian ownership, companies such as Cessna and Beech were being set up to create aircraft for the growing band of enthusiastic amateur pilots.

The 1930s can be considered a classic period for light aviation, encompassing designs from such luminaries as Luscombe, Piper, Stinson and Waco. It fostered an interest in aviation that has remained undiminished: today the USA can boast an aircraft

population of more than 300,000.

Post-war, many governments saw aircraft as an easy way of maintaining contact with the outposts of their Empires. The French had lost no time in

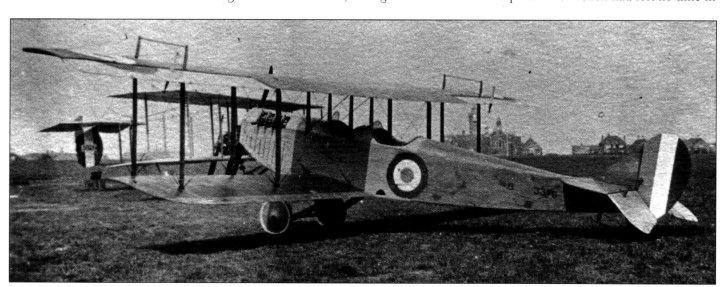

inaugurating flights to their African colonies, and in 1924 KLM began long-distance trial flights to their Dutch East Indies colony. The British Empire, covering around one quarter of the globe, presented its own problems: as well as the physical distance of Australia, Canada, South Africa, and India from the UK, the countries themselves were huge and transport around them posed difficulties, often exacerbated by the extreme weather conditions met there. Aircraft were also used for exploring then-uncharted territory, making ideal camera platforms for the infant science of aerial photography, and enabling government officials to cross huge swathes of inhospitable territory with relative ease.

As well as setting up attention-grabbing long-distance flights, aircraft were used for polar exploration. One of the first to realize the benefit of aircraft was the veteran Norwegian explorer Roald Amundsen, first man to the South Pole. On May 21 1925 he and a crew of five took off from

Spitzbergen to aim to be the first to fly over the North Pole, but poor weather forced their two Dornier Wal flying boats to land around 150 miles (240km) short of their goal. Amundsen did not return to Spitzbergen until July 16, having spent nearly a month building a runway on the ice for the return flight.

The following year, Amundsen was at Spitzbergen again, this time with an airship. Taking off on May 11 1926, the cross-polar flight of 2,485 miles (4.,000km) to Teller, Alaska, took 70 hours and marked the first crossing of the entire Arctic as well as the first airship visit. Amundsen was beaten to the accolade of being the first person to reach the North Pole by air by Lieutenant-Commander Richard Byrd of the US Navy, who had already made a name for himself as an arctic explorer. Taking off from Spitzbergen on May 9 in

the specially adapted Fokker F.VII-3m *Josephine Ford*, he orbited the Pole before turning to Spitzbergen at the end of a 16-hour flight. Two years later, Hubert Wilkins and Carl Ben Eielson made the first crossing of the Arctic by aeroplane, landing their Lockheed Vega at Spitzbergen on April 21 1928 after an eventful six-day journey, five days of which were spent on an island just five miles (8km) from Spitzbergen when they were forced down by storms. Not until 1951 would anyone succeed in crossing the Arctic solo.

Byrd, by now promoted to Commander, took on the South Pole in 1929, flying from Little America to become the first man to fly over both Poles. Using the Ford 4-AT Trimotor *Floyd Bennett* for this record, he dropped a stone from Bennett's (his partner on his Arctic flight) grave at the South Pole, wrapped in the American flag.

ABOVE: Byrd's Fokker F.VII-3m trimotor is prepared for take-off. Byrd became the first person to fly over the North Pole and later the South Pole.

TOP: Air-to-air refueling – 1929 style. Dale Jackson and Forrest O'Brien set a world record for longest endurance flight between July 13–30 1929.

RIGHT: The ungainly Armstrong-Whitworth Argosy entered service with Imperial Airways on July 1927 when G-EBLO *City of Birmingham* flew from Croydon to Paris.

By the middle of the 1920s, airliner construction was definitely entering its second generation. Gone were the small, cramped cabins of the immediate post-war years. Air travel was still mainly the preserve of the wealthy and, as they demanded comfort from cars and trains, so they demanded it from airliners. In-flight catering had begun in a small way with British Handley Page Transport's three-shilling (15 pence) picnic hamper and cabin heating had been introduced soon afterwards. German airlines went one further during 1925 and offered in-flight entertainment – airborne film shows. This was still the era of the silent movie and these suited airlines down to the ground, for nobody would have heard a soundtrack above the noise of the aircraft's engines.

BELOW: An Imperial Airways de Havilland DH.66 Hercules is refueled at Karachi. Imperial's seven Hercules were predominantly used on routes between Cairo and Karachi.

British-built second-generation airliners were still biplanes, but rather large ones for all that. Imperial Airways had been formed on April 1 1924 as an amalgamation of four smaller airlines:

Daimler, Instone, British Marine Air Navigation (BMAN) and Handley Page Transport. The British national airline, its role was seen as providing communication with the outposts of Empire, and its aircraft requirements were correspondingly different to other commercial companies. It was dominant in the market and government-backed, and so British manufacturers deferred to its requirements. As a rule, Imperial Airways' airliners were opulent but slow.

Two contemporary British airliners were the Armstrong Whitworth Argosy and de Havilland DH.66 Hercules. The three-engined Argosy was a typical Imperial aircraft – square and functional, with steel tube and fabric fuselage, and wood and fabric wings. It carried 20 passengers in its cabin and had a crew of two in an open cockpit (Imperial didn't believe in spoiling its aircrew). Large windows gave travelers a panoramic view of the countryside they were cruising over at the stately speed of 95mph (153km/h). The Argosy's range was around 330 miles (531km), ideal for Imperial's longer European routes. It was an extremely reliable machine, so much so in fact that Imperial ordered a further four to go with their original three. Entering in service in July

1926, the Argosy remained in use until the 1930s, when the six survivors were retired; one had been lost in a fatal accident in Belgium on March 28 1933.

The Hercules was intended for use further from home, specifically on the flights between Cairo and Karachi in the Middle East. The route had been added to Imperial's schedules at the behest of the government, which had used the RAF to fly communications in the area but came to the conclusion that it would be cheaper to offer a subsidy to the airline. The first of Imperial Airways' five Hercules entered service in December 1926 and proved sturdy and reliable. Seating seven passengers and carrying a hefty chunk of mail at a cruising speed of 110mph (177km/h), they had a long career. Four DH.66s had been bought by Australian Airways for use between Adelaide and Perth, and a further two acquired by Imperial to replace crashed examples to gave a production run of 11. The last two survivors were eventually chopped up in South Africa in 1943.

Handley Page's second-generation triumphs were the HP.42 and HP.45 airliners, distinctively shaped biplanes to say the least. Before they entered service they were obsolete by European standards but they suited Imperial Airways well. Eight were built – four HP.45s (designated HP.42W by the airline) for use on European routes, and four HP.42s (designated HP.42E) for Far Eastern routes. They entered service in 1931 and remained in use up to the outbreak of the Second World War, when the seven survivors were impressed for military use; the last was dismantled in 1941.

The activities of Imperial Airways in Great Britain were matched by other national airlines throughout the world. Deutsche Luft Hansa (DLH), flagbearer for Germany, was formed on January 6 1926 as the last step in a chain of mergers. Its two main components were Deutscher Aero Lloyd and Junkers Luftverkehr

and by the time it began operating under its own name on April 6 it had more than 100 aircraft in its fleet, including Dornier flying boats for services over water. DLH (which dropped the "Deutsche" from its name on January 1 1934) began expanding services immediately, adding new destinations all over Europe, many in partnership with other airlines.

The US spreads its wings

The first American international airline was Aeromarine Airways, which started services from Key West, Florida to Havana, Cuba on November 1 1919. In the United States, no operator was able to claim to be the national airline and fierce competition saw companies come and go with regularity. Some aircraft manufacturers had their own airlines, of which Boeing became the strongest, also including enginemakers Pratt and Whitney and aircraft manufacturers Chance Vought in a massive empire that included Hamilton, Standard, Sikorsky and United Air Lines.

One of the biggest American airlines was Pan American Airways (Pan Am), which was formed on March 14 1927 and nearly didn't make it to the

ABOVE: The last word in luxury – the ladies' cabin aboard Imperial Airways' Handley Page HP.42 G-AAGX Hannibal. The HP.42 entered service in November 1931 and remained in use until the outbreak of the Second World War.

TOP: Flying the flag around the Empire: HP.42 G-AAGX makes a stop-over for fuel and mail at Entebbe, Uganda. While the Hercules operated in Asia, the HP.42s were used on routes in Africa.

RIGHT: The world's first airline stewardesses were employed by United Air Lines in the spring of 1930, for $125 a month.

BELOW: Imperial Airways Short S.8 Calcutta G-EBVG visited the Thames for three days in August 1928 to enable Members of Parliament to inspect the aircraft.

end of the year, coming within an ace of having its mail contract to Cuba rescinded and its $25,000 deposit confiscated. Disaster was averted at the last minute and Pan Am's reputation was saved. The airline was taken over by charismatic Juan Trippe in June 1928 and eventually became a massive force in international airline transport before descending into bankruptcy and ceasing operations in December 1991. Pan Am's competition included American Airlines, which was created by the merger of no fewer than 12 small independent airlines in 1930, and United Air Lines, the latter being the first airline to introduce female flight attendants in a (then) daring move in May 1930. Its early stewardesses were all nurses. Transcontinental and Western Air (TWA) was another product of a series of mergers and was officially formed in July 1930. Fourth of the "big four" American airlines was Eastern, created in January 1930.

Swissair, the national airline of Switzerland, also came into being as the result of a merger, this time between Balair and Ad Astra, though it had a rather smaller fleet of aircraft: six Fokker F.VIIbs. Despite its size it was at the forefront of aviation development and in 1934 it became the first European airline to employ air stewardesses. Aeroflot, the massive Soviet Union airline, was created in 1932 and immediately became the world's largest civil aviation operator, tasked with duties such as firefighting, pipeline patrol, surveying, aerial photography, cropdusting and ambulance work as well as the more mundane carriage of passengers. The French state airline Air France was officially launched on October 31 1933, again as the result of a series of amalgamations and takeovers, principally of Air Orient, Air Union, CIDNA and SGTA. As a result Air France's fleet at inception consisted of 259 aircraft of no fewer than 35 different types!

Overwater operations

Acting in consort with Imperial Airways' long-range airliners was its fleet of flying boats. Airliners

were fine for crossing long stretches of desert and jungle, but overwater operations demanded flying boats. Shorts, based on the River Medway at Rochester and the oldest British aviation company, was preferred by Imperial Airways for much of its flying boat fleet; their *Singapore* was the first commercial flying boat to enter airline service. Other designs such as the *Calcutta* followed, culminating with the 'C' Class Empire flying boats of 1936. Carrying 17 passengers and 2 tons of mail, they were the last word in refinement and enabled Imperial to improve journey times to destinations' such as Egypt, South Africa, India, Malaya and Australia. Extra fuel tanks saw services to Canada added to the network in 1937. Shorts also produced the unique Short-Mayo *Mercury/Maia* composite flying boat for Imperial; the small *Mercury* mailplane being launched from the top of the larger *Maia* in flight; the mailplane could be loaded up well past its own maximum take-off weight. In this configuration, *Mercury* had a range of more than 6,000 miles (9,656km).

Pan Am also followed the flying boat route to service its Latin and South American routes; the Sikorsky S-42 was designed specifically to Pan Am's requirements. Martin M-130s were also used on Pacific airmail routes from 1935 onwards, covering over 8,000 miles (12,875km) in four days. Passenger services to the Philippines began in October 1936, and in June 1937 Pan Am teamed up with Imperial Airways to offer services from Bermuda to New York. Pan Am and Imperial also began discussions regarding flights from the USA to Europe. Pan Am's Boeing 314 flying boat *Yankee Clipper* made the first passenger-carrying flight on May 20 1939, taking three days. Imperial's service began in August, using Short S.30 flying boats, by which time Imperial was close to being consigned to history – a merger between it and smaller British Airways created the British Overseas Airways Corporation (BOAC) which came into being that November. By that time, however, Adolf Hitler had rather upset the schedules.

In Germany, Junkers had followed up its smart

F 13 with a whole series of corrugated airliners, progressing in size through the 16-passenger G31 to the W33 and W34, replacements for the F 13. Both proved popular and Junkers turned out 199 of the W34 and no fewer than 1,791 W34s, including several as light bombers. Fokker, building on its F VII success, continued to increase the size and performance of its trimotors and concentrated much of its efforts in setting up American production lines, where it correctly foresaw the largest market for airliners. Its 32-passenger F 32, for example, used four Pratt & Whitney Hornet radials mounted in pairs on the main undercarriage legs to give two tractor and two pusher powerplants. Although it was not a great success due to overheating engines, the F 32 did feature a rudimentary form of sound proofing, with balsa wood stuffed into the fuselage walls. Fokker's influence in the airliner market was eventually to decline as the company clung to its high-wing layouts. Junkers, meanwhile, went from strength to

ABOVE: Pan American Airways System rapidly became the United States' major intercontinental operator, using flying boats to transport passengers and mail on its South American routes. The Sikorsky S-42 entered service in August 1934.

LEFT: Pan American began non-stop transatlantic mail services on May 20 1939 using Boeing 314 Clipper flying boats.

ABOVE: The Junkers Ju 52/3m marked the pinnacle of Junkers' commercial airliner success and was used by more than 30 airlines on both sides of the Atlantic.

BELOW: Henry Ford acquired the Stout Metal Airline Company in 1925; the following year the Ford 4-AT Trimotor appeared, followed in 1928 by the improved 5-AT shown.

strength and was shortly to produce the Ju 52, a classic among airliners. First it had to suffer the ignominy of its giant G 38, a four-engined monster of which only two were built in 1929-30.

Like the Fokker F VII, the Junkers Ju 52 initially appeared as a single-engined airliner. Of conventional layout, it was built of Junkers' trademark corrugated duralumin. Power for the first six examples was provided by the 725hp (541kW) BMW VIIA inline engine, but the seventh was fitted with a BMW 132 license-production version of the Pratt & Whitney Hornet, and the eighth aircraft was fitted out as a trimotor. The first trimotor made its maiden flight in April 1931 and entered service with Lloyd Aereo Boliviano in early 1932. The Ju 52 remained in production throughout the war, and in service much longer. Several examples are still airworthy today.

In the USA, airliner production was much more of a piecemeal affair, and it was not until the automotive genius Henry Ford got involved in the aircraft manufacturing business that the Americans had a successful airliner they could call their own. Ford, recognizing that aviation was an up and coming market, bought out the Stout Metal Airplane Company to diversify his interests. The Ford 3-AT wasn't a success, but the 4-AT proved a versatile aircraft, representing as it did the marriage of Fokker's trimotor technology with Junkers' metal construction combined with the newly developed Pratt & Whitney Wasp radial engine. Built on a production line, the 4-AT initially entered service with Ford's own airline, but was soon in use with airlines the length and breadth of the country. A total of 78 4-ATs was produced, followed up by 116 larger 5-ATs. Even today the Ford Trimotor earns its keep, mainly on tourist flights.

Arguably the world's most successful airliner producer, Boeing entered the field in July 1927 with the Boeing 40, also powered by the Wasp. Used for mail flights, the Model 40 would also carry two passengers; the improved Model 40B carried three. A total of 82 was built, a modest start to a company that could later claim

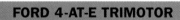

FORD 4-AT-E TRIMOTOR

Wingspan	74ft 0in (22.56m)
Length	49ft 10in (15.19m)
Powerplants	3 Wright Whirlwinds rated at 300hp (224kW);
Passenger capacity	11
Maximum speed	130mph (209km/h)
Range	570 miles (917km)
Date of entry into service	1926
Number built	78

JUNKERS Ju 52/3m

Wingspan	95ft 11.5in (29.25m)
Length	92ft 0in (28.04m)
Powerplants	3 BMW 132A-1s rated between 600hp and 830hp (447kW and 619kW); other powerplants were also used
Passenger capacity	Up to 17
Maximum speed	180mph (290km/h)
Range	795 miles (1,279km)
Date of entry into service	1932
Number built	At least 4, 845

the runway at Roosevelt Field, New York. His heavily overloaded Sikorsky S-35 failed to get airborne and, in the attempt to abort, Fonck escaped, but two of the four-man crew were killed in the ensuing fireball.

Fonck's disaster did not deter others. During 1927, no fewer than 24 attempts were made, starting with Davis in his Keystone on April 26, again with tragic results: he and co-pilot Stanton Wooster crashed on take-off from Langley Field, Virginia, and were killed instantly. Two weeks later on May 8 Charles Nungesser and François Coli took off from Le Bourget in their Levasseur PL-8 White Bird. Reported off Ireland at

BELOW: Charles A. Lindbergh's Spirit of St Louis. When the Ryan NYP (New York–Paris) touched down at Le Bourget on the evening of May 21 1927, he had flown 3,614 miles (5,816km) in 33 and a half hours and was $25,000 richer.

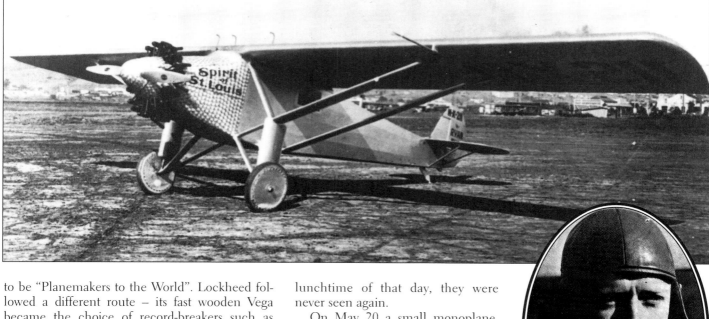

to be "Planemakers to the World". Lockheed followed a different route – its fast wooden Vega became the choice of record-breakers such as Wiley Post, Ruth Nichols and Amelia Earhart. But though both Boeing 40 and Lockheed Vega were fast they had one drawback – neither was particularly large.

New York–Paris competition

The mid-1920s witnessed many long-distance flights as previously inaccessible parts of the globe were opened up. Although the Atlantic had been crossed by Alcock and Brown in 1919, by the mid-1920s no solo effort had succeeded. As a natural barrier between two halves of the civilized world, it was ripe for crossing. A prize of $25,000 had already been offered for the first non-stop flight between Paris and New York by hotelier Raymond Orteig. The race really got underway in the summer of 1926. One of the first serious contenders was Richard Byrd, fresh from his success over the North Pole, while Noel Davis announced plans to make the trip in a modified Keystone biplane bomber. Not to be outdone, French war hero Charles Nungesser announced that he too would attempt the journey, starting from the eastern side of the Atlantic. As it turned out, another French war hero, René Fonck, was first away. Unfortunately, he got no further than the end of

lunchtime of that day, they were never seen again.

On May 20 a small monoplane took off from Roosevelt Field, New York, bound for Paris. On board the Ryan NYP (New York–Paris) monoplane was 2,700 pounds (1,225 kg) of fuel, and Charles A. Lindbergh. A reserve officer in the US Army and a pioneer of Robertson Aircraft Corporation's air mail service, Lindbergh was confident that he would be able to make the flight which had already killed so many. His aircraft had been designed specially for the attempt – the only unknown quantity was himself. Thirty-three hours, 30 minutes and 29.8 seconds after leaving Roosevelt Field, the NYP came down on the grass at Le Bourget to make Lindbergh the 92nd person to cross the Atlantic by air, but the first to do it solo.

Once Lindbergh had broken the ground, the Atlantic lost some of its mystery. Two weeks later Clarence Chamberlain and Charles Levine crossed in a Bellanca and Richard Byrd's Fokker C-2 made the trip on June 29. But it was still a dangerous undertaking; of the 24 attempts in 1927, only five were successful. Meanwhile, the French were attacking the South Atlantic successfully – Costes and Bellonte's Breguet XIXGR Nungesser et Coli crossed from Senegal to Brazil

ABOVE: Lindbergh (1902–1974) became a national hero overnight in 1927 and spent his entire career in aviation. Initially a barnstormer, he later flew the US mail and, after his transatlantic flight, became a consultant with Pan American Airlines.

RIGHT: The honor of being first across the Pacific Ocean fell to Australians. In front of their Fokker F.VIIb-3m are (left to right) navigator Harry Lyon, pilots Charles Ulm and Charles Kingsford Smith and radio operator James Warner.

RIGHT: Amelia Earhart's eventual fate remains a mystery. The first woman to fly solo across the Atlantic and from California to Hawaii, she and co-pilot Fred Noonan went missing over the Pacific on July 2 1937, during an attempted circumnavigation of the world.

on October 15 and in 1930 the pair made the first direct east-west crossing of the Atlantic. The first woman to fly across the Atlantic was arguably the United States' best-known female aviator – Amelia Earhart, part of a three-person crew that landed a Fokker F.VIIb-3m at Barry, South Glamorgan, on June 18 1928 after a 24-hour crossing from Newfoundland.

On the other side of the world, two Australian pilots were setting about the Pacific Ocean.

Charles Kingsford Smith and Charles Ulm were first to complete a Pacific crossing, again in a Fokker F.VIIb-3m. Taking off from San Francisco on May 31 1928, they made stops at Hawaii and Fiji during the ten-day, 7,316 mile (11,774km) flight to Brisbane. In September, they claimed another first when they, along with a navigator and radio operator, crossed the Tasman Sea between Australia and New Zealand in treacherous weather conditions.

Britain's favorite airwoman, Amy Johnson was catapulted to fame in 1930. Taking off from Croydon on May 3 in a DH.60 Moth, she arrived at Darwin on the 24th to become the first woman to fly to Australia, collecting a £10,000 prize from the *Daily Mail* in the process. Having captured the hearts of the British public, Amy Johnson went on to achieve other records, flying to Tokyo the following year, and (with husband Jim Mollison) took part in the historic England-Australia air race in 1934, retiring in India. Her next epic flight was a return trip from London to Cape Town in just over three days during May 1936, using a Percival Gull. After the outbreak of the Second World War, Amy Johnson joined the Air Transport Auxiliary, ferrying aircraft from manufacturers to front-line units, but was killed when the Airspeed Oxford she was flying ran out of fuel over the Thames Estuary on January 5 1941.

Amy's biggest rival in the eyes of the British public was Jean Batten, a New Zealander who beat Amy's England-Australia time by four days in May 1934. Also flying a Moth, Jean Batten later switched to a Percival Gull Six for a new England-Brazil record in November 1935 and used the aircraft, named *Jean* on her record-breaking England-New Zealand record in October 1936. Unlike so many record-breakers of the age, Jean Batten survived to reach old age.

Lockheed around the world

With the Pacific and Atlantic Ocean conquered, the next logical step was to circumnavigate the globe. First to take the honors was Wiley Post, flying a Lockheed Vega. Post, accompanied by Harold Gatty, departed from Roosevelt Field, New York, on June 23 1931 on the first leg of a flight that took in the UK, Germany and the entire breadth of the Soviet Union before crossing to Alaska and home through Canada and the mainland USA. The 15,474-mile (24,903km) trip took 8 days, 15 hours and 51 minutes to accomplish, slicing nearly 168 days off the previous round-the-world record set in 1924 by the US Army Air Service's Douglas World Cruisers. In 1933 Post repeated the feat in a solo circumnavigation. Sadly, he was to lose his life in an aircraft accident in Alaska on August 15 1935 when his seaplane's float hit the surface of a frozen lake. Less than three months later, Charles Kingsford Smith went missing while flying from India to Singapore.

The Lockheed Vega was also the favorite mount of Amelia Earhart for her early record-breaking flights – she became the first woman to cross the Atlantic solo in one on May 20-21 1932 and the first woman to cross the USA non-stop in the same aircraft that August. By 1935, she had turned her attentions to the Pacific and became the first woman to fly solo from Hawaii to San Francisco on January 12, 1935. A round-the-world attempt using a Lockheed Electra ended after a tire blew-out on take-off from Honolulu on March 20 1937. Her second attempt that summer culminated in the aircraft's disappearance over the Pacific Ocean in July 1937, shrouding her eventual fate in mystery.

Howard Hughes, director of the classic film *Hell's Angels*, had the money to develop his own aircraft thanks to inherited wealth. His H-1 racer smashed the world speed record six times in a

single day during September 1935, taking it to 352.38mph (567km/h) before it crashed into a field, fortunately without injury to Hughes himself. He was not averse to using other manufacturers' aircraft, though – on January 14 1936 he set a new USA coast-to-coast record of 9 hours 26 minutes and 10 seconds using a Northrop Gamma. On February 19 1937, back in his repaired H-1, he lowered it further to just under 7½ hours. Hughes was eventually to smash the round-the-world record set by Wiley Post to 3 days 19 hours and 8 minutes, this time with a Lockheed 14N Super Electra. Hughes' fascination with aircraft continued and culminated in the *Spruce Goose*, which made just one flight in November 1947. His aviation interests also included ownership of TWA.

While airliners were being developed apace, interest in airships had waned a little. The Royal Air Force had been experimenting with aircraft launches from airships, and the US Navy and French Army also maintained small fleets. The

ABOVE: Lockheed's chief test pilot Wiley Post (right) and Harold Gatty pose alongside the Lockheed Vega *Winnie Mae* after completing a record-breaking flight around the Northern hemisphere.

BELOW: Britain's pin-up girl of the 1930s was Amy Johnson, a secretary who took flying lessons, bought herself a de Havilland DH.60 Moth and became the first woman to fly solo to Australia.

ABOVE: The Vickers
R.100 was the last
pre-war British
airship. It first flew
in December 1929
and flew to Canada
in 1930, crossing
the Canadian coast
on July 31.

BELOW: The world's
largest airship, the
LZ 129 *Hindenburg*
joined the LZ 127
Graf Zeppelin in
service across the
Atlantic Ocean; the
journey took around
four days.

big drawback with airships was the gas used to
inflate them: the French airship *Dixmunde* (an
appropriated Zeppelin taken as war reparation)
was lost with 52 crew in December 1923 over the
Mediterranean, probably as the result of an
explosion. The US Navy's *Shenandoah* went
down in a violent storm on September 3 1925
with the loss of 29 of its crew, breaking up as a
result of the forces exerted by the weather.
Shenandoah was unusual for its time, being filled
with non-explosive helium rather than the more
usual – and highly flammable – hydrogen.
Germany, at the forefront of airship technology
before the First World War, continued to produce dirigibles, and the 775 foot (236m)-long
Graf Zeppelin, at the time the world's largest airship, went into service during 1928 and started
services between Friedrichshafen and Lakehurst,
New Jersey, that October. *Graf Zeppelin* went on
to become the first airship to circumnavigate
the world in August 1929, completing the
21,150 mile (34,038km) flight in an impressive
21 days; flying time was 12 days 12 hours and 40
minutes to give an average speed of 70.23mph
(113km/h).

Demise of commercial airships

Britain's answers to the *Graf Zeppelin* were two
equally massive airships. Though they were sister
ships, the R.100 and R.101 were built by two different companies, the former by Vickers using
private funding and the latter by the government-
funded Royal Airship Works. The R.101 left
Cardington on a proving flight to Egypt and India
on October 4 1930 but got no further than
Beauvais in northern France before disaster
struck. The airship had been struggling against an
engine problem and poor weather conditions
when it dived into the ground, killing 48 of its 54
passengers and crew in the worst British aviation
disaster to that date. Among the dead were the
Secretary of State for Air, Lord Thomson, and
Director of Civil Aviation, Sir Sefton Brancker,
who had been responsible for much of Britain's
post-war aviation development. The demise of the
R.101 sounded the death knell for the R.100,
which had been flying since December 1929 and
had performed without fault, thereby ending
Britain's flirtation with airships for half a century.

German airship development reached its
zenith with LZ.129 *Hindenburg*, an 803.8ft

(245m) long monster which made its first flight on March 4 1936. After shake-down trials it embarked on a series of flag-waving publicity flights before beginning transatlantic services on May 6, flying from Friedrichshafen to Lakehurst in around two and a half days. *Hindenburg* met a fiery end at Lakehurst on May 6 1937, its hydrogen gas exploding while coming in to moor and killing 36 of the 97 passengers and crew. Commercial airship operations were over for the foreseeable future.

By the mid-1930s, the American market for "larger" airliners had been effectively shaken up by two companies that went on to be giants in the field: Boeing and Douglas. First into service was the Boeing Model 247, which made its first flight on July 1 1933. The unique DC-1 was delivered to TWA in December and an improved 14-seat DC-2 was put into service the following May. As far as its passengers were concerned, it had one major advantage over the Boeing 247 – no wing spar to negotiate in the cabin! Determined to keep up with the forefront of technology, American Airlines approached Douglas for an enlarged version of the DC-2 to accommodate sleeping berths, and the Douglas Sleeper Transport was born. First flown on December 17 1935, the day version of the DST was to become the world's most popular airliner – the DC-3. Its popularity was such that by the outbreak of the Second World War it was estimated that nearly 90 per cent of the world's airliner passengers flew in DC-3s.

BELOW: The *Hindenburg* meets a fiery end at Lakehurst, New Jersey, on May 6 1937. Thirty-six passengers and crew lost their lives in the conflagration.

on February 8 1933. It entered service just one month later with United Air Lines. A derivative of the company's successful B-9 bomber, 75 were built, all but five being for United. Almost immediately it made a coast-to-coast crossing of the USA in 19¾ hours, knocking more than 6 hours off the time offered by TWA's Ford Trimotors. Other refinements for its 10 passengers included air conditioning, soundproofing, reading lights and a toilet. The Boeing 247 also pioneered in-flight de-icing and at the end of its career, the RAF's sole example became the first aircraft to make a true blind landing.

As Boeing's production line was taken up for many months to come, when TWA wanted new aircraft it was forced to look elsewhere. Accordingly, it turned to Douglas Aircraft. The result of this partnership was the 12-seat Douglas Commercial 1 or DC-1, first flown

While the larger Boeing and Douglas airliners were plying their trades, other manufacturers still found a ready market. In the USA Lockheed produced a series of twin-engined high-speed

LEFT: The 1934 Douglas DC-2, which cruised at 170mph (272km/h) and carried 14 passengers.

Wingspan	95ft 0in (28.96m)
Length	64ft 6in (19.66m)
Powerplants	2 Wright Cyclones or 2 P&W Twin Wasp rated between 1000 and 1200hp (746 & 895kW) on take off
Passenger capacity	32 maximum
Maximum speed	230mph (370km/h)
Range	2,125 miles (3,420km)
Date of entry into service	25 June 1936
Number built	10,654 by Douglas plus at least 2,485 under license production in Japan and the Soviet Union

ABOVE: Douglas DC-3 G-AMPY has had a typically checkered career: built for service in World War II, it was later sold to the civilian market and has earned its keep ever since.

RIGHT: Only ten Boeing 307 Stratoliners were built: four for Pan Am, five for TWA and one for Howard Hughes. It was the first airliner with a pressurized interior, and led indirectly to the Stratocruiser.

Electras, and Curtiss, which had been producing biplanes such as the T-32 Condor, came up with the CW-20 in 1940. On the other side of the Atlantic de Havilland introduced the DH.84 Dragon and DH.86 Express, both of which featured the graceful de Havilland lines and became popular feederliners. Germany's airliner aspirations were tempered by their clandestine need to serve more nefarious purposes. The Dornier Do 17, for example, was an unsuccessful airliner design before it became an extremely successful bomber, and the same can be said for the Junkers Ju 86 and Heinkel He 111. In Russia, Tupolev tended to go for larger aircraft, culminating in the ill-fated ANT-20 Maxim Gorki, which would have carried 80 passengers had it not been destroyed in an air-to-air collision in 1935.

The next logical step for American manufacturers was to increase the range and size of their products. Douglas and United Air Lines got together in 1935 to put ideas on paper for an airliner that would have twice the capacity of the soon-to-appear DC-3. Developmental costs were high and it was not until March 1936 that the finance was raised; five of the largest airlines each contributing $100,000 to the development of what eventually appeared as the DC-4E. When the aircraft was finally completed in May 1938 the design brief had undergone many changes, and when the resulting aircraft entered service the following year it was not what United Air Lines actually wanted. Sold on to Japan, it was dismantled by Nakajima and formed the basis of the company's G5N1 Shinzan heavy bomber.

Boeing's answer to the four-engine quandary was the Boeing 307 Stratoliner, partly financed by Pan American and TWA after they had withdrawn support from the DC-4E. Entering service in July 1940, only ten had been built by the time the USA entered the Second World War and all were commandeered for military service. Despite its small numbers and short service period, the Stratoliner was considered a success and formed the basis of Boeing's post-war 377 Stratocruiser.

In Europe, the three main four-engined airliners were built by Armstrong Whitworth, de

Havilland and Focke Wulf. The high-wing AW.27 Ensign and sleek low-wing DH.91 Albatross and Fw 200 were all eyecatchers. The Ensign, which entered service in 1938, was slowest of the three with a top speed of 208mph (335km/h), while the wooden DH.91 could reach 225mph (362km/h) and the Fw 200 was fastest of all at 261mph (420km/h). None was built in any great quantity, although the Condor in its military guise earned itself the epithet "The Scourge of the Atlantic", its long range enabling it to prey on naval convoys far out in the Atlantic Ocean. The outbreak of the Second World War effectively ended airliner development in Europe and it was not until the closing stages of that conflict that thoughts turned to post-war civilian transport.

Wartime airliners

Throughout the war, airlines continued to operate on a low-key level. BOAC flew at night to neutral countries such as Sweden, performing vital courier tasks. In the United States, airlines continued to offer services the length and breadth of the country. Long-distance routes were flown by airlines such as QANTAS, which operated what was then the longest non-stop scheduled service in the world, flying over 3,500 miles (5,600km) from Perth in Western Australia to Colombo in Ceylon (now Sri Lanka). The journey took an average of 27 hours in the airline's Catalina flying boats and was used mainly for mail – few passengers had the stamina to attempt it! When the Catalinas were superceded by Liberators, the flight time came down to a mere 17 hours, and a stop was added at Exmouth Gulf, some 600 miles (960km) from Perth.

Lockheed's graceful Constellation, originally designed for TWA, actually entered service not with the airline but with the US Army Air Force, serving as a troop carrier. Post-war, it reverted to its

civilian duties, remaining in service with some airlines until the mid-1970s. TWA got its own Constellations in 1944 and immediately set about reducing the transcontinental crossing time from the 13 hours 40 minutes it took using Stratoliners to around seven hours.

The D-Day invasion of France on June 6 1944 opened up a real possibility of international air travel in Europe, and it was not long before British airlines began to operate once again, mainly using pre-war aircraft types such as the DH.84 Dragon and DC-3 Dakota. On the other side of the conflict, Lufthansa was kept busy serving outposts of German occupied territories and neutral countries; it was forced to stop operating only on May 5 1945, just three days before VE-Day.

Although civil aviation took a back seat during the Second World War, its development at the end of the conflict was still given some consideration. In Britain, a committee was formed on December 23 1942 under the chairmanship of Lord Brabazon of Tara to consider the country's needs for civil aircraft in the post-war period.

While the Brabazon committee discussed and planned brand new airliner designs, aircraft had to

ABOVE: The Boeing Stratocruiser, developed from the wartime Boeing B-29 Superfortress, entered service with Pan Am in April 1949, BOAC's 17 aircraft, delivered from the end of 1949 onwards, were withdrawn from service at the end of 1958.

LEFT: BOAC Stratocruiser G-AKGH *Caledonia* descends to land at Heathrow at night using an instrument landing system (ILS), thanks to improvements in air traffic control and radar.

RIGHT: Post-War, airliners were urgently needed as air transport grew. One temporary solution was the conversion of bombers, such as the Avro Lancaster. Lancastrian G-AGMD flew with BOAC and carries the airline's "speedwing" logo on its nose.

opened for business on January 1 1946; on the same day it was announced that British European Airways (BEA) would emerge from under the wing of BOAC that summer.

For manufacturers, "bigger is better" were the keywords to the immediate post-war period in both military and civil projects. The Lockheed Constitution, planned before the war but shelved for the duration of the conflict, first flew on November 9 1946 and was capable of carrying 200 passengers. Biggest of all was the Hughes H-4 Hercules. Nicknamed the *Spruce Goose*, it made just one hop and covered around one mile on November 2 1947 – it never flew again. Equally unsuccessful was the Saunders-Roe *Princess* flying boat. Though it made many flights, the largest all-metal aircraft in the world at the time never went into service, being obsolete before it ever got off the water on its maiden flight on August 21 1952.

The first fruits of the Brabazon committee's deliberations appeared on September 25 1945 in the shape of the de Havilland DH.104 Dove, a small twin-engined airliner intended to replace the Dragon Rapide. Seating eight passengers, the

ABOVE: The graceful Lockheed Constellation was built in response to a 1939 request by TWA but USAAF was first to put the type into service. L-749 N91207 was delivered to TWA in June 1948.

be found to fill immediate requirements. Smaller aircraft such as the Lockheed Electra and transport aircraft like the DC-3 were one answer; another was the conversion of redundant bombers for passenger duties. Avro Lancastrians, converted from Lancasters, went into service with BOAC immediately after the war, flying as far afield as Australia and South America; the airline also made good use of seaplanes such as the Short Sunderland. A third option was the production of aircraft using parts from bombers, typified by the Vickers Viking. Scheduled transatlantic flights by landplanes, unheard of before the war, began in October 1945, flown by ex-military C-54s of American Overseas Airlines. TWA's Constellations began scheduled services to Paris at the beginning of 1946 and Heathrow Airport officially

Dove initially met with some opposition as it was more expensive to purchase and operate in a market that relied on low overheads keeping companies solvent, but eventually 542 were produced over a 23-year period. A less successful committee product was the Bristol Brabazon; aimed at carrying 100 passengers over the Atlantic, it was already obsolete when the first prototype made its maiden flight on September 4 1949. Only two were built.

The committee had more success with the Vickers Viscount, aimed at the medium-range route; the prototype first flew on July 16 1948. Vickers believed that turbine-engined airliners offered greater promise than a pure jet type in the closing years of the Second World War and as a business decision this was to prove sensible for 445 Viscounts and 43 of its Vanguard successors were

eventually built and it was the only one of all the new aircraft designs to appear as a result of the Brabazon committee's deliberations to sell well in the United States. It also offered growth potential and the last Series 800 aircraft carried 65 passengers, double the prototype's 32. The Viscount entered service with BEA on July 29 1950. That flight, from Heathrow to Paris, was the world's first scheduled commercial passenger service using a turbine-engined aircraft.

One aircraft category considered but discarded by the Brabazon committee on account of its role being filled adequately by the Lockheed Constellation was that of an airliner in the 100,000lb ((45,360kg) class. Post-war, BOAC required an aircraft roughly to this specification and contacted Bristol, which suggested the purchase and conversion of a number of Constellations. Horrified at the potential expenditure, the Treasury refused to countenance such a move, and so Bristol began work on an aircraft design to fill the gap. The result was the Bristol 175 Britannia, a medium-range turboprop airliner which first flew on August 16 1952. After a long

and tortuous testing programme, the Britannia entered service with BOAC on February 1 1957, initially flying to Johannesburg and later to Sydney. Rights to license production were granted to Canadair, which produced the design as the CL-28 Argus for the Royal Canadian Air Force and the CL-44 for both military and civilian use; the latter's tail unit swung open to allow freight to be easily loaded.

The Brabazon committee's greatest technological success was the DH.106 Comet, built by de Havilland at Hatfield. When it first flew on July 27 1949 it made history as the world's first jet airliner. Relatively small – the Comet 1 seated only 36 passengers – it set several records while undergoing testing. The privilege of operating the world's first jet airliner service fell to BOAC, which started with freight flights to South Africa in January 1952. Passenger-carrying flights began on May 2 1952 with a service to Johannesburg, reducing the journey time by half. European and Commonwealth airlines lined up to buy the Comet and its future looked assured.

Then disaster struck. In a twelve-month period

ABOVE: The Vickers Viscount, the world's first turbine-engined passenger aircraft, was built in quantity and broke into the American market, a major challenge for European manufacturers.

BELOW: Proving that bigger isn't necessarily better, the Hughes H-4 Hercules makes it maiden flight on November 2 1947. It never flew again.

ABOVE: The world's first jet airliner, DH.106 Comet, was first flown on July 27 1949. It's early career was blighted by metal fatigue, then very much an unknown quantity.

BELOW: The world's most popular jet airliner, the prototype Boeing 737 took to the skies on April 9 1967. Thirty years later it's still going strong.

between May 1953 and April 1954 three BOAC Comets were lost in mysterious circumstances. All the Comets were grounded while intensive investigations into the crashes were carried out. Using the salvaged remains of one of the lost aircraft and four complete aircraft, aircraft accident investigators were able to pinpoint the problem. During flight one corner of the ADF window had failed, depressurizing the aircraft and causing it to rip open in flight like a tin can. The Comet 1's square windows, coupled with buffeting from the exhausts of its engines, were to blame. Though the Comet 1's career came to an abrupt end, the design itself, suitably modified, was reasonably successful and a total of 115 airframes was completed, the last two becoming prototype Nimrod maritime patrol aircraft. The Nimrod is just about to undergo a new "facelift", which will see it remain in service until the year 2025.

De Havilland's loss was Boeing's gain. The big American manufacturer had chalked up success

DOUGLAS DC-8

Wingspan	142ft 5in (43.41m)
Length	187ft 4in (57.10m)
Powerplants	4 Pratt & Whitney JT3D rated at 18,000 – 19,000lb (80.1 – 84.5kN) thrust
Passenger capacity	259
Maximum speed	529mph (851km/h)
Range	5,755 miles (9,262km)
Date of entry into service	September 1959
Number built	556 of all models

Data generally applies to the DC-8-61

with its Stratoliner family post-war, but needed something new to catapult it back into supremacy. Boeing had gained useful experience with its B-47 Stratojet program for the United States Air Force, and it was able to apply the lessons it had learned to the new Boeing 367-80, so designated to mislead the competition into thinking it was a variant of the C-97/377 Stratocruiser. Boeing's privately funded gamble paid off on July 15 1954 when the prototype, N70700, first flew from the company's Renton, Washington, airfield. The swept-wing airliner was an immediate success – the prototype reached speeds of up to 600mph (960km/h) in testing, the United States Air Force ordered examples for use as aerial tankers and on October 13 1955 Boeing was able to announce the largest order for a civil aircraft at that time: $296 million from Pan American Airways. From that moment onwards, Boeing began to dominate the jet airline market, later adding the three-engined Boeing 727 and twin-engined Boeing 737 – the world's most popular airliner with over 3,600 ordered and still going strong – to its range. By June 6 1967 Boeing had delivered 1,000 jet airliners of all models, and by January 1996 had passed the 8,000 mark. Deliveries for 1997 were about 340, or nearly one aircraft per day.

Boeing didn't have the market to itself, however. Douglas Aircraft, with a long tradition of producing outstanding airliners, countered with the superficially similar DC-8. Caught a little on the hop, Douglas opted to ascertain what the airlines wanted and then go straight into production rather than build a prototype, and the first aircraft first flew on May 30 1958. The early DC-8s later gave way to stretched examples. And eventually 556 DC-8s of all models were sold between 1958 and 1972. Douglas followed up the DC-8 with the medium-range DC-9 competitor to the Boeing 737, which found favor worldwide with airlines and continues in production today, albeit in the state-of-the-art MD-90 series. Convair, building on the success of its Model 240, 340 and 440 medium-range turboprops, first flew the jet-powered 880 on January 27 1959 but built only 65, followed by 38 of the model 990 Coronado.

World-wide competition

While Western companies were competing for orders from the burgeoning airlines, behind the Iron Curtain it was a completely different story. The Soviet Union was able to keep up with the West thanks to a variety of methods – these included pirating parts of aircraft supplied during the Second World War, such as the B-29, blatant government-encouraged infringement of Western patents, and industrial espionage. The first Soviet jet airliner, the Tupolev Tu-104, first flew on June 17 1955 and visited the West for the first time the following spring. Later Russian airliners included the Ilyushin Il-62 and Il-96 and Tupolev Tu-204.

In western Europe, the French aerospace industry had gone from strength to strength in the post-war era and first flew its first jet airliner, the Sud-Est SE.210 Caravelle, on May 27 1955. The Caravelle sold relatively well and 280 of various models were built before production at Toulouse ceased in 1973. Elsewhere in Europe, Fokker was

experiencing some success with its F.27 Friendship, intended to replace the ubiquitous DC-3, and later ventured into jet airliner production with the F.28 Fellowship. Improved versions of the two models were still in production when disaster struck Fokker in January 1996 and the company was forced into bankruptcy when its major backer, Deutsche Aerospace, pulled the financial plug. De Havilland's DH.121 Trident also chalked up some success (117 examples), as did the British Aircraft Corporation's BAC 1-11 (242 built) and the Vickers VC-10 (62 including 14 for the Royal Air Force). Sadly for European companies, the market was dominated by the American aerospace industry, which had not been afflicted so much by the upheavals of the Second

TOP: The Soviet Union followed its own path into the jet age. The Tupolev Tu-104 first flew on June 17 1955.

ABOVE: First flown in November 1955 the Fokker Friendship has enjoyed an unrivaled career which came to an end in early 1997.

RIGHT: The best-known passenger aircraft in the world. Air France Concorde F-BVFA prepares to touch down after another supersonic flight. Though only 20 were built, Concorde provided spectacular proof that collaboration was the way forward for European airliner manufacturers.

BAC/AEROSPATIALE CONCORDE

Wingspan	83ft 10in (25.55m)
Length	203ft 9in (62.10m)
Powerplants	4 Rolls-Royce/SNECMA Olympus 593 turbojets rated at 38,050 (169kN) thrust
Passenger capacity	Up to 128
Maximum speed	Mach 2.2
Range	4,090 miles (6,582km)
Date of entry into service	January 1976
Number built	20

World War and was able to press home its advantage. The only way for European companies to compete was to amalgamate, giving larger financial backing for new projects.

The first example of this co-operation in the airline field came in 1962, when the British and French governments gave their backing to plans to create a new supersonic airliner. Jointly built by BAC and Sud-Aviation with engines manufactured by Bristol Siddeley and SNECMA, the airliner was intended to fly at twice the speed of sound and cross the Atlantic in less than four hours. Both countries had been working on transonic and supersonic projects for many years, but it required their combined efforts to bring the aircraft to reality.

That aircraft is Concorde, and despite only 20 being built, it is probably the most famous airliner in the world to the man in the street. The leading edge technology built into Concorde made it Europe's most talked-about engineering project – while the Americans were busy planning to get a

man on the Moon, the Europeans were keeping their feet firmly on the ground! Concorde was so ahead of its time that its sales team had difficulty in convincing sceptical airlines that it would indeed happen. BOAC and Air France were naturally first in the queue for aircraft, and Pan Am also took out an option to buy six aircraft in June 1963, followed by Continental, American Airlines, TWA and QANTAS.

Pan Am's interest in Concorde encouraged President John F. Kennedy to commit the United States to a supersonic transport program and Boeing, Lockheed and North American all submitted possible designs. Of these, the latter was eliminated and Boeing and Lockheed went forward into a second round of tendering, culminating in Boeing receiving a contract for further design work. By 1970, Boeing had accumulated orders for 126 aircraft from 22 different operators for its proposed 250-seater Boeing 2707, but the US public was not convinced of the need for the aircraft and the program fizzled out.

Tupolev, with full government backing, was already working on its own supersonic transport. The Tu-144 owed its genesis to design studies undertaken in the late 1950s and its undoubted advantages to the state airline of a country covering half the width of the globe were tremendous. The Tu-144 was the first supersonic airliner to get into the air, flying for the first time on December 31 1968. A great deal of redesign work continued throughout the aircraft's test life, and it eventually entered service on December 26 1975 on freight services from Moscow to Alma Ata, a journey of 2,000 miles (3,218km) which it covered in two hours. Passenger services began on November 1 1977 but ceased on May 30 1978 after an aircraft was lost in flight. Aeroflot appeared to lose interest in the Tu-144 and the surviving aircraft were stored and in many cases scrapped. The Tu-144 has recently been dusted off and re-engined as the Tu-144LL in a joint US-Russian project.

Concorde, in the meantime, was progressing nicely with only minimal disagreements between the partners. The honor of the first flight fell to the French prototype, serialled 001 which took to the air on March 2 1969 at Toulouse, followed on April 9 by the British prototype 002 from Filton. An intensive period of testing and route proving

ABOVE: The Soviet answer to Concorde was the Tupolev Tu-144; 15 were built and the aircraft beat Concorde into service.

Up to the mid-1960s, narrow-bodied airliners were the order of the day, seating people in six-abreast seating with a single aisle. Airlines considered that aircraft had just about reached the limits of size practicable with the engines available, yet they needed to carry more passengers. Talks between Pan Am and Boeing in 1965 resulted in the go-ahead for the Boeing 747 project, a widebody airliner capable of carrying around 490 people, twice the capacity of the Boeing 707. The

LEFT: Washington-Dulles plays host to Concordes of BA and Air France, which inaugurated services to the US on May 24 1976, and to mark the occasion the aircraft landed simultaneously on parallel runways.

followed before the aircraft entered scheduled service. This was delayed until January 21 1976, when Air France's inaugural Concorde flight left Charles de Gaulle for Rio de Janeiro, simultaneously with British Airways' flight to Bahrein. The event was considered of such significance that it was shown on live television in both countries. Anti-noise legislation meant that Concorde was unable to operate to New York in its early days and was instead redirected to Washington DC's Dulles Airport, some 15 miles (24km) out of the city.

Despite the relatively healthy order book of the late 1960s, Air France and British Airways have remained the only operators of supersonic transport aircraft in the world, unless you count Braniff's brief flirtation between January 1979 and May 1980. A new generation of supersonic airliners are on the drawing boards around the world. Most major aerospace players are presently carrying out studies, though whether any of them could make a financial success of the project remains clouded.

project's roots lay in Boeing's unsuccessful bid for the USAF's C-5 programme, won by Lockheed. Boeing decided to power its new "baby" with turbofan engines, which were quieter and cheaper to operate and had been used to great effect on the 727 and 737 families, but at that time had not powered anything larger. Enginemakers Pratt &

BELOW: The shape of things to come? Aerospatiale's Alliance proposal for a second-generation supersonic transport.

BOEING 747	
Wingspan	211ft 5in (64.44m)
Length	213ft 0in (64.92m)
Powerplants	4 turbofans rated between 56,750 and 62,000lb (252 & 276kN) thrust, depending on airline requirements
Passenger capacity	524
Maximum speed	Mach 0.85
Range	8,170 miles (13,148km)
Date of entry into service	January 1970
Number built	1,192 by December 1995; deliveries continue

data generally applies to the Boeing 747-400

ABOVE: Most successful of the "jumbo" jets. Boeing produced the first Boeing 747 widebody airliner in 1969. So far over 1,000 have been delivered and orders continue to roll in.

RIGHT: McDonnell Douglas's widebody competitor was the three-engined DC-10, of which 386 were built before the company switched to the MD-11, an improved and updated version which remains in production today.

McDONNELL DOUGLAS DC-10

Wingspan	165ft 4in (50.39m)
Length	181ft 7in (55.35m)
Powerplants	3 General Electric CF-6 turbofans rated between 49,000 and 52,500lb (218 & 234kN) thrust, depending on airline requirements
Passenger capacity	Up to 380
Maximum speed	Mach 0.82
Range	4,690 miles (7,548km)
Date of entry into service	August 1971
Number built	386 plus 154 MD-11s; production continues

data generally applies to the DC-10-30

Whitney produced the JT9D turbofan, four of which powered each aircraft. Boeing needed a new factory in which to build the aircraft, and an area of land at Paine Field, Washington, was bought, where Boeing erected the world's largest building by volume to house the production line. Pan Am's initial 1966 order for 25 aircraft was worth $525 million and enabled Boeing to develop the 747 protected from financial problems.

Inside the Boeing 747, there was much work to be done on the cabin infrastructure – feeding and entertaining nearly 500 people needed careful planning. However, by September 30 1968 all the glitches had been ironed out and the aircraft was

revealed to the world. On February 9 1969 it made its first flight, entering scheduled service on January 21 1970 with a flight from New York-JFK to Heathrow. Boeing's "Jumbo" Jet had arrived and remains an important player on the world scene today, with more than 1,000 delivered and a healthy order book for some time to come.

Boeing had again stolen a march on other manufacturers, though both McDonnell Douglas – formed by the merger of McDonnell and Douglas in 1967 – and Lockheed countered with their own jumbo airliners. Both were trijets and first flew in 1970: the DC-10 on August 29 1970 and the Lockheed 1011 TriStar on November 16 1970. Both have proved relatively successful, although TriStar production ended in 1983 after 250 had been built. After a poor start when several were lost or damaged in accidents, the DC-10 gained ground and was later improved to become the MD-11. It remains in production today and the company builds around nine per year; it is particularly popular with freight operators.

A new generation of airliners was born with the arrival of the Boeing 757 and 767. Both featured a state-of-the-art "glass" cockpit mainly comprised of cathode-ray tube instrumentation and a flight deck crew of two, the flight engineer's workload being carried out by the two pilots. The medium-range 767 made its first flight on September 26 1981, followed by the short-range 757 in February 19 1982; nearly 1,000 of each have been sold to date. Boeing followed up these successes with the long-range 777, which first flew on June 12 1994. The company's recent take-over of McDonnell Douglas makes it the world's largest aircraft manufacturer, a position which it intends to consolidate over the coming years.

The early 1970s saw the emergence of credible European competition to the might of the Americans. The Airbus Industrie consortium was formed in December 1970 to bring together France, Britain, Germany and Spain to produce a wide-bodied airliner. First flown on October 28 1972, the Airbus A.300 made steady progress in racking up sales, though only with difficulty did it break into the partisan American market – the first US customer was Eastern Air Lines, which began

A.340 are closely related, differing mainly in the number of engines and their related systems; they are built on the same production line. Airbus has recently gone one step further with its Airbus A3XX programme for an ultra-high capacity airliner capable of carrying up to 850 passengers. The company recently delivered its 1,500th Airbus, an A.319 to Lufthansa, and has orders for another 750 aircraft on its books.

Smaller airliners

Although bigger aircraft took most of the limelight, many smaller airliners have been introduced over the past four decades, many as replacements for the irreplaceable Douglas DC-3.

BELOW: Boeing's newest airliner is the 777, which entered service in June 1995 with United Airlines. Cathay Pacific's aircraft are powered by Rolls-Royce Trent engines.

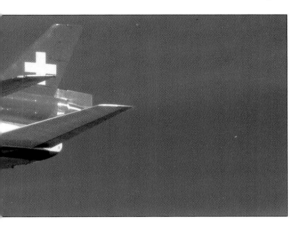

operations with leased aircraft in November 1977.

The four-engined A.300 was followed by the two-engined A.310, which intended to compete with the 767. First flown on April 3 1982, it went into service with Swissair and was followed by the Airbus A320. First flown on February 22 1987, the A.320 was the world's first airliner to be designed using Computer Aided Design techniques and has since been joined by the shorter but basically similar A.319 and stretched A321. Airbus's newest designs, the two-engined A.330 and four-engined

Among the many smaller, third-level feeder airliners to hit the market over the past 30 years or so have been the British Britten-Norman Islander and the Brazilian Bandeirante. In Canada, the exacting terrain presented de Havilland Canada with very specific problems. Its range of bushplanes such as the DHC-3 Otter and DHC-4 Buffalo have led on to the DHC-6 Twin Otter, at home on skis, floats or

AIRBUS A.300

Wingspan	147ft 1in (44.83m)
Length	177ft 5in (54.08m)
Powerplants	2 turbofans rated between 56,000 and 61,500lb (249 & 274kN) thrust, depending on airline requirements
Passenger capacity	Up to 375
Maximum speed	Mach 0.82
Range	4,775 miles (7,685 km)
Date of entry into service	May 1974
Number built	462; deliveries continue

data generally applies to A.300-600

wheels. The turbine-powered DHC-7 and DHC-8 have both been in service for some time as feederliners, while Canadair's Regional Jet also fits the bill for companies such as Lufthansa. British Aerospace's BAe 146 also proved popular with smaller airlines around the world, as did the SAAB 340 and 2000; the multinational AI(R) company has also captured a reasonable share of the market with its ATR.42 and ATR.72 family.

As more and more passengers took scheduled

ABOVE: The Airbus Industrie A330, one of the company's newest designs, seats 335 passengers on medium- and long-haul routes.

ABOVE: The Beech Starship was one of the most futuristic shapes in the sky; perhaps too futuristic, as only 53 were built before production ceased in 1995.

RIGHT: Going up! Research suggest that air shows are the second largest spectator sports in the world. Throughout the summer months, display teams criss-cross countries and continents to show off their aerobatics prowess.

FAR RIGHT: An Embraer EMB-201A Ipanema makes short work of spraying a field of crops. As well as pest control, agricultural aircraft like this can be adapted to carry water to use against forest fires.

services to more and more destinations, more and more companies and businessmen have invested in their own aircraft. De Havilland (later Hawker Siddeley) blazed the trail with the HS.125, still marketed today as the Hawker 1000, and Bill Lear came up with the innovative Lear Jet in the early 1960s, and is also still in production. Cessna, with a strong background of producing both light and business aircraft, introduced the Citation family of business jets, while in France the Falcon series, which started life as the Mystère, has grown in size and range over the past 30 years. More recently, the market for executive helicopters has expanded to get executives from the airport to – in some cases – the office.

Recreational flying received a kick start after the Second World War thanks once again to a surplus of wartime trainer and liaison aircraft. In Britain, owners had received an unpleasant knockback at the outbreak of war when all pri-

vately owned aircraft capable of serving some useful purpose were impressed, for which compensation of one shilling (£0.05, about 10 cents) was paid; post-war they could buy their aircraft back, if it had survived – at market prices!

The post-war market was flooded with war-surplus aircraft; in Europe the Tiger Moth and Auster were found just about everywhere, while in the United States Aeroncas, Luscombes, Stinsons and Piper Cubs formed the backbone of the general aviation revival. Around the world light aircraft manufacturers struggled to keep going; some, like Beech, Cessna and Piper, were able to expand; others were hard put to keep their heads above water; all have been badly hit by the recessions of the last decade. As proof of the popularity of flight as a recreational hobby, it is estimated that there are over half a million aircraft in civil ownership throughout the world today.

Microlight aircraft came along at the end of the 1970s and provided a whole new market; cheap to buy, operate and maintain, they have rapidly found a niche. Hot-air ballooning, the oldest form of powered flight, has made a comeback over the past 20 years; technological advances mean that they can be built in almost any shape under the sun, and balloons in the shape of houses and beer cans are just two of those gracing the skies – an advertising agency's dream come true!

Wartime improvements in air traffic control also filtered through to post-war civil aviation The International Air Transport Association (IATA) was inaugurated on April 19 1945 to oversee airline operations and safety matters. Radar was still, relatively speaking, in its infancy and few aircraft were fitted with it. Airliners still crashed in bad weather, despite aids such as ground-controlled approach radar, although IATA strove to improve the situation. Pan Am began trials of weather radar in early 1955; improvements continued over the past 40 years mean that all airliners are fitted with it.

Airline deregulation in the late 1970s helped expand the number of airlines trading, though some struggled to survive and others went under – Pan Am was the highest-profile airline to go into receivership when it filed for bankruptcy in January 1991. Low-cost airlines appeared worldwide to cater for the package holiday market and many disappeared just as quickly. A new market also grew up: no-frills travel reduces the cost of airline flights dramatically.

Airports have grown to accommodate the massive numbers of people able to fly for the first time. Heathrow rapidly became Europe's busiest airport, but lagged behind Chicago-O'Hare, Illinois, where by the end of the 1950s half-a-million flights were made annually, carrying over 10 million passengers. In Paris, Le Bourget had lost its number one slot to Orly; the city's third international airport, Charles de Gaulle, opened for business on March 13 1974 after eight years of development. The seven airports coming under the aegis of the British Airports Authority handled 974,012 airline movements carrying 98 million passengers in the 1996/97 financial year, representing a quarter of a million air travelers each day. Chicago-O'Hare handles well over 60 million passengers a year; New York's three airports are coming close to 100 million. In all, we travel around 1.5 billion miles by air each year. Airports are major industries in themselves, providing employment for thousands, from the airline captain and the air traffic controller to the runway sweeper and the ticket check-in operator.

Questions for the future

But what of the future? There are major problems at many airports due to insufficient landing slots. Business aircraft have been all but banned from many international airports worldwide; there are simply insufficient landing slots to cater for all those airlines who wish to use the airport. Do we invest in larger airliners or do we extend airport opening hours? Some airline routes will not sup-

port larger aircraft, so should short-haul and commuter airlines suffer at the expense of the big players? Will the existing infrastructure cope with aircraft delivering more passengers per hour? After all, there's no point in putting up to 1,000 people on an aircraft if they then have to wait two hours to retrieve their luggage!

Airline travel has become so commonplace for so many; for most of us it's as simple (and as routine) as boarding a bus or a train. Nevertheless, while the early romance may have waned, traveling by air still holds an aura of excitement.

ABOVE: Airliner congestion at Gatwick Airport as Virgin Atlantic Boeing 747s await another load of passengers. The growth of air travel over the past decade has imposed a strain on airports.

PASSENGERS CARRIED BY IATA MEMBERS 1949-1993

	Domestic	International	Total
1949	20,300,000	–	20,300,000
1955	9,350,000	42,411,000	51,721,000
1965	35,357,000	105,756,000	141,098,000
1975	87,327,000	229,859,000	317,186,000
1985	154,244,000	311,206,000	465,429,000
1993	303,788,000	686,716,000	990,505,000

Source: *IATA*

FREIGHT (in tonnes) CARRIED BY IATA MEMBERS 1949-1993

	Domestic	International	Total
1949	429,000	–	429,000
1955	821,000	–	821,000
1965	3,416,000	–	3,416,000
1975	2,590,000	2,389,000	4,979,000
1985	2,911,000	4,777,000	7,688,000
1993	6,407,000	8,989,000	15,396,000

Source: *IATA*

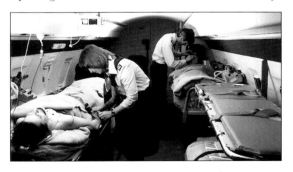

ABOVE: Although aircraft have been used by the emergency services for decades, there has been a boom in the use of business jets as ultra-fast air ambulances.

IATA MEMBER EMPLOYEES 1949-1993

1949	225,000
1955	274,000
1965	577,000
1975	796,000
1985	939,000
1993	1,462,000

Source: *IATA*

CHAPTER THREE
Aerial Warfare

RIGHT: Balloons were widely used during the American Civil War, balloons were widely used. This photo dates from 1862 and was probably taken during the Richmond campaign of that year. Observation, reconnaissance, and spotting for the guns were the main tasks.

RIGHT CENTER: The British Army first used a balloon in Bechuanaland in 1884. Not used in action, it impressed a local chief who, after a flight in it declared: "We would have worshipped them and served them. The English have indeed great power!"

Beginnings

Even as man has always dreamed of flying, so his dreams have been translated into military action. In 200 BC, the Chinese general Han Sin used kites to measure the distance to enemy fortifications, using simple triangulation methods. Then in 1670, Fr. Francesco de Lana-Terzi postulated a flying ship which could drop nasty substances on the enemy. Although a strange interest for a Jesuit priest, it should however be remembered that alone among religious orders, the Society of Jesus has always been at the forefront of scientific knowledge. In August 1709, another Jesuit, Fr. Bartolomeu de Gusmão, designed and flew a model hot-air balloon in Portugal.

It is therefore hardly surprising that the first military use of the air was by balloon. This was at the Battle of Fleurus in 1794, when Capitaine Jean-Marie-Joseph Coutelle took the tethered hydrogen balloon *Entreprenant* aloft to relay information on the progress of the battle against the Austrians to French Army commander General Louis Jourdan.

In those days a hydrogen balloon was not suited for quick reaction. There were no cylinders of compressed gas; first a kiln had to be built. The gas was then produced, which took 50 hours. Once *Entreprenant* had been inflated, it was marched 30 miles (50km) to the battlefield by 20 men holding ropes, at a height which allowed cavalry to pass beneath it. The effect on the horses was not recorded!

Fleurus was a French victory, aided to a degree by aerial observation. Its value was proved again at Ourthe later that year, but the combination of logistical problems in inflating balloons and getting them to where they were most needed, and communications between the observers and the commanders on the ground, were enough to cause Napoleon Bonaparte to display a marked lack of interest. The French balloon service was disbanded in 1799.

Whilst of limited value to an aggressive and fast-moving commander like Bonaparte, the balloon had much greater potential for observation in a defensive battle. For the decisive Battle of Borodino in 1812, the Russian supreme commander Mikhail Kutuzov asked for the use of Leppisch's observation balloon. Unfortunately for

Balloons were widely used by the Union in the Civil War, not least for directing artillery fire, but they were insufficiently appreciated, and the Union Balloon Corps was disbanded in 1863. The Confederates, far weaker in resources, used balloons on a very limited scale.

The next military use of the balloon came in the Franco-Prussian War of 1870/71. Paris was besieged, but maintained contact with the outside world by balloons filled with coal gas, which was more readily obtainable than hydrogen. In all, 66 balloons were despatched, with passengers, and over 3,000,000 messages, which were microfilmed. Most got through, but the service was at the mercy of the wind; the *Jacquard* was last seen disappearing over the Atlantic, while the *Ville d'Orleans* ended up in Norway! It was of course a one-way service, and few of the outbound carrier pigeons returned to the beleaguered capital

The 20th Century saw radical changes in military aviation. At first, the lighter-than-air craft, typified by the steerable airship, or dirigible, looked to be the obvious way ahead, but the controllable heavier-than-air airplane, first flown by the Wright Brothers in December 1903, soon made gigantic strides to catch up. It was followed in 1907 by Paul Cornu's helicopter, but this aerodynamically inefficient device took many years to become a practical proposition and even longer to become a fully-fledged weapon of war.

The first war flight of an airplane took place on February 12 1911, when Charles Hamilton flew a reconnaissance mission over Ciudad Juarez in Mexico. On November 1 of that year, Italian Giulio Gavotti dropped small bombs on Turkish forces in Libya, in the first ever offensive mission. He was answered with rifle fire, but this was ineffective.

The First World War

The beginning of the First World War in August 1914 saw many air arms equipped with airplanes. Reconnaissance was the primary task, and most were two-seaters carrying a pilot and an observer. As aerial reconnaissance proved increasingly valuable to the ground forces, it became inevitable that attempts would be made to deny the enemy the same facility.

him it failed to arrive in time. Had it done so, the information it provided might just have turned the tide against the Grand Armèe.

A more offensive use came in 1849, when the Austrians attacked Venice with a number of hot air balloons each carrying a 30lb (14kg) time-fuzed bomb. This scheme was naturally at the mercy of the elements; little damage was caused, and when the wind changed the Austrians came under threat from their own weapons!

Reconnaissance was obviously still the primary mission of balloons, but a major problem was communication between air and ground. In June 1861, in the early days of the American Civil War, the first telegraphic message was sent from a balloon by Thaddeus Lowe. Shortly after, he made an untethered ascent to establish that Confederate forces were not advancing towards Washington.

ABOVE: Paul Cornu at the controls of his helicopter at Lisieux in 1907.
He made the first controlled helicopter flight in November of that year, but technical problems delayed its use as a practical flying machine by 25 years.

RIGHT: The prototype BE. 2 was first flown in 1912 by Geoffrey de Havilland (seen here). A product of the Royal Aircraft Factory at Farnborough, it was a very stable airplane, but this made it unmaneuvrable.

OPPOSITE TOP: The best early German reconnaissance machines were Aviatik B types. Seen here is the Aviatik CIII two seater, which was developed from the B variants. The CIII first entered service in 1916.

BELOW: The prototype Sopwith Tabloid in 1913. A prewar racing biplane, it carried a small load of 20lb (9kg) bombs, and was used by the RNAS to raid airship sheds at Cologne and Dusseldorf on October 8 1914.

Consequently airplanes began to fight each other, although at first they had little idea as to how. On August 25 1914, three British BE. 2as hounded a German two-seater to earth by aggressive flying. On the following day, Russian pilot Piotr Nikolaevich Nesterov rammed an Austrian biplane with his Morane-Saulnier M over Sholkiv, in Galicia, killing both himself and his opponent, Baron von Rosenthal.

Neither method was a practical long-term proposition, and various methods of arming airplanes were tried. Many were exotic, such as grapnels with grenades attached, or even blunderbusses, even though it was obvious from the outset that the most suitable weapon was the fast-firing machine gun.

Many early machines were so underpowered that the added weight and drag of a machine gun, its mounting and ammunition, significantly reduced both speed and rate of climb. Unless it was exceptionally well placed, with a height and position advantage at the time of the encounter, it was almost impossible to close to within effective

shooting range. By the same token, it was equally difficult for it to escape from a determined opponent with a better airplane.

The alternatives were the rifle, the carbine, or the pistol, all of which were single-shot weapons. On the ground, all were deadly in the hands of a marksman, but accurate firing from the cockpit of an unstable and vibrating airplane while battling with an 80mph (129km/h) slipstream, was another matter. Deflection shooting was an art well-known to many country-bred observers, but bullet trail (caused by the gyrations of the observer's aircraft); and precession (caused by the relative speeds of firer and target) were at first unknown quantities. Even at close quarters, encounters between airplanes with single-shot weapons were pretty harmless.

The typical machine gun of the day could spew out ten or more bullets per second, which vibration (gun mountings were far from rigid) tended to disperse, giving a cone of fire with a far greater chance of scoring a hit or two.

Even with a machine gun, air combat victories

contained an element of luck. On October 5 1914, Wilhelm Schlichting and Fritz von Zangen flew a reconnaissance mission near Reims. Engrossed in their task, they failed to notice the approach of a French Voisin III.

The interception was quite fortuitous. The Voisin, flown by Josef Frantz and Louis Quénault, was significantly slower than the German Aviatik biplane, and in the normal way of things would have been unable to catch it. But the Frenchmen had the initial advantage of height and position, and Frantz dived his ungainly mount to the attack. Rudely made aware that he was not alone, Schlichting tried to dive away, but Frantz maneuvered his Voisin "chicken coop" to give Quénault a firing position. His shots struck home and the Aviatik went down in flames; the first air combat victim in history.

The development of the fighter

The victory of the two young Frenchmen was the exception that proved the rule. Over the following months, air combats remained rare and victories even rarer. The fact was that the airplanes of the day were not really suitable for fighting. What was needed was an airplane designed for the task, and this depended on two things: greater performance to force battle on an opponent or to disengage when circumstances were unfavorable, and the means to shoot directly ahead.

The latter was possible using an airplane with a pusher configuration. With the engine and propeller mounted at the rear of a central crew nacelle, this allowed a clear field of fire ahead. The drawback of this was that it was aerodynamically inefficient. The tail surfaces had to be carried on an arrangement of booms, heavily strutted and braced, all of which caused excessive drag and reduced performance. Two other faults of the pusher layout were reduced rearward visibility, and the fact that if the engine broke free in a crash-landing, it was liable to pulp the crew.

Aerodynamically, the tractor (engine in front) layout was far superior and, power for power, handily outperformed the pusher. But the propeller, whirling round directly in front, prevented guns being fired directly forward. Gun armament was handled by the observer, usually from the rear cockpit. While this was fine for beating off an attack from astern, it was difficult to act offensively with a gun that could only be used in the rear arc.

There were two ways of obtaining greater performance. The first was of course to develop more powerful engines; the second was to increase the power/weight ratio by minimizing weight.

A specialized air combat machine, or fighter, would not require an observer. Therefore it could be made a single-seater, saving the weight of the observer. Without the second cockpit the fuselage could be made smaller. With less weight to lift, the wings could also be made smaller. Considerable savings in weight could be made, with a consequent increase in power/weight ratio and thus

performance. Translated into "the smallest possible airframe wrapped around the biggest possible engine", this principle dominated high-performance fighter design for the next half-century.

The next step was to allow the pilot to use the gun while simultaneously flying the airplane. This was achieved by using a fixed gun aimed by pointing the whole airplane at the target.

Attempts had been made pre-war to develop a

BELOW: The Voisin pushers were rugged if unmaneuverable and slow biplanes, mainly used for bombing and strafing. The first ever air combat victory was scored by a Voisin 1914.

synchronization gear which would allow a gun to shoot through the propeller disc without hitting the blades, but for technical reasons this had not succeeded. Early in 1915, French pilot Roland Garros fitted steel wedges to the propeller of his Morane-Saulnier, to deflect the few bullets which might otherwise have damaged it.

Thus equipped, Garros took to the skies. On April 1 1915 he downed a German Albatros. It was a fateful move. Over the next two weeks more German airplanes fell to his guns, but on April 19 he force-landed at Courtrai, behind the German lines.

The publicity accorded Garros ensured that the Germans knew well who he was. They discovered the deflectors on his propeller, and determined to manufacture something similar. The task was given to Dutch designer Anthony Fokker. Aware of prewar work on synchronization gear in Switzerland, Fokker adapted this and fitted it to his new monoplane, the Fokker E.1 Eindecker. Thus armed, the Eindecker, which was immediately ordered for the Luftstreitkräfte, can truly be described as the world's first real fighter airplane.

The Eindecker, which was given more powerful engines, and two, or even three guns during its operational career, scored its first victory, a Morane-Saulnier, on July 1 1915. The successful pilot was Kurt Wintgens.

Ironically, in view of what came next, the performance of the Eindecker was unexceptional for its day. Maximum speed was just 87mph (140km/h), it took a full half-hour to reach 9,843ft (3,000m), and its ceiling was 11,484ft (3,500m). For lateral control it used wing-warping, a system which even then was beginning to fall into disuse in favour of ailerons, while the rudder and tail surfaces were all-moving slabs, making handling rather sensitive.

On the other hand, the Eindecker had its virtues, the main one being of course the ability to fire straight ahead through the propeller disk. It was agile, although not exceptionally so, and was strong. Unlike many of its contemporaries, it could be dived at a steep angle without shedding its wings!

The Eindecker gained its deadly reputation largely through the exploits of two young German pilots. Max Immelmann, later known as "The Eagle of Lille", flew mainly against the British. He is remembered today primarily for the maneuver that bears his name, although extensive research has failed to reveal precisely what it was. All that can be said with any certainty is that it was a pull-up after a diving attack, followed by a rolling turn which left him well-placed to dive again. He therefore appears to have been the first fighter pilot to maneuver in the vertical plane rather than in the horizontal. He was killed in combat on June 18 1916, his score fifteen. Precisely how is unclear.

Oswald Boelcke was to earn undying fame as "The Father of Air Fighting". Whilst he and Immelmann were friendly rivals, Boelcke's attention quickly turned to tactics. Recognizing that war is not a form of sport, as some of his colleagues and many of his opponents seemed to think, he set about developing a set of rules. In these, the so-called "Dicta Boelcke", he stressed the seeking of advantages before attacking. The chief of these was the surprise attack. The Eindecker lent itself to this. End-on, the small monoplane was far more difficult to spot than a biplane, while in normal flight, its slender lines gave it the appearance of "fairly streaking across the sky", to quote high-scoring British ace James McCudden.

Surprisingly, Boelcke's rules stand up very well today, more than eight decades later, despite the technological changes that have taken place in the intervening years. He also seems to have been the first to closely study, and if possible fly, captured British and French machines, seeking out possible weak points. He also addressed the problems of formation tactics in some detail.

In wars between nations with comparable resources, no technical advantage can be sustained for long, and the Eindecker reached its zenith at the beginning of 1916. The British and French were slow in developing their own syn-

chronization gear, and thus used other means of firing directly ahead. Their new aircraft started to reach the front in numbers. The British introduced the Airco D.H. 2, a single-seater pusher with a fixed forward-firing gun. The D.H. 2 had only a marginal performance edge over the Eindecker, but was far more maneuvrable. The new French fighter was the Nieuport 11, the fixed gun of which was mounted on the top wing to fire over the propeller disk. Fast and agile, it totally outclassed the German monoplane in all departments.

Although their lead was fast slipping away, Boelcke and Immelmann continued to fly and fight. It should of course be remembered that

ABOVE: Oswald Boelcke, the first man to define methods of air combat. The strain is obviously showing; here he looks far older than his 25 years. At the time of his death in action in October 1916, he was the top-scoring fighter pilot in the world.

their opponents were not always the new fighters; reconnaissance machines and artillery spotters were far more valuable targets. But with Immelmann's death in June 1916, Boelcke, the German top-scorer with 18 victories, was rested.

He was recalled in August to form Jagdstaffel (Jasta) 2, one of the new fighter units. Its fighters, a mix of Fokker and Albatros single-seater biplanes, the latter with two Spandau machine guns, started to arrive from September 1.

During the working-up period for the Jasta, Boelcke flew alone, the superiority of his new mount allowing him to add to his score. He started to lead Jasta 2 operationally from September 17, initially with great success. On October 25 he gained his fortieth victim, but was killed three days later as the result of a dogfight. A minor mid-air collision with one of

FOKKER EINDECKER

Wingspan	32ft 2⅜in (9.52m)
Length	23ft 7½in (19.66m)
Power	One Oberursel rotary engine rated at 100hp.
Maximum speed	87mph (140km/h)
Endurance	2¾ hours
Armament	One spandau m.g
Date of entry into service	June 1915
Number built	c200

LEFT; The first true fighter was the Fokker Eindecker. Performance was not outstanding, but its ability to shoot straight ahead through the propeller disk enabled it to outfight Allied types from mid-1915. It was countered from February 1916 by new Allied fighters.

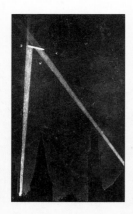

ABOVE: A Zeppelin held by searchlights over London. Against these raiders anti-aircraft fire had little effect, while slow defending fighters such as the Avro 504 and the BE. 2 were hard-pressed to catch them.

MAIN PICTURE: The Germany Navy used Zeppelins to scout for the fleet, but with little success. Most were switched to take part in night raids on British targets in conjunction with the German Air Service.

his own pilots weakened the wings of his fighter. Boelcke spiralled down, seemingly under control, but at low level his wings crumpled and he crashed to his death. This was ironic, as one of his tenets was: "When the fight breaks up into a series of single combats, take care that several do not go for one opponent." It was however his sixth sortie that day, and there can be little doubt that fatigue had weakened his concentration.

Airships at war

Air warfare does not exist in isolation; it is an integral part of the main conflict. From the outset, reconnaissance airplanes proved invaluable to the surface forces. Once the initial communications problems had been ironed out, artillery spotters became very effective force multipliers. It was equally obvious that airplanes could provide more direct support by attacking ground targets with suitable weapons, as the Italians had demonstrated in Libya.

The warplane of 1914/15 was in general "barely able to carry a box of matches the length of a football field", to use the modern idiom. To be truly effective, three things were needed: a larger weapons load, longer range, and greater reliability. The need had been foreseen; several nations started to develop multi-engined long-range bombers, but these took time to mature enough to enter service. The airship with its phenomenal lifting powers, long range, endurance, and reliability, looked a far safer bet. Reliability stemmed from a relatively benign flight profile. Whereas airplane engines ran at high or maximum revolutions for most of their operational life; the same engine in an airship chugged along comfortably at perhaps 60 per cent. Consequently strain on the engine was less, and it lasted longer.

The term "Zeppelin" soon became synonymous with all German airships regardless of origin and force (both the German Army and Navy operated airships on bombing raids). The first attempt came on August 6 1914, when Zeppelin LZ 21 tried to attack Liege with eight converted artillery shells, but was hit by ground fire and driven off, force-landing near Bonn. Other raids followed, but it was soon found that Zeppelins were vulnerable to ground fire, especially near the front lines, which were rich in artillery pieces. They were big; the early ones were rather longer than a football pitch and one third of its width in diameter, dwarfing a modern Boeing 747. Later models were considerably larger. At sedate speeds of about 50mph (80km/h) they took more than seven seconds to fly their own length. This combination made them good targets for the guns in daylight. They reverted to night raiding.

The first raid on England took place on the night of January 19/20 1915, when two Imperial Navy Zeppelins headed for the Humber and one for the Thames Estuary. The latter turned back with engine trouble; the other two missed the Humber by 80 miles (129km) and bombed inconsequential targets.

This fiasco highlighted the difficulty of navigating over the trackless sea, and the even greater diffi-

culty of locating one's whereabouts over a strange blacked-out country. It was almost three months before the Zeppelins tried again. Had this not been a war, the results would have been comical. Not until the giant gasbags were unleashed against London, where the moonlit Thames was a certain landmark, did the English fully realize they were under attack.

Zeppelin threat spawned a whole family of airplanes dedicated to the task – such freaks as the rocket-gun armed Parnall Scout and the PB 31E Night Hawk, with a three-man crew, a trainable searchlight, and a traversable Davis gun which was 7ft (2m) long! None succeeded.

While the Zeppelin raids did little to directly damage the British war effort, they were probably justified by the huge resources deployed to stop them. In the end they were defeated, not by the more exotic solutions proposed, but by the increasing efficiency of the fighter defenses. The tide turned on September 2/3 1916, when William Leefe-Robinson, patrolling in a BE. 2c, shot down SL11 (a wooden-framed Schutte-Lanz) over Cuffley in Hertfordshire. LZ 32 and LZ 33 followed on September 24/25, and eight nights later Kapitän-Leutnant Heinrich Mathey, the doyen of Zeppelin commanders, went down in LZ 31 over Potters Bar, Middlesex.

From this point on, the defenders had the

LEFT: This BE. 2C was flown by William Leefe-Robinson on the night of September 2/3 1916, when he shot down the Schutte-Lanz SL.11 over Cuffley in Hertfordshire. This was the first victory over the night raiders.

Night defense against air attack posed almost intractable problems. Even a huge Zeppelin was easily lost in the vast wastes of the night sky. High-angle guns and searchlights in potential target areas proved only a partial answer, while the fighters of the day, selected for tractability rather than fighting qualities, were inadequate. Reaching interception altitude took too long; once there, seeing the Zeppelin was difficult, and armament inadequate. The first interceptions occurred on May 17, but in each case the Zeppelins, LZ 38 and 39, escaped with damage. The first success was scored by Reginald Warneford, who blundered across LZ 37 over Belgium and dropped his bombs on it.

The next victory was long in coming. One thing was certain; machine gun fire was ineffective, and incendiary ammunition did not become available until the following year. A plethora of anti-Zeppelin weapons was developed – bombs, mortars and grenades – but, as these relied on the airplane being able to climb above the monsters before attacking, they were foredoomed. The

measure of the raiders, culminating in a brilliant victory on October 19/20 1917, when five out of eleven Zeppelins were lost. The airship had been defeated. But as it went down in blazing ruin, it passed on the baton of strategic bombing to the airplane.

ABOVE: Zeppelin LZ.33 sustained heavy damage from anti-aircraft fire on the night of September 23/24 1916. Limping home, it was intercepted near Chelmsford by a BE.2c flown by Alfred Brandon of 39 Squadron, who inflicted further damage. It lost height and crashed near West Mersea.

ABOVE: The world's first four-engined bomber was the Ilya Mourometz, the brainchild of Russian designer Igor Sikorsky. Endurance was five hours and it carried up to half a tonne of bombs. out of the 80 built, only one was lost to enemy fighters.

BELOW: German Gotha G IV and G V bombers are best remembered for their raids on London and the south of England in 1917/18. A Gotha G V is seen here being bombed up. From spring 1918 they were operated at night.

The Strategic bomber

The first long-range airplane capable of carrying a heavy payload was the four-engined Ilya Mourometz (named after a 10th Century Russian folk hero), a transport aircraft designed by Igor Sikorsky, which first flew on December 11 1913. On February 14 1914, Tsar Nicholas II ordered it as a long range bomber for the Imperial Russian Air Service.

After the outbreak of war, the first attacks by Ilya Mourometz bombers took place on February 15 1915, when targets in East Prussia were attacked. Interceptions by German fighters were frequent, but the huge Russian aircraft proved very survivable. On June 6, a single bomber was attacked by several German fighters and repeatedly hit. Despite this, it returned to base on two engines. When operations ceased on February 17 1918, they had flown 442 missions and dropped 65 tonnes of bombs, for the loss of just three in action, only one of them to fighters.

The next country to introduce strategic bombers was Italy. The Caproni Ca 33 was a tri-motor biplane, used to cross the Alps and attack targets in Austria with a 1,000lb (454kg) bomb load.

The most famous German bombers of the war were the Gotha G.IV and G.V; twin-engined machines with a three-man crew, a maximum

speed of 87mph (140km/h) and a range of 305 miles (490km). Maximum bomb load was 1,102lb (500kg), although to allow a bombing altitude of 14,765ft (4,500m) this was normally reduced to 661lb (300kg). A specialist bombing unit, the England Geschwader, was formed with Gothas in the spring of 1917.

Defensive armament was two pairs of Parabellum machine guns, one pair in the nose, the other amidships. Provision was also made for firing into what would otherwise have been the blind spot beneath the tail. Realizing that the massed cross-fire from a close formation of bombers could offer considerable protection against fighter attack, commander Ernst Brandenburg drilled the Geschwader in various formations, which could be changed at will on his signal.

The Gotha made its debut against England on May 25 1917 with a raid aimed at London, but heavy cloud in the area prevented bombing. Brandenburg then swung his 21-strong force south towards Folkestone, inflicting heavy damage on the town center. At bombing altitude they were above the reach of anti-aircraft fire, while the combination of altitude and speed made them difficult to intercept. Only one home-based fighter made contact, damaging a bomber, although British and French fighters based in France managed to shoot a Gotha into the sea. A second Gotha crashed near Brugge in Belgium, killing its crew.

Other raids followed, and again the defense was ineffective. On June 13, a school was among buildings hit. This was hardly deliberate; it underlined the difficulties of high-level bombing. If a target area could be located (difficult), and a specific military objective identified (very difficult), hitting it with a bomb dropped from a fast-moving airplane from nearly three miles (5km) up, with the crude sighting systems of the day, was close to impossible.

The effective end of the daylight bombing campaign came during August. On the 18th, 28 Gothas took off for England in poor weather, but turned back when in sight of the English coast. The winds worsened; two Gothas crashed in the sea, two strayed over Holland and were shot down by Dutch gunners, while five crashed on landing. Then on August 22, 15 Gothas set out to bomb coastal targets; five were forced to turn back with mechanical trouble. The remainder were met by

LEFT: The F.E. 2b entered service as a fighter in the late winter of 1916. This example is an F.E. 2d of 20 Squadron, with the 250hp Rolls Royce Eagle engine and a fixed gun for the pilot. Defense to the rear was provided by a Lewis gun on the top plane.

heavy gunfire and by 15 fighters, and the protective formation broke up. Ground fire accounted for one, while fighters got another two. Such losses could not be sustained; daylight bombing was abandoned. Night raiding commenced on September 3/4, with an attack on Chatham by four Gothas. Then on September 28/29, two huge four-engined Staaken Riesenflugzeuge, which carried a far greater bombload, joined the fray.

While high performance fighters such as the Camel and SE5a were introduced to the British night defense squadrons, few bombers were lost to this cause; far more fell to the weather or accidents. The strategic bombing campaign was a failure, due to its inability to inflict significant damage, either to materiel or morale.

Whilst the British paid lip service to strategic bombing, the idea was never fully taken up. Independent Force RAF attacked targets in Germany from June 1918 until the end of the war, but the vast majority of its airplanes were short-ranged tactical machines such as the F.E. 2d and D.H. 4. The few multi-engined Handley-Page 0/100s and 0/400s also flew mainly tactical missions, with transport, coal, steel and chemical plants as the main objectives. By the end of the war this situation was about to change, as the British had developed the Handley-Page V/1500, which could reach Berlin. Given the difficulty which the Germans experienced in finding their way over blacked-out Britain at night over much shorter distances, it is probably as well that the Berlin raid was not attempted.

Lone wolf aces

Single combat in the clear blue sky, or a lone flyer battling against odds, seemed a world apart from trench warfare. It carried an aura of glamor; of chivalry even. In times of strife, nations need heroes to inspire them, and in the Great War, the mantle of the knight of old fell upon the fighter pilot.

BELOW: The first British heavy bomber was the Handley-Page 0/100 which entered service in 1916. Its maximum bomb load of 16 112lb (51kg) or one 1,650lb (748kg) bomb, was exceptional for its day.

ABOVE: Charles Nungesser with his Nieuport 17 with his macabre coat of arms. Notable as much for his serious injuries as his victories, he survived the war with a score of 45. He was lost at sea while attempting to cross the Atlantic in 1927.

At first the most successful were the "lone wolf" flyers. Immelmann and Boelcke have already been mentioned. The first great British ace was Albert Ball who, between March 1916 and his death in action on May 7 1917, was credited with 44 victories. He was the master of the stealthy stalk to very close range, but was not averse to attacking from head-on, where his iron nerve usually forced his opponent to break first. The most successful RFC lone flyer was undoubtedly Canadian Billy Bishop who, once he learned a modicum of restraint, survived the war with 72 victories.

Ball's French counterpart was Georges Guynemer, who became a byword for reckless-ness, attacking at every opportunity and from all angles. In June 1917 he encountered Ernst Udet, who survived the war as the second highest German scorer. The combat was inconclusive, but Udet later recorded that Guynemer, flying a SPAD XIII, had anticipated all his moves. The Frenchman was killed in action on September 11 1917, his score at 53. In achieving this, he had himself been brought down eight times.

Even more reckless was Charles Nungesser. Wounds and injuries sustained in crashes ensured that he spent as much time away from the front as

ABOVE: The best British fighter of the war was the SE.5a. Very fast and easy to fly, it lacked the maneuvrability of rotary-engined types, but compensated for this with sheer performance, especially rate of climb. Most leading RFC/RAF aces flew the type.

at it, but astonishingly he survived the war, his personal tally 45, only to die years later in an attempt to fly the Atlantic.

What was a fighter ace? In the most basic terms he was a pilot credited with five or more aerial victories. This system was started by the French, who lionised their heroes. It was only tacitly accepted by the British, while the Germans demanded ten victories to qualify as an Oberkanone. The Germans gave wide publicity to their top scorers, even to the point of producing postcards of them.

At a deeper level, an ace was usually, but not always an outstanding aircraft handler, able to outfly an opponent and get in close enough to minimize the problems of air to air gunnery, even though most were good marksmen. They were generally long-sighted, which helped them avoid being surprised, with excellent depth perception. One notable exception to this last was Welshman Ira Jones, who survived the war with 40 victories. Aces had their share of luck, but also a quality known as situational awareness. Difficult to define accurately, this is the ability to keep track of fast-moving events; an awareness of space and time in a dynamic situation. While it can be developed to a degree with combat experience, with some pilots it seems innate.

During 1916, the Eindecker menace was in part defeated by greater numbers, initially three machines to protect one on a reconnaissance mission. As the Allies regained control of the skies, the Germans also started to use formations. These were mainly of fighters, tasked with protecting photo machines and artillery spotters. The air superiority mission was born, and formations of a dozen or more airplanes became ever more frequent.

Encounter battles

Under such circumstances, seeing the enemy formation first was vital. The first move was to gain a position higher and upsun, before maneuvring to come plunging down from astern. If the attackers could remain unseen, they might easily send two or three enemy machines down in the first pass, throwing the rest into disarray.

If they were seen, the enemy formation would turn into them for a head-on pass; all cohesion would be lost, and a dogfight would ensue; two

dozen fighters whirling around, each trying to take up a shooting position on another's tail. With the fighters of the day able to turn through up to 45 deg/sec, it became almost impossible for one man to keep track of events. The dogfight was a very dangerous place to be. Both survival and success lay in teamwork, each pilot giving his fellows mutual support, while relying on coincidental support to offset unseen threats.

Performance versus manoeuvrability

Much depended on the capabilities of individual machines viz-a-viz those of the enemy. Even as the Eindecker was outfought by the D.H. 2 and the Nieuport 11, so they in turn were outclassed by the newer German fighters; the Albatros D.III and the Pfalz. And so it went on: the French SPAD XIII and Nieuport 27; the British S.E.5a, Camel, and Bristol F.2b; the German Albatros D.V and the Fokker D.VII. First one had the advantage, then the other. Only in the final months of the war did the situation more or less stabilize.

From the beginning, engine development had taken two distinct paths, and this resulted in two

basic fighter families with markedly different characteristics. The rotary engine was very short, and its cylinders, to which the propeller was bolted, rotated around the fixed crankshaft. This arrangement precluded any reasonable form of carburation, consequently the rotary had only one speed: flat out. In combat this was rather limiting; to slow down, the pilot had to "blip" the engine with a switch which cut off the ignition.

At higher altitudes, the rotary engine lost power quickly, which placed another combat limitation on fighters so engined, but it had one enormous advantage. It was so short that all the heavy weights could be placed close together: engine, pilot, fuel and guns. This gave a short moment arm longitudinally, conferring tremendous maneuvrability. The Sopwith Camel was tricky to fly, but could out-maneuver anything in the sky, particularly if turning with the torque of the engine. Yet another rotary-powered machine was

LEFT CENTRE: The Pfalz D.III was an adequate if not outstanding fighter when it entered service toward the end of 1917. In some ways inferior to the Albatros D.V, it handled better. This example was captured intact in December 1917.

ABOVE: Pilots and ground crew of No 1 Squadron RAF, seen with their S.E.5a fighters at Clairmarais, near St. Omer, on July 3 1918. It took a lot of people to keep a single squadron in the air.

the Fokker Triplane, favored by Manfred von Richthofen and Verner Voss among many others.

The alternative was the rather heavier and longer water-cooled inline engine. It gave much greater performance if less maneuvrability than a rotary, was fully throttleable, and maintained power much better at altitude.

These contrasting power plants to a degree determined tactics. Compared with the Camel, the S.E.5a was much faster, climbed and dived better, was a more stable gun platform, was much

ability, for few of its opponents could be outrun. The correct tactics for the Camel pilot were to turn, turn, and turn again, giving an inferior opponent the option of disengaging or being shot from behind.

Which was most important – performance or maneuvrability, was in the tactical battles over the Western Front – largely a matter of personal preference. The question was finally resolved many years later, when bomber performance started to outstrip that of the fighter. When this

RIGHT: The most agile British fighter of the war was the Sopwith Camel. As can be seen here, all the weights are concentrated in a small space, making for a short moment arm. This 46 Squadron Camel carries bombs for a ground attack mission.

SOPWITH CAMEL F.1

Wingspan	28ft 0in (8.53m)
Length	18ft 9in (5.71m)
Power	Clerget rotary rated at 130hp
Maximum speed	115mph (185km/h)
Endurance	2½ hours
Armament	Two Vickers m.g
Date of entry into service	Mid-1917
Number built	5,490

easier to fly, and had a higher ceiling. In the traditional horizontal circling combat it was at a disadvantage against a rotary engined opponent, and this had to be avoided if possible. Correct tactics in the S.E.5a were to gain an altitude advantage, keep speed high, which aided the achievement of surprise as it reduced the time between the first sighting and the attack, and once battle was joined, to fight on the climb and dive wherever possible. Able to dive at more than 200mph (322km/h), the S.E.5a could force battle on most of its opponents, and was fast enough to disengage at will.

By contrast, the Camel was unstable in all axes, unforgiving of a ham-fisted pilot and, if caught in a dogfight, salvation lay in its incredible turning

happened, the need to intercept and to escort bombers became paramount, and performance took precedence over maneuvrability. But in 1917/18, matters were less clear-cut.

The Red Baron era

The creation in 1916 of specialized fighter units by all the major combatants changed the nature of aerial conflict. Whereas before, the more experienced pilots often went up to hunt alone, against the larger formations encountered this gradually became almost suicidal. There were of course exceptions; Billy Bishop was one, while James McCudden had a predilection for stalking high-flying reconnaissance machines, for which he had a specially tuned engine in his S.E.5a. But these were few. By and large, the most successful air fighters in the final 18 months of the war were team players.

From the time that he formed Jasta 2, Oswald Boelcke became the great fighter leader, formulating tactics and methods, and leading by example. Of the 25 victories scored by Jasta 2 in the final fortnight of September 1916, the maestro accounted for ten! He has however been eclipsed in the public mind by one of his pupils, Manfred von Richthofen.

Credited with 80 victories, Richthofen was the top-scorer of the entire war. A master marksman, he was apparently not a particularly outstanding flyer; it is generally agreed that Werner Voss was far superior. Neither was he a tactical innovator, following Boelcke's precepts faithfully during his time in command. His score, although impressive, was surpassed by more than 150 German fighter pilots in World War II, most of whom are almost unknown to the general public. Richthofen's enduring fame has a slightly mysterious quality about it.

The answer appears to lie in glamor. Richthofen was a member of the minor nobility, a Freiherr (a bit lower than a real baron, but the latter name stuck), and therefore inherited the mantle of the Teutonic Knights as of right. To reinforce the image, he was a cavalryman before he became a flyer. Finally, he led the largest fighter formation of the war: Geschwader, JG 1, which consisted of four Jastas, and which became known to the Allies as the Flying Circus.

The soubriquet (and legend) of the Red Baron is instantly memorable. It derived from his habit of flying an all-red fighter, to make himself easily recognizable in the air. He was not of course the first to do this; that distinction goes to French ace Jean Navarre. Finally, he was killed in action in April 1918, at the height of his powers. The fact remains that he has become the most famous fighter pilot of all time.

The second highest scorer of the war was Frenchman René Fonck. A fantastic marksman, whose economy with bullets was unsurpassed, his own airplane was rarely hit. Fonck's almost clinical approach to air fighting was not the stuff of heroes, and although he survived the war with an official score of 75, his exploits never caught the public imagination as had those of Guynemer or Nungesser.

The RFC/RAF top-scorer was Edward Mannock, with a score of 73. As a candidate for the title of greatest patrol leader of the war, he has few equals. A slow starter, he is reputed to have faulty vision in one eye. His efforts to overcome his own inadequacies made him sympathetic towards novice pilots, and his efforts to gain advantages for his men could not have been bettered by Boelcke himself. He was a master of ruses and of careful preparation. When leading 85 Squadron, it was said of him that, by the time they took off, his patrol even knew what the Germans had for breakfast! He was shot down by ground fire on July 26 1918, having survived McCudden (57 victories) who died in a flying accident, by less than three weeks.

One fact emerged from this phase. The scores of the handful of aces were out of all proportion to the units with which they flew. Ernst Udet of Jasta 4 accounted for 39 out of 71 victories in less than five months, while Karl Degelow of Jasta 40 scored 26 out of 49. Similar figures can be found in Allied units. The ace legend had been born.

LEFT: The Red Baron, Manfred von Richthofen, seen after suffering a severe head wound when shot down by the gunner of an F.E.2d of 20 Sqn Another fraction of an inch and he would not have become the top-scoring ace of the war.

BELOW: The two-seater Bristol F.2b was one of the most remarkable fighters of the war. A 275hp Rolls-Royce Falcon engine enabled it to match the German single-seaters, while a gunner guarded the tail.

RIGHT: The Avro Anson, which entered service in March 1936 was the first monoplane in the RAF, and the first to have a retractable main gear. Used by Coastal Command, it carried out the first attack of the war on a U-boat. As a trainer, it remained in service until June 1968.

OPPOSITE CENTER: The Polikarpov I-16 Mosca was the most advanced fighter in the world when it entered large-scale service in 1935, with an enclosed cockpit and retractable main gears. Formidable in the Spanish Civil War, it was outclassed by 1941.

RIGHT: One of the most famous transports of all time, the Junkers Ju 52 tri-motor was also used as a bomber from 1934. As a transport it played a major part in the invasions of Norway, the Low Countries, and Crete.

The end of the Great War saw the Luftstreitkräfte disbanded, and the air forces of the victorious Allies reduced to a fraction of their former strength. At the same time many valuable tactical lessons were forgotten. The Vic of three or five aircraft became standard, even though the pair, consisting of leader and wingman, had been widely used during the final year of the war. Reasons for this were not hard to find. Communication in the air was by means of visual signals, by hand, by Very Light, or by aircraft movement. In the Vic the leader flew in front, with the others stepped up and back, where they could easily see him and his signals. For bombers, this was well-suited to give the defensive crossfire needed for mutual protection. For fighters it was less suitable, although it lent itself to maintaining formation integrity when penetrating cloud.

The armchair strategists were active at this time. A prime theory was that wars could be won entirely by strategic bombing. Based on the assumption that the bomber could always get through, which was not too far off the truth, it failed to take into account what constituted a sustainable level of attrition. It also presupposed a level of accuracy and destruction that would be hard to attain at the present day, three quarters of a century later. In short, bombers became fashionable.

The late 1920s and early 1930s saw enormous advances in aviation technology. The water-cooled inline engine was further developed to give greater power, while the air-cooled rotary engine was supplanted by the radial with fixed cylinders, which had the advantage of being fully throttleable. Then, whereas engines lost power in the attenuated air at high altitudes, this was restored to a degree by supercharging. Variable pitch propellers were used to give greater efficiency. The quest for increased performance led to the widespread adoption of the monoplane configuration, which was of far less drag than the biplane. Other drag-reducing measures were the enclosed cockpit, and the retractable landing gear. While the latter imposed its own penalty in weight and complexity, this was more than offset by the reduction in drag. Metal stressed-skin monocoque construction gave greater strength for lighter weight than canvas and wood.

Whereas fighters had traditionally outperformed bombers, the newest monoplane bombers of the mid-1930s reversed this trend, and became almost uninterceptable by the biplane fighters of the day. A new breed of fighters was developed to

counter them, in which speed, rate of climb, and ceiling were stressed at the expense of maneuverability. Most biplane fighters of the era had maintained the First War tradition of just two rifle-caliber machine guns. The need to knock down a fast, metal-construction bomber in a single brief burst called for much heavier armament. Many nations settled on the 20mm cannon; others the heavy (12.7mm) machine gun. Britain was unique in demanding eight rifle caliber machine guns for its fighters. While not as destructive as larger guns, a two-second burst contained over 300 rounds, giving a high probability of scoring multiple hits.

For fighters, the most important advance was high-frequency radio-telephony, which enabled pilots to communicate with each other and with the ground over distances and in circumstances impossible with visual signals. This greatly increased tactical flexibility. Reception was not

Initially, so few Messerschmitt Bf 109s were available that they had to be flown in pairs, rather than three-ship Vics. The pair was found to be a far more flexible formation, and retained even

always clear, but this was largely overcome by the use of codewords as a form of verbal shorthand. These were selected on the basis of being difficult to mistake; for example, bandit for enemy airplane; bogey for unidentified airplane etc. Unit callsigns were adopted on the same basis.

The proof of the pudding

However convincing the theory, the crucible of battle is needed to prove it. Two wars in the late 1930s gave vital combat experience to five major nations.

The Spanish Civil War saw Fascist forces, aided by German and Italian contingents, opposed by Russian-backed Republicans. Most air operations were in direct support of the ground forces, and the German Legion Kondor was able to refine its close air support tactics. It also, rather fortuitously, made considerable advances in fighter tactics.

when more '109s became available. Under the impetus of Werner Mölders, the crossover turn, which was used in the Great War, was reinvented, and a whole new tactical system established.

The Italians learned little during the Spanish Civil War; their Fiat biplane fighters survived by virtue of their agility, and this became an essential part of Italian tactical thinking.

Opposing the '109s with their Polikarpov I-16 monoplanes, the Russians also adopted the pair as the basic fighter formation but, as most of their successful pilots were purged by Stalin shortly after their return, the Soviet Air Force reaped no lasting benefit.

On the far side of the world, an unseemly brawl developed between China and Japan. To the Japanese, maneuvrability in the dogfight was the primary asset of a fighter. Consequently, their airplanes were agile but, with little protection, were not very survivable. They quickly got the upper

TOP: Bearing Spanish insignia, this is a Messerschmitt Me 109B of the Legion Kondor, where it flew with Jagdgruppe 88. Shortage of aircraft led to the Rotte or pair, the Schwarm or four, and a radical improvement of Luftwaffe fighter tactics.

RIGHT CENTER: Ely's
daring bore fruit.
The next 25 years
saw the aircraft
carrier become an
indispensable part
of the fleet. Seen
here are Fleet Air Arm
Fairey Swordfish
dive- and torpedo
bombers ranged on
the deck of their
carrier.

hand of the Chinese, but then the Russians joined the fray. The I-16 was much more heavily armed and armored than the Japanese fighters, and while the latter used tight turns as their main tactical ploy the Russians fought on the dive and zoom. Overclaiming was a feature of this conflict, and this served to disguise the fact that this campaign was a hard-fought draw. Admitted losses were 207 Russians; 223 Japanese: far less than the claims of either side.

The carrier comes of age

Admirals of the major seafaring nations were swift to see the advantages of air power in the scouting role. Experiments in flying off and landing on ships began in the USA in 1910, but it was some considerable time before this became a practical proposition. Meanwhile, land-based air, and in particular the long-ranged airship, provided eyes for the fleets.It soon became obvious that what was really needed was a dedicated airplane-carrying ship, the aircraft carrier, with virtually the whole of the deck as a flying area, and the deck below as a hangar. While obviously not the most seaworthy of vessels, its advantages were enough to offset the handicaps.

Scouting, or maritime reconnaissance, as it is now called, was but one function. Fleet air defense against air attack from land- or ship-based forces was of primary importance, while enemy fleets could be attacked from far beyond the gun range of even the largest battleships. This sounded the death-knell of the battleship, although many Admirals were slow to admit it.

The author first saw an aircraft carrier from the air in 1952. His reaction; "However can anyone land on that matchbox?" This problem also exercised aircraft designers. Landing speeds had to be slow, and even then, arrester gear had to be used to slow the airplane within the available space in what amounted to a controlled crash.

The result was that naval airplanes were designed primarily for safe carrier operation, rather than suitability for their mission. Stressed for deck-landings, with a tailhook, and with wing-folding to make the most of the restricted space in the hangar, they were heavier than their land-based counterparts, and performance suffered accordingly.

Main picture: On the morning of January 18 1911, Eugene Ely landed his Curtiss pusher on a specially prepared deck on USS *Pennsylvania*: the first ever deck landing. He is seen here taking off a few hours later.

LEFT: The Imperial Japanese Navy, with the wastes of the Pacific on its doorstep, took an early interest in carrier aviation. The Nakajima B5N torpedo bomber seen here first flew in 1935 and entered service three years later.

By 1939 only Britain, America, and Japan had carrier forces. The quality of their airplanes differed widely. The main British carrier airplane was the Blackburn Skua, a two-seater monoplane which doubled as fighter and dive bomber. Its maximum speed of 225mph (362km/h) was too slow to allow it to catch the faster bombers of the era, and its main armament of four .303 caliber machine guns was inadequate.

The USN fielded the Grumman F3-F3 biplane fighter, which was even worse. A top speed of 256mph (425km/h) was backed by just two .30 caliber machine guns. On the other hand, the USN had two monoplanes in service; the Douglas Devastator torpedo bomber and the Vought Vindicator dive bomber; both of which were slower than the Grumman fighter.

The fastest carrier fighter of the time was the Japanese Mitsubishi A5M2, an open cockpit monoplane with fixed landing gear, capable of 273mph (439km/h), but armed with only two .303 caliber guns. The best Japanese attack airplane was the Nakajima B5N torpedo bomber, which was capable of 235mph (378km/h).

British carrier aircraft saw action from 1939, the Americans and Japanese from December 1941, by which time new and better machines had entered service.

Blitzkrieg

Blitzkrieg, or Lightning War, was a fast-moving all-arms assault spearheaded by air power. Initially successful in Poland, Denmark and Norway, it was launched against the West in May 1940. Starting with a glider-borne assault on the Belgian fortress of Eben Emael, and backed by paratroop landings in Holland, the German forces swept all before them.

Numerically strong, the Luftwaffe provided close air support for the ground armies as they raced forward. French ground control, never very good, was quickly over-run and rendered impotent, after which the combined French and British air forces were badly handicapped. The pace of the advance was such that the defending British and French air units were forced to retreat continually as their airfields were threatened, which reduced their effectiveness. By the end of May, the British armies were cut off at Dunkirk, but for the first time this brought the Luftwaffe within range of British-based fighter units, which fought hard to cover what became one of the epic evacuations of all time. But within a matter of days, France capitulated.

The Battle of Britain

The Luftwaffe had been built as a tactical force. Efforts to produce a strategic bomber had been countered by the comment, "The Führer will not ask what; he will only ask how many!" As a result, the assault element consisted of single-engined dive bombers, the Ju 87 Stuka, and twin-engined level bombers, the Heinkel He 111, Dornier Do 17, and Junkers Ju 88, all with limited bomb loads.

Having over-run France, the Luftwaffe now faced England with a force that was never intended to mount a strategic campaign. Having said that, it is only fair to admit that RAF Fighter Command had been equipped and trained to counter an assault by large formations of un-escorted bombers. But now, with German fighter bases just across the Channel, they were faced with a totally different task.

The defenders had however one tremendous advantage. The coast of south and eastern England was ringed with radar stations able to detect approaching formations at more than 100

BELOW: he Legion Kondor was a proving ground for the Luftwaffe. A Heinkel He 111B unloads over the target in the Spanish Civil War. Developed to the H, K, and P models, the He 111 was part of the Luftwaffe Blitzkreig spearhead.

RIGHT: A Heinkel He 111K over England in 1940. It proved very vulnerable to frontal attack, as its glazed nose offered no protection. From late 1940, it operated mainly as a night bomber, and was used by KGr 100, the German pathfinder Gruppe.

miles (160km). Inland, this was backed by a network of observer stations. Set up and practised long before the war, the defensive system could detect and track approaching raids with a fair degree of accuracy, and position fighter squadrons to intercept.

What followed became known as the Battle of Britain, the first air campaign in which surface forces took no part. The task of the Luftwaffe was to gain air superiority over south-eastern England to allow an invasion to take place. RAF Fighter

HEINKEL He 111H

Wingspan	74ft 1½in (22.60m)
Length	53ft 9½in (16.40m)
Power	Two Junkers Jumo 211F rated at 1,340hp
Maximum speed	258mph (415km/h)
Range	1,740 miles (2,800km)
Bomb load	5,510lb (2,500kg)
Date of entry into service	Late 1936
Number built	c7,000

Command had to inflict unacceptable losses on the German bombers while remaining in being as a viable fighting force.

The main German fighter was the Messerschmitt Me 109E. While superior to the British Spitfire and Hurricane at high altitude, most fighting took place at medium levels, where performance was more even, and where the RAF fighters could comfortably out-turn the '109.

As the Duke of Wellington said after Waterloo, it was a damned close-run thing. As the aggressor, the initiative lay with the Luftwaffe; all Fighter Command could do was to respond to the German raids. The Me 109s generally had the advantage of height, position and numbers, plus a superior tactical formation honed in the Spanish Civil War.

The priority of the British fighters was to inflict an unacceptable level of attrition on the German bombers, but this often left them vulnerable to the lurking '109s, which cut a deadly swathe through their ranks. This notwithstanding, the British squadrons often broke through to the bombers. Casualties inflicted on the Stuka units caused them to be withdrawn from the battle in late August, while the twin-engined Me 110 long-range fighter also proved too vulnerable to be effective.

An all-out assault on British fighter airfields from August 13 failed to achieve its aim. Luftwaffe intelligence was faulty; many raids were wasted against non-fighter airfields, while too little effort was expended against the vital radar stations. The sophisticated British ground control system allowed the hard-fighting squadrons to be where they were most needed, and this was enough to turn the tide.

RIGHT: A Heinkel He 111 over London's East End on September 7 1940. The defending fighters were absent on this occasion. Expecting a heavy attack on their airfields, they were wrong-footed.

MESSERSCHMITT Me 109E

Wingspan	32ft 3½in (9.85m)
Length	28ft 3½in (16.40m)
Power	Daimler-Benz DB 601a rated at 1,100hp
Maximum speed	354mph (570km/h)
Range	575 miles (925km)
Armament	Two 20mm cannon, two 7.92mm m.g
Date of entry into service	1937
Number built	c35,000 all variants

Discouraged by their failure to reduce Fighter Command, the Luftwaffe began a series of raids against London. These resulted in heavy losses. With the British still undefeated, Hitler called off the invasion, and the Battle of Britain drew quietly to a close at the end of October, aided in part by bad weather.

The Blitz

Defeated by day, the Luftwaffe turned to night bombing. This was a far more difficult problem for Fighter Command; the night sky was huge, and finding a bomber in it was worse than trying to find the proverbial needle in a haystack. Whereas in daylight a lone bomber could be seen at a range of five miles (8km), at night this was reduced to perhaps 2,000ft (600m) in moonlight, and barely 450ft (137m) in starlight.

Radar could place the night fighter within about three miles (5km) of a bomber, but this was not enough. The answer was the radar-equipped night fighter, able to make contact at well beyond night visual range. This duly emerged as the Bristol Beaufighter; twin-engined, fast enough to overhaul a bomber in a stern chase, and with four 20mm cannon, able to knock it down with a single burst.

Night interception was still far from easy, but gradually teamwork between aircrew and ground controllers improved. In January 1941, British night fighters flew 486 sorties, gaining 78 contacts, which resulted in 11 combats, of which only three were successful. In May, 1,988 night fighter sorties were flown, with 371 contacts; 196 combats, and 96 victories. During this time, German losses went from a minuscule 0.02 per cent to a far more effective 3.93 per cent. Had it not been for the fact that at this point many German units were transferred eastwards for the invasion of Russia, the attrition percentage would quickly have risen to unacceptable levels.

Nightmare over the Reich

Well before the war, the RAF had invested heavily in strategic bombers. Bomb loads were greater than those of any other force, while to enable them to fight their way past defending fighters they were fitted with multi-gunned power-operated turrets.

Operational experience soon showed that unescorted bombers were far too vulnerable to fighters in daylight, and RAF Bomber Command reverted almost exclusively to night operations. But operating over a blacked-out continent brought its own problems. The difficulties of navigation were compounded by distance, and finding the target area, let alone a specific target, proved almost impossible.

The bombers, twin-engined Wellingtons, Whitleys and Hampdens, were gradually

ABOVE: The angular lines of the Messerschmitt Me 109E were a familiar sight in the skies over England in the summer of 1940. Short operational radius was its greatest failing, which allowed a mere 10 minutes combat over London.

LEFT: The spirit of the Battle of Britain was often shown in nose art. Douglas Bader, commander of 242 Squadron, admires the irreverent heraldry on his Hurricane. He is flanked by Eric Ball (6 victories – left), and Willie McKnight (17 victories – right). Bader's own score was 20 plus four shared.

ABOVE:
The Bristol
Beaufort was
used by RAF Coastal
Command as a
minelayer and
torpedo bomber
until 1943. The
Beaufighter night
fighter was based on
it, and this also
superseded the
Beaufort in the anti-
shipping role.

BELOW: The mighty
Avro Lancaster was
the spearhead of
Bomber Command's
night offensive
against the Third
Reich. Docile to fly, it
carried the heaviest
bomb loads of any
aircraft during the
entire war.

replaced by more effective four-engined Stirlings, Halifaxes and Lancasters, but the problems of accurate bombing remained. In the first months of 1942, only one crew in three managed to place their bombs within five miles (8km) of the target. Even in daylight, dropping bombs from a fast-moving airplane three miles (5km) up, was an inexact science. At night the difficulties were greatly increased! The inherent inaccuracy of night raiding caused the policy of area bombing to be adopted, simply because there was no alternative.

Each crew, having been assigned a target, made its own way there in its own good time. The German night fighter force, increasingly assisted

by radar and ground control, was tailored to meet this threat with a line of defensive boxes. Bomber losses rose, and the future of the force seemed at stake.

At this point, command of the bombers passed to Air Marshal Bert Harris. An electronic navigational device code-named Gee had entered service, which for the first time made it possible to concentrate the bombers along a single route, closely spaced in time. Thus was born the bomber stream.

Its first use was Operation Millennium, the Thousand Bomber Raid on Cologne at the end of May. The bombers crashed through the line of defensive boxes on a narrow front. The few night fighters in that sector had more targets than they could possibly deal with, and the vast majority of bombers passed unharmed. For the first time, widespread damage was caused to a German city.

Raids of this size taxed Bomber Command to the utmost, and were replaced by forces of a hundred or more, three or four times a week. But accuracy was still not good. What was needed was a force to find and mark targets for the main body of the raid. This duly emerged in August 1942 as the Pathfinders, an elite force of four (later greatly expanded) squadrons. Led by the Pathfinders, bombing became more concentrated, but better aids were needed to allow targets to be found if they were hidden by cloud.

Two blind bombing devices were introduced at the beginning of 1943. The first was Oboe, which worked on a system of signals from ground stations in England. Of limited range, it allowed Pathfinders to put down markers on an unseen target to an average accuracy of 1,200ft (366m). The second was H_2S, a primitive ground mapping radar carried by the bombers. The radar picture took skill to interpret correctly, and average accuracy was about four times worse than that of Oboe, but it did allow an unseen target area to be bombed. To back up Oboe and H_2S, target indicators were introduced, which produced bright pools of colored fire on the ground, and at which the main force aimed its bombs. If cloud was too thick for the glow from these to be seen, sky markers, colored parachute flares, were used. While these tended to be very inaccurate, they were much better than nothing.

Meanwhile the German night fighters had become an increasing threat. To counter them, devices were introduced to jam their radars and their communications. Electronic countermeasures (ECM), which over the next three years became ever more sophisticated, was born.

A high spot was reached on July 24 1943. Chaff, metallic strips sized to jam German radar, was first used during a raid on Hamburg. The

AVRO LANCASTER B.1

Wingspan	102ft 0in (31.09m)
Length	68ft 11in (21m)
Power	Four Rolls-Royce Merlins rated at 1,390hp
Maximum speed	270mph (434km/h)
Range	2,230 miles (3,588km)
Bomb load	14,000lb (6,350kg)
Date of entry into service	March 1942
Number built	7,374

BOEING B-17G FLYING FORTRESS

Wingspan	103ft 9½in (31.63m)
Length	74ft 4in (22.65m)
Power	Four Wright Cyclone radials rated at 1,380hp
Maximum speed	300mph (483km/h)
Range	1,850 miles (2,977km)
Bomb load	8,000lb (3,630kg)
Date of entry into service	August 1937
Number built	12,723 (all models)

bomber losses fell dramatically to just 0.7 per cent The night war over the Reich was as good as won.

USAAF in Europe

When the first heavy bombers of the USAAF arrived in England in 1942, the strategic doctrine was to place bombs accurately on target. They regarded the night area bombing policy of RAF Bomber Command as wasteful of resources, and in any case their primary bomber, the Boeing

defending guns, searchlights and night fighters were rendered impotent, and of the 746 heavy bombers involved only 12 were lost. The complete German defense organization was in disarray, and remained so for several weeks. Only gradually, with the introduction of radars which operated on a different wavelength, more flexible tactics, and devices which could home on British radars, notably H_2S, did it again become a serious threat.

The first quarter of 1944 saw Bomber Command suffer its heaviest defeats, culminating in the disastrous Nuremburg raid on March 30/31, when 94 bombers went down. At this point it was perhaps fortunate that Bomber Command was switched to support the forthcoming invasion.

For the final two years of the war, RAF intruders played an increasing part in the assault on Germany. Initially, they did little more than patrol known German night fighter airfields, usually without success. Then the first radar-equipped British night fighters had been released to fly bomber support missions over the continent. The first of these, the Beaufighters of 141 Squadron, carried Serrate, a device which could home on German night fighter radars, with deadly results.

Beaufighters were soon replaced by the superb Mosquito, which had already given sterling service as a light bomber. Fast and agile, with a state-of-the-art radar and passive homing devices, it outflew and outfought the Luftwaffe night fighters.

In July 1944, a captured Ju 88G yielded its secrets. The result was new British ECM, and, in the Mosquito, radar-homing devices and a gadget which triggered the German identification system. These things took a while to enter service in quantity. When they did, German night fighter losses soared to 114 in the final month of 1944, for a mere 60 victory claims. At the same time, British

B-17 Flying Fortress, carried a far smaller bomb load than the RAF heavies. This made it essential that their bombs should not be wasted.

Accurate bombing could be carried out only in daylight, when the target could be clearly seen and positively identified. The British felt that, given the strength of the German day fighter defenses, this was suicidal, and urged the Americans to join them in the night bombing campaign. The USAAF 8th Air Force, its bombers heavily defended by .50in (12.7mm) heavy machine guns, longer ranged and with greater hitting power than the British .303s (7.7mm), was not convinced. The Americans determined to try it their way, starting with raids on Occupied France.

ABOVE: A Boeing B-17F en route for German targets. The Flying Fortress was able to defend itself with cross-fire from a close formation, but on deep penetration raids this was found to be less than successful.

LEFT: Close formation bombing had its hazards. The first bomb from the Fortress from which the picture was taken broke off the left stabilizer of the aircraft below. The lower aircraft did not return from this mission.

Above: Consolidated
B-24 Liberators also
took part in the
assault on Germany.
More modern than
the B-17, and with a
rather faster cruising
speed, the ceiling of
the B-24 was lower,
and it was more
difficult to handle at
high weights
and altitudes.

Faith was shaken on November 17 1942, when St. Nazaire was bombed in mistake for La Pallice, over 100 miles (160km) away. This was the very thing that daylight operations were supposed to eliminate. Then just four days later, only 11 out of 76 B-17s managed to find Lorient!

The lesson learned was that the cloudy skies of Europe were a far cry from California. Weather was the enemy that the USAAF never really mastered. The first raid on Germany, Vegesack on January 27 1943, was foiled by cloud, and results against the alternative target of Wilhelmshaven were unimpressive.

Meanwhile the Luftwaffe fighters honed their tactics against the American four-engined heavies, and losses rose. It quickly became clear that, unless the German fighter force could be reduced, losses would be prohibitive. The only answer was a long-range escort fighter, but at the time, this didn't exist. RAF Spitfires were too short-legged; American P-38 Lightnings were no match for the German Me 109s and FW 190As; while the P-47 Thunderbolt could barely reach the German border.

August 1943 saw the notorious first raid on Schweinfurt/Augsburg, in which the first wave turned south to land at airfields in North Africa. Whilst the bombers fought their way through to the target against heavy odds, 60 were shot down, while a further 55 remained in North Africa, too badly damaged to return. Another 60 bombers went down on the second Schweinfurt raid on October 14, more than 20 per cent, and another 138 were damaged. Such losses were unacceptable.

Blind bombing aids, the British Oboe and H_2S, were adopted, which at least allowed attacks to be made, even though accuracy fell to the same level as RAF night operations. Another British device, Carpet, a jammer effective against radar-laid flak, also entered service.

The air battles over Germany were far from a one-way street. The B-17, and its stablemate the B-24 Liberator, were capable of absorbing a con-

siderable amount of battle damage, and the Luftwaffe was hard-pressed to counter them. Among the various stratagems tried were air to air bombing and 21cm mortars, both of which were bedevilled by aiming problems. The Luftwaffe finally introduced the Sturmbock, a heavily armed and armored FW 190A, able to endure the return fire from the bombers, and capable of knocking down a four-engined bomber in a single pass.

The turning point came at the end of 1944. The North American P-51B Mustang was a happy marriage of an American airframe and the British Rolls-Royce Merlin engine. The equal of its Luftwaffe opponents in performance and maneuverability, it had the range to escort the bombers to Berlin.

February 1944 saw "Big Week", a concerted

RIGHT: North
American B-25
Mitchell bombers
set out for a target
in Occupied Europe.
Fast and heavily
armed, they were
the main tactical
bomber in the ETO,
and were widely
used in the Pacific.

attempt to cripple the German aircraft industry. In six days, 3,800 bomber sorties were flown against a dozen aircraft plants. USAAF losses were 226 bombers and only 26 escort fighters. Estimated German production losses were more than 1,000 fighters. This was however not so critical. More important was the loss of 225 pilots during the month, with a further 141 wounded. The German fighters were bleeding to death.

Berlin was first attacked in force in daylight on March 6 1944. Cloud made bombing results problematical, and 69 heavy bombers and 11 escort fighters were lost. The Luftwaffe met this incursion in force, but of the 370 sorties which made contact, 66 were lost; an unacceptable 17.8 per cent.

With the Allied invasion of Normandy looming, the strategic bombing campaign, spearheaded by 8th AF in England and 15th AF in Italy, concentrated on German oil production. From 175,000 tons in April 1944, it dropped to a minuscule 7,000 tons in September. The fuel-starved Luftwaffe was denied enough to carry out normal operations; bomber units were disbanded while fighter training was severely curtailed. The German fighter force, a few veterans who were very experienced and dangerous, backed by a lot of novices with little idea, gradually shrank.

The Americans had proved their point, albeit only with the aid of the Mustang, a single-engined single seater fighter with a range that at first no-one thought possible. Target-finding in often appalling European weather had not entirely been solved; as late as March 1945 Basel and Zurich in neutral Switzerland were bombed in error.

The other limitation of the USAAF in Europe was the size of bomb carried. Design limitations ensured that they were never able to deploy weapons such as the 8,000lb (3,600kg) block-

buster, let alone the 12,000lb (5,440kg) Tallboy or the 10 ton Grand Slam, as carried by the British Lancaster.

Tactical air power

The best fighters in service in the final year of the war in Europe were the British Supermarine Spitfire XIV and Hawker Tempest V; the American Republic P-47D and North American P-51D; and the German Messerschmitt Me 109G and Focke Wulf FW 190D. In combat conventional fighter performance had increased to the practicable limit possible with the reciprocating engine. Maximum speeds and ceilings had increased by almost one third; climb rates nearly doubled, even though maneuverability suffered. Firepower increased considerably; in 1945 the Tempest V had four times the weight of fire of the 1940-vintage Spitfire.

NORTH AMERICAN P-51D MUSTANG

Wingspan	37ft 0in (11.28m)
Length	32ft 3in (9.83m)
Power	Rolls-Royce Packard Merlin rated at 1,695hp
Maximum speed	437mph (703km/h)
Range	2,080 miles (3,347km) with drop tanks
Armament	Six .50in (12.7mm) m.g.
Date of entry into service	1942
Number built	14,819 (all models)

SUPERMARINE SPITFIRE XIV

Wingspan	36ft 10in (11.23m)
Length	32ft 8in (9.96m)
Power	Rolls-Royce Griffon rated at 2,050hp
Maximum speed	448mph (721km/h)
Range	850 miles (1,368km)
Armament	Two 20mm cannon, two .50in (12.7mm) m.g.
Date of entry into service	June 1938
Number built	22,884 (all models incl. Seafires)

ABOVE: P-51D Mustangs over Berlin signaled the beginning of the end for the Third Reich. The Allied bombers were now never without escort fighters, and the Jagdwaffe was ground down by sheer weight of numbers.

RIGHT: With underslung fuel tank for extended range, a Mitsubishi A6M2 Zero speeds down the deck of *Akagi* on its way to Pearl Harbor. The agility of the Zero came as a great shock to the Allies.

Tactically, the once-rampant Luftwaffe fighters had been defeated on all fronts. In Russia they had been swamped by sheer numbers. Over Malta, where they had held the advantages of height and position, they had been held off by sheer determination, while in North Africa and Italy they had been ground down by a combination of numbers and quality.

Over France and the Low Countries, they had to a large degree held their own, but from 1944 were again ground down by superior numbers. In the nine weeks prior to the invasion of Normandy in June 1944, three Allied fighter sorties were flown for every German one. The 13 weeks following saw the ratio more than double and, while there was little difference between the number of victories per hundred sorties, the loss ratio at this time reached 44:1!

The difference lay less in aircraft quality than in pilot quality. But at this point, German jet fighters entered the fray, with a speed advantage of 100mph (160km/hr) over conventional Allied fighters.

Had the German jets become available in large numbers, the course of the air war might just have been altered. As it was, there were never enough

MITSUBISHI A6M6 ZERO-SEN

Wingspan	36ft 1in (11m)
Length	29ft 9in (9.07m)
Power	Nakajima Sakae NK1P rated at 1,210hp
Maximum speed	346mph (557km/h)
Range	1,130 miles (1,818km)
Armament	Two 20mm cannon, three (12.7mm) m.g.
Date of entry into service	July 1940
Number built	10,938 (all models)

of them. The Messerschmitt Me 163 rocket fighter had limited endurance, and was confined to the point defense role; the twin-engined Me 262 had pushed the German state-of-the-art metallurgy far beyond its limits, to the point where its engines were short-lived and unreliable. Once again numbers were decisive; the Me 262s were shot from the skies by Mustangs, Spitfires and Tempests.

Despite the experience of the Great War, carrier air power remained an unproven quantity for many years. Then on November 11 1940, a handful of antiquated Swordfish aircraft of the Fleet Air Arm attacked the Italian fleet in its sup-

RIGHT: A Zero about to "come aboard" the battleship *USS Missouri* on April 28 1945. Kamikaze attacks were very difficult to defend against, and did much damage to the US fleet. The armored deck of British carriers made them less vulnerable.

posedly secure harbor of Taranto.

The 21 elderly British biplanes attacked by night, aided by flares. Eleven were armed with torpedoes, the rest with bombs. The attack was a tremendous success; one Italian battleship was sunk; two more and two heavy cruisers were badly damaged. For the loss of just two Swordfish, the crew of one of which survived, the Italian fleet was out of the war.

War in the Pacific

The Imperial Japanese Navy was impressed by the victory of Taranto, which had clearly demonstrated the vulnerability of capital ships to air power. American economic sanctions on Japan led to a pre-emptive strike against the US Pacific Fleet at Pearl Harbor, in December 1941. The strike force comprised six carriers and the first attack wave consisted of 120 Nakajima B5Ns and 51 Aichi D3As, escorted by 43 Mitsubishi Zeros.

Surprise was complete. The B5Ns attacked what was known as "battleship row", while the D3As went for the USAAF bases. An hour later, a second wave of 55 B5Ns and 80 D3As, escorted by 36 Zeros, compounded the assault. The USN battleships and cruisers were virtually eliminated as a viable force, and 92 USN and 96 USAAF airplanes were destroyed. Japanese losses were just 25 airplanes.

While the raid on Pearl Harbor appeared to be a striking Japanese victory, it carried within it the seeds of eventual defeat. While it clearly demonstrated the vulnerability of battleships to air attack, underlined three days later by the sinking of the British *Prince of Wales* and *Repulse*, it forced the USN Pacific Fleet to continue the fight with its carriers. As luck would have it, these were away from Pearl Harbor at the time, and escaped the attack.

The vast wastes of the Pacific, liberally studded with islands and atolls on its western margin, demanded mobility and, for this, control of the seas was vital. The campaign was marked by a series of fleet actions fought by carrier-borne aircraft, in which only rarely did surface units so much as see each other.

The first was the Battle of the Coral Sea in May

1942. The USN fleet carriers, *Yorktown* and *Lexington*, were opposed by the IJN fleet carriers *Shokaku* and *Zuikakau*, and the light carrier *Shoho*. This inconclusive action showed errors of judgement and poor ship recognition by both sides. *Shoho* was discovered by chance and sunk on May 7. On the following day, *Shokaku* and *Yorktown* were badly damaged, while *Lexington* sank, primarily due to faulty damage control.

The first decisive carrier battle of the war was Midway, in early June. Midway was an air and sea base east of the Hawaian Islands, control of which

BELOW: A Wildcat lines up for takeoff on USS *Ranger* in October 1942. The Grumman F4F Wildcat was the primary carrier fighter of the US Navy during the early war years.

was strategically invaluable. The Japanese object was to take the island, then destroy the USN carrier force when it tried to intervene.

With just three fleet carriers, eight cruisers and 16 destroyers, the Americans could not afford a surface action against the numerically and qualitatively stronger Japanese fleet. The only chance was to stand off and use air power, backed by Marine and Army Air Force units on Midway itself.

The Japanese attack on Midway began shortly after dawn on June 4 1942 and the defenders were badly mauled. Having established the position of the Japanese vanguard, American strikes were launched against it. But instead of the carefully co-ordinated attack by dive- and torpedo-bombers needed to split the defenses, the Japanese squadrons arrived in dribs and drabs. The first

BELOW: Mitsubishi G4M bombers run the gauntlet of anti-aircraft fire at Guadalcanal to attack transport shipping in 1942. Two of them are barely skimming the surface as they pass.

ABOVE: USS *Wasp* blazes furiously after being torpedoed. Carriers were valuable assets, and at the same time high value targets. Aviation fuel and munitions made them vulnerable when hit.

RIGHT: The fastest naval fighter of the war, the Vought F4U Corsair was not ideal for carrier landings. Forward view was poor, and the oleo legs had a built-in bounce. The Royal Navy was the first service to take it aboard carriers; only later was it accepted by the USN.

arrivals were cut to pieces by the defending Zeroes before they could inflict any damage. But the series of actions pulled all the Japanese fighters down to low level.

At this point, Dauntless dive bombers arrived at medium level, and hurtled to the attack unopposed. Three of the four Japanese carriers were mortally hit; *Hiryu*, the only survivor, launched a counter-strike at noon which crippled *Yorktown*. *Hiryu*'s triumph was short-lived; later that day she was found and bombed into oblivion. With its carrier force destroyed, the Japanese fleet retired, defeated.

Midway was the turning point of the Pacific War. For the IJN, the loss of four carriers was bad, but the loss of so many experienced flyers was far worse. From this point, the level of expertise of Japanese pilots fell markedly, never to recover. Another factor, generally unremarked, was the loss of "face" so dear to the oriental nations.

After Midway, American forces pursued a two-pronged strategy in the Pacific. Whilst the US Army and Army Air Force worked their way up New Guinea and through what is now Indonesia, the US Navy and Marines specialized in island-hopping. The result was that the Japanese never knew where the next attack was coming; flexibility, to a large degree conferred by carrier air power, provided the key. Not every Japanese-held island was invaded; many were bypassed and cut off from supplies, at the same time giving easy targets for new squadrons to gain experience.

The fifth and last major carrier battle of the war was the Battle of the Philippine Sea, in June 1944. Nine Japanese carriers, assisted by land-based air units, sallied forth against seven fleet carriers and eight light carriers of the USN. The air battle that followed became known as the Marianas Turkey Shoot. In two days, 476 Japanese aircraft were lost, against 76 American. At the end of the battle, only 35 Japanese aircraft were operational.

In the first Pacific battles, the agility of the Zero fighter, flown by very experienced and capable pilots, had posed all sorts of problems for the Americans in their sturdy Grumman F4F Wildcats. Only teamwork and tactics allowed them to hold their own. But this was soon to change. While the IJN introduced better and more powerful Zeros, these were outmatched from 1943 by two new American fighters: the Grumman F6F Hellcat and the Vought F4U Corsair. Although unable to turn with the Zero, their performance was vastly superior. In addition, the thoroughly trained USN pilots were more than a match for Japanese novices.

In the final months of the war, the USN was able to put more than 1,000 carrier aircraft over the Japanese home islands in a single raid. Naval air power had finally proved itself!

Finale

With the capture of bases in the Marianas, the Japanese home islands came within reach of Boeing B-29 strategic bombers. Raids commenced on November 24 1944, but the most devastating attack of all was a raid on Tokyo on the night of March 9/10 1945, when 334 B-29s carried out a fire raid, burning out nearly 16 square miles (25km²). Other fire raids followed, on a further 58 cities. But the worst was still to come.

On August 6 1945, a lone B-29 dropped Little Boy, the first operational nuclear bomb, on Hiroshima. The damage from this single weapon was horrendous; over 70,000 people were killed and a similar number injured, while 49,000 buildings were destroyed. The Japanese were aghast. Three days later, another lone B-29 dropped Fat Man on Nagasaki. Faced with obliteration, Japan surrendered.

The nuclear shadow

The end of the Second World War was greeted with relief. Germany and Japan were occupied by Allied forces, and the future seemed to con-

VOUGHT F4U-4 CORSAIR	
Wingspan	41ft 0in (12.5m)
Length	33ft 8in (10.26m)
Power	Pratt & Whitney R-2800 rated at 2,100hp
Maximum speed	446mph (718km/h)
Range	1,005 miles (1,617km)
Armament	Six .50in (12.7mm) m.g.
Date of entry into service	October 1942
Number built	10,447

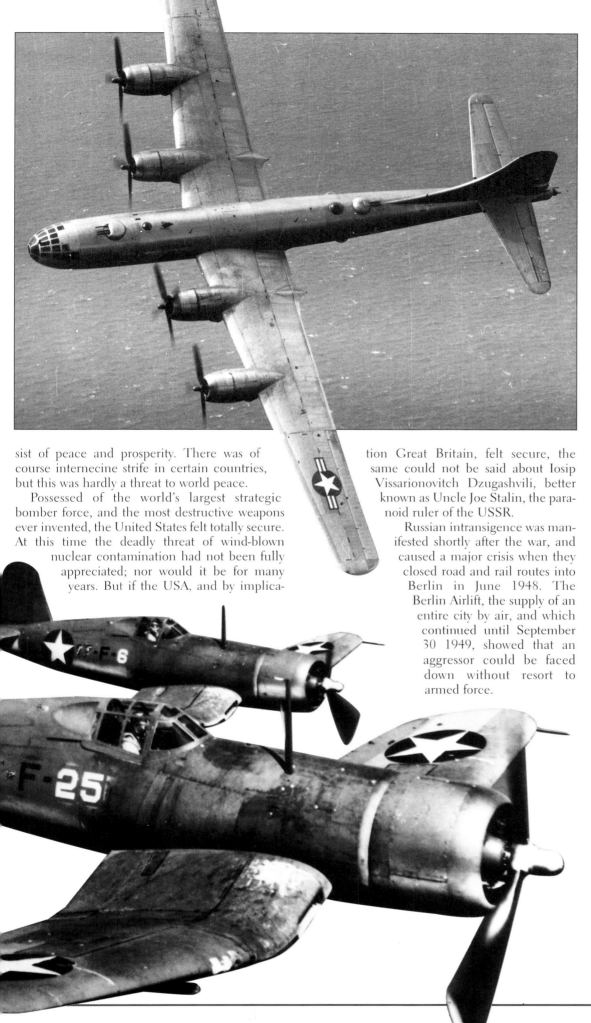

LEFT: The Boeing B-29 Superfortress was by far the biggest bomber of the Second World War. It had a range of about 3,700 miles (5,954km) while carrying a bomb load of 12,000lb (5,443kg). Aircraft of this type carried out the nuclear attacks on Hiroshima and Nagasaki.

sist of peace and prosperity. There was of course internecine strife in certain countries, but this was hardly a threat to world peace.

Possessed of the world's largest strategic bomber force, and the most destructive weapons ever invented, the United States felt totally secure. At this time the deadly threat of wind-blown nuclear contamination had not been fully appreciated; nor would it be for many years. But if the USA, and by implica-

tion Great Britain, felt secure, the same could not be said about Iosip Vissarionovitch Dzugashvili, better known as Uncle Joe Stalin, the paranoid ruler of the USSR.

Russian intransigence was manifested shortly after the war, and caused a major crisis when they closed road and rail routes into Berlin in June 1948. The Berlin Airlift, the supply of an entire city by air, and which continued until September 30 1949, showed that an aggressor could be faced down without resort to armed force.

ABOVE: The US Marines used the Corsair in the close air support role, a mission in which it was very effective both in the Second World War, and in Korea where this picture was taken.

By mid-1950, the USA had about 300 nuclear weapons, and roughly 840 bombers capable of delivering them. Western intelligence estimated that at this time the USSR had about 24 nuclear weapons and 200 suitable bombers. A nuclear war looked a distinct possibility.

The destructive power of atomic weapons seemed to indicate that bombing accuracy was a thing of the past. But, at the Bikini Atoll tests in 1946, the battleship *Nevada* was the aiming point. Although it was painted bright red, the bombardier on the B-29 still managed to miss it (on a clear day) by a sufficiently wide margin for it to survive!

The jet age compounded the problems. Whereas the B-29 or its Russian Tu-4 clone could carry nukes at 300mph (483km/h) and 30,000ft (9,144m); the new breed of jet bomber could manage 500mph (805km/h) at 40,000ft (12,191m). The obvious next move was to supersonic bombers such as the Mach 2 B-58 Hustler and the Mach 3 XB-70 Valkyrie (which never

ABOVE: Speed brakes out, a Grumman F9F Panther lets fly with a rocket at a ground target in North Korea. Carrier aircraft flew tens of thousands of close air support missions during the war, and accounted for several MiGs in air combat.

entered service), which would make fighter interception even more problematical.

Given the destructive capability of nuclear-armed bombers, not one could be allowed to slip through. High speeds coupled with the restricted maneuvrability at high altitude reduced the value of the traditional stern interception; the necessity of jockeying for position could be avoided by a collision course attack from the front quarter. The fighter was vectored towards its target, locked up its radar, and armed the weapons system. The computer then launched the weapons automatically when the target came within range.

The gun was totally inadequate for this task. It was first replaced by batteries of unguided rockets, then later by homing missiles. Automated interception reached its apogee with the Convair F-106 Delta Dart. This had a fire control system and autopilot tied to ground control via data link. The interception could thus be guided from the ground, with the pilot reduced to the status of system manager. The Soviet equivalent was the MiG-25 Foxbat, of similar concept but even higher performance.

From 1958, long-range high-altitude surface to

air missiles (SAMs) entered service, with an anticipated kill probability of around 90 per cent. Against this, high-speed high-altitude bombers did not look such a good bet. Their response was to switch to low-level subsonic penetration, under the radar coverage.

Miniaturization was another factor. This gave rise to small tactical nuclear weapons carried by fighter-bombers, the short range of which meant that the mission was essentially a one-way ticket. Attack airplanes were specifically designed for this role, with radar navigation devices to tell the pilot where he was at all times.

Deterrence worked, and nuclear conflict between east and west was subordinated to a series of limited wars in which the major powers confronted each other indirectly, mainly through surrogate nations. The first of these was Korea from 1950-1953.

MiG Alley

Korean air combat had three distinct aspects. Daylight strategic bombing was carried out by B-29s, but even with fighter escorts, casualties

counter it, the USAF introduced the swept-winged F-86 Saber. From this point, the air war took on an artificial aspect.

Sabers patrolled high over the battlefield to protect the attack airplanes. The MiGs, reluctant to concede the traditional advantage of superior altitude, flew even higher. In doing so they distanced themselves from the ground war, and were rarely able to intervene over the battlefield. The result was a fighter war in the stratosphere almost entirely divorced from the main conflict, over an area known as MiG Alley.

Powered by a jet engine developed from the British Roll-Royce Nene, the MiG-15 was a simple no-frills fighter with a superb high altitude performance and rate of climb which the Saber could not match. Maximum speeds were similar, but whereas the F-86 could reach supersonic speed in a dive the MiG became unstable and snaked at speeds above Mach 0.86, while the dive brakes deployed automatically at Mach 0.92. Although outclassed by the MiG-15 at very high altitudes, the rather heavier and more sophisticated Saber handled much better, thanks to its advanced flight control system. A radar-ranging gunsight was another advantage, although its armament of six 0.50in (12.7mm) Brownings lacked hitting power against jets, which were considerably tougher than their piston-engined forebears.

Fighting in the stratosphere posed unique problems. In the thin air at 40,000ft (12,191m), stall speeds more than doubled. In anything other than gentle turns, the pilot risked "dropping it", which in combat could be embarrassing. When avoiding action was needed, often the only way to go was downwards. Under these circumstances, achieving a valid shooting position called for very fine judgement.

LEFT: Superfortresses unload on Korean targets. The sheer speed of the opposing MiGs allowed them to penetrate the screen of escorts, and the B-29s suffered heavy losses. Shortly after they were relegated to night bombing.

BELOW: The problems of interception were made ever more difficult as bombers got faster and higher. The ultimate was reached with the Convair B-58 Hustler, able to make a Mach 2 dash over the target.

were too high to be sustained. The Russian MiG-15, armed with two 23mm and one 37mm cannon, had been designed as a bomber destroyer, and when the shooting started it proved very effective.

The major aspect of the war was interdiction, fighter-bombers attacking communist supply routes. While this played an important part in the ground war, it was partly negated by two previously unconsidered factors. Firstly, the communists had almost unlimited manpower available for repair work. Secondly, the communist forces were primitive; a Chinese division needed only a fraction of the supplies required by its Western equivalent.

Korea was the first conflict in which jet fought with jet. Russian-flown MiG-15s appeared at the front late in 1950, and outclassed the straight-winged American jets in the theater. To

In the very clear air at high altitudes, there was little on which the pilot's eyes could focus, which aggravated the problems of keeping a sharp lookout. Accounts of the period often contain the words "they jumped into focus!"

Finally, large throttle movements could easily cause the engine to flame out. In combat, it was best left well alone, but this caused difficulties in keeping station. The leader had to fly in such a manner as to allow his flight to maintain formation integrity.

USAF records show that the Saber pilots logged a kill/loss ratio of nearly 7½:1 over the MiGs. Given the superior altitude performance of the Russian fighters, this can only be attributed to the superior fighting skills of the Saber pilots, many of whom had flown in the Second World War.

Air-to-air guided missiles

As combat speeds increased, so did the distance at which the average pilot could bring his guns to bear. The inaccuracy of unguided rockets, despite reports to the contrary, made them all but useless. What was needed was a homing system which would enable a projectile to follow its target.

Initially only two guidance systems were adequate: Semi-Active Radar (SARH), in which the fighter focussed its radar on the target and the missile homed on the reflected energy, and Infra-Red (IR), in which the missile homed on heat from the jet efflux of the target.

The latter was intrinsically very accurate, and quite a small warhead was needed to ensure destruction. On the other hand it was indiscriminate; the pilot had to be certain that his target was an enemy. Consequently it was a visual range weapon.

SARH missiles were less accurate; to give a good chance of destruction the warhead was large. This made for a large missile, which meant that it was easy to build-in longer range. Electronic means used for target identification made it theoretically easy to intercept from beyond visual distance.

The first use of homing missiles took place on September 24 1958, when 14 F-86Fs of the Taiwanese Air Force clashed with MiG-15s of the Air Force of the Chinese People's Republic. Ten MiG-15s were claimed destroyed, four by AIM-9B Sidewinder heat-seekers. Thus began a new phase of air warfare.

In the gun era, attacks could be avoided by diving away out of range. Missiles like the Sidewinder made this form of evasion distinctly unprofitable, as was shown in the Indo-Pakistan War of 1965. The primary Indian fighter was the Hawker Hunter which, although less maneuverable, had a significant performance advantage over Pakistani Sabers. But about one quarter of the Sabers carried Sidewinders, and this forced the Indian Hunters to turn rather than extend away, negating their performance advantage.

ABOVE: A North American F-86 Saber launches a high-velocity aircraft rocket (HVAR) over the range in the Nevada desert. Speed brakes are deployed while the missile accelerates clear of the fighter.

Guns resurgent

The foundation of the State of Israel in 1948 was greeted with hostility by its Arab neighbors. Border incidents were frequent, and culminated in all-out war in June 1967.

The Israeli Air Force was badly outnumbered, with only 170 fighters, 72 of them modern Dassault Mirage IIICJs, with which to oppose more than 600 Arab fighters, including 200 MiG-21s.

To reduce the odds, the Israelis launched a pre-emptive strike at Egyptian and Syrian airfields, destroying more than 300 aircraft on the ground on the first day. This notwithstanding, many air combats took place over the six days of the war, and the Israelis claimed 58 victories against losses of at least six. Curiously, these were all claimed with gunfire in close combat, although it is known for certain that missiles were used.

Three conclusions were drawn from this conflict. The most important was the vulnerability of aircraft on the ground. Within weeks, hardened shelters proliferated throughout Europe in an attempt to reduce vulnerability to surprise attack. The second was a reappraisal of the gun as a valid fighter weapon.

David versus Goliath

The air war over Vietnam was the most protracted of modern times, lasting from mid-1965 to January 1973. Although the full might of the USA could have secured a quick victory, this was politically unacceptable. Instead, a policy of escalation was adopted, gradually stepping up pressure to indicate the strength of American resolve. This was however interpreted as weakness, to the detriment of all involved. The result was a David versus

LEFT: A Boeing B-52 Stratofortress salvoes its bombs over a North Vietnamese target. The eight-engined monster was designed for the delivery of nuclearweapons, but until 1972 was assigned tactical targets in Vietnam.

Goliath combat, with Goliath blind-folded and with one hand tied behind his back.

The two main areas of conflict were the in-country war against the Viet Cong partisans, and to a lesser degree the North Viet-namese army; and the semi-strategic war against the north which supported them. A fre-quently expressed American sentiment of the period was "bomb them back to the stone age!"

Against a sophisticated, high-tech opponent, this attitude might have been valid. But, as the Korean War had shown, against a primitive oppo-nent the difference was minimal. Sending a multi-million dollar fighter-bomber to wipe out a few trucks was far from cost-effective, even if it suc-ceeded.

The other strange thing about the conflict in South-East Asia was that for many years tactical aircraft carried out strategic missions, while gigan-tic eight-engined B-52 strategic bombers flew mainly tactical missions, flattening huge areas of jungle where the Viet Cong were thought to be lurking.

For attacks on the North, the USAF operated mainly from bases in Thailand, a distance equiva-lent to London/Berlin. This made it dependent on in-flight refueling, with an extended period under communist radar surveillance. Its major types were the F-105 Thunderchief, which was an opti-mized nuclear strike machine with an internal bomb bay and a Doppler-radar navigation system. Fast but heavily wing-loaded, it was rather less than perfect for putting conventional "iron" bombs accurately on target.

DASSAULT MIRAGE IIIC

Wingspan	27ft 0in (8.23m)
Length	48ft 5½in (14.77m)
Power	SNECMA Atar 9B afterburning turbojet rated at 13,320lb (59.2kN) static thrust
Maximum speed	Mach 2.15
Range	c994 miles (1,600km)
Armament	Two 30mm cannon; two or three AAMs
Date of entry into service	July 1961
Number built	1,420 (all models, incl. 5 and 50)

MIKOYAN MiG-21F-13

Wingspan	23ft 5½in (7.15m)
Length	44ft 2in (13.46m)
Power	Tumansky R-11 afterburning turbojet rated at 13,670lb (60.8kN) static thrust
Maximum speed	Mach 2.05
Range	808 miles (1,300km)
Armament	One 30mm cannon; two AAMs
Date of entry into service	1959
Number built	12,000 (all models, incl. Chinese F-7s)

ABOVE: Designed as a tactical nuclear bomber, the Republic F-105D Thunderchief carried out mainly strategic raids in Vietnam until 1968, with iron bombs carried externally. Only rarely did it use its supersonic capability.

ABOVE: The F-4 Phantom has been the subject of many upgrades. The IAI Phantom 2000, powered by two Pratt & Whitney P.1120 turbofans, seen here, has been developed for the Israeli Air Force.

McDONNELL DOUGLAS F-4E PHANTOM II

Wingspan	38ft 5in (11.71m)
Length	63ft 0in (19.20m)
Power	Two General Electric J79-17afterburning turbojets rated at 17,900lb (79.6kN)
Maximum speed	Mach 2.20
Range	cl,750 miles (2,816km)
Armament	One 20mm Vulcan cannon; eight AAMs
Date of entry into service	1962
Number built	5,195

The main escort fighter, which also took over the attack role from the F-105 in the final years of the war, was the F-4 Phantom. A twin-engined two-seater, originally developed as a fleet air defense fighter, its standard armament was four AIM-7 Sparrow SARH missiles, and four AIM-9 Sidewinder heat seekers. No gun was carried.

USN carriers operated from the Gulf of Tonkin, standing offshore. As in the USAF, the primary fighter was the Phantom, backed in the attack role by the A-7 Corsair and the all-weather A-6 Intruder, which had been designed to a requirement emanating from Korean experience.

By contrast the North Vietnamese Air Force was comparatively tiny, operating Russian-built MiG-17s and MiG-21s and, in the final two years, Chinese F-6s, a reverse-engineered MiG-19. It was trained by Russian instructors, and operated under Russian-style close ground control. Too weak to even think of inflicting a decisive defeat on the US forces, it settled for a policy of air deniability, remaining in being as an effective force and thus making the Americans waste a lot of resources in providing fighter escort and electronic countermeasures for their strikes. In this the Vietnamese were aided by their adversaries; for a long while American rules of engagement forbade attacks on North Vietnamese airfields, and even on SAM sites unless these fired first.

Two theories were shattered by the Vietnam War. The advent of homing missiles which could be launched from far beyond visual range, combined with the overwhelming performance of the latest fighters, were thought to herald the end of the dogfight, while the cheap and cheerful communist fighters were supposedly outclassed by the sophisticated American weapons systems.

These assumptions were quickly proved wrong. After a couple of unfortunate incidents, visual recognition became mandatory, and from this point virtually all combats took place at visual range. Nor was the fashionable Mach 2 maximum speed ever used. The records show that, during the entire war, supersonic flight totaled just a few hours, and that Mach 1.6 was never reached. Virtually all air combat took place at high subsonic speeds which put a premium on maneuverability. This was to the advantage of the austere but agile Russian "sports car" fighters.

Nor did the all-singing, all-dancing missiles perform as advertized. Sparrows achieved a probability of kill (Pk) of about 8 per cent; Sidewinders were rather better with 15 per cent. Both had a rather long minimum range, and opponents within this were safe from attack. The gun was re-

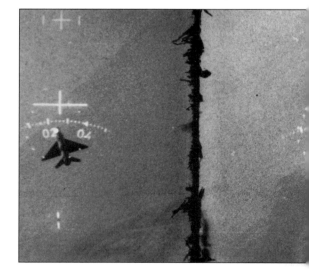

RIGHT CENTER: Camera gun film from the October War of 1973. An Egyptian MiG-21 is caught in the sights of an Israeli fighter and catches fire as the shells strike home, first in the port wing and fuselage, then in the starboard wing.

introduced for close-range combat, in pods on most Phantoms, internally on the later F-4E.

Far more dangerous than the North Vietnamese fighters were the SAMs. It was however found that these could be outmaneuvered if seen in time, while at a later date jamming provided a partial answer. The best counter of all was the Wild Weasel, a specially equipped airplane with missiles which could home on SAM radars.

Statistically, the fighter war over Vietnam was a sideshow, with just 200 victories and 78 losses to show for ninety months of combat. This notwithstanding, the failure to even approach the Korean victory/loss ratio forced the Americans to address the neglected art of maneuver combat once more – Top Gun by the USN, the Aggressor program by the USAF.

Other wars

The October War in the Middle East in 1973 once more saw Israel heavily outnumbered, this time by roughly 4:1. Another pre-emptive strike was politically unacceptable, and a classic defensive action resulted. The main adversary fighter was still the MiG-21; the Israelis had by now acquired about 128 Phantoms to back their Mirages and Neshers, armed with Sparrows, and the indigenous Shafrir IR missile. Total Arab air combat losses were 277, and unlike in the Six Day War four-fifths of these fell to AAMs. Israeli air combat losses were roughly 20. Friendly fire was a feature of this conflict, and many "own goals" were scored.

The Israelis were next in action over Lebanon in June 1982. By now they were largely equipped with the latest American fighters, the F-15 Eagle and F-16 Fighting Falcon, backed by Hawkeye E-2C airborne early warning aircraft.

The first Israeli move was to detect and take out the SAM batteries. Syrian ground radar was then rendered impotent by a combination of attacks and jamming. When the Syrian fighters, MiG-23s and MiG-21s, reacted, they had no help from the ground. Thus blinded, they were ambushed from radar shadows by F-15s with

Sparrows, then engaged at close quarters by the F-16s. A total of 84 Syrian fighters were claimed, for no Israeli losses.

A totally different conflict took place in the South Atlantic at about this time. Argentina occupied the Falkland Islands, and a British task force was sent to recover them. This saw the combat debut of the Sea Harrier jump jet. Heavily outnumbered by the combined Argentine Air Force and Navy aircraft, the Sea Harriers were firmly subsonic, with pulse radar only, with no lookdown mode. In theory they could perform unconventional maneuvers with thrust vectoring, but in

ABOVE: A Sea Harrier soars off the ski-jump of HMS *Hermes* in the South Atlantic in 1982. The war with Argentina proved conclusively the value of short takeoff and vertical landing aircraft, without which the Royal Navy would have had no fighter cover.

LOCKHEED MARTIN F-16C FIGHTING FALCON	
Wingspan	31ft 0in (9.45m)
Length	49ft 3in (15.01m)
Power	Pratt & Whitney F100 or General Electric F110 afterburning turbofan rated at 29,000lb (129kN)
Maximum speed	Mach 1.8
Range	840 miles (1,353km) with drop tanks
Armament	One 20mm Vulcan cannon; four AAMs
Date of entry into service	January 1979
Number built	4,000 plus (production continues)

ABOVE: Helicopters
have proved
invaluable air assets
for many years. This
is a Bell AH-1W
Whiskey Cobra of
the US Marine
Corps. Whiskey
Cobras provided
close air support to
theground forces in
the Gulf War of
1991.

practice this was never used. They had two main advantages: their ability to land vertically allowed them to operate in weather conditions that no other carrier fighter could match, and they were armed with the latest AIM-9L Sidewinders.

The main fighter opposition was the Mach 2 capable Mirage III, armed with French R.530 or R.550 Magic AAMs, but in the event nearly all air combat took place when fighter-bombers were intercepted. In all, 20 Argentine jets were shot down by Sea Harriers, for no British air combat losses.

The Gulf War, 1991

The war to liberate Kuwait in 1991 was to a degree a proving ground for the most modern technology and tactics. The Iraqi air defenses could be accounted strong by any standards: a detection, command and control system backed by an estimated 7,000 SAMs of French and Russian origin and 9-10,000 anti-aircraft guns. The Iraqi Air Force was numerically strong, with many good if not particularly outstanding fighters, of which the MiG-29 was very much an unknown quantity to the West.

Iraq was opposed by a Coalition of many nations, air power for which was supplied by the USA, Britain, Canada, France, Italy, and of course the host country, Saudi Arabia. Underpinning the entire Coalition effort was the biggest strategic airlift in history. Most of this was conducted by the USAF, with Lajes in the Azores playing a critical if largely unsung role as a staging post, and as a

base for refueling tankers. Without such speed of reaction, the war might have been lost by default.

The Russians have a saying about radar detection, command and control systems: destroy one third, jam one third, and the rest will collapse on its own. This was precisely what the Coalition set out to do. Hostilities were opened by a helicopter raid which took out two radar stations, opening up a corridor through which attack aircraft poured. To the east, USN carrier aircraft were preceded by drones with the radar signatures of real airplanes; these decoys soaked up much of the initial Iraqi response.

The attack aircraft were escorted. Fighters, notably the F-15 Eagle, ranged ahead and on the flanks; EF-111 Ravens of the USAF provided dedicated jamming inland; while F-4G Wild Weasel Phantoms hunted for and killed SAM radars. For the US Navy, EA-6B Prowlers provided jamming and SAM suppression for the carrier strikes. Within 72 hours the Iraqi defense system was rendered almost completely impotent.

While Coalition air power enjoyed a qualitative advantage from the outset, nowhere was this so marked as its ability to operate during the hours of darkness, and not only operate, but carry out first pass blind strikes against ground targets. The Iraqis had no equivalent to this, nor any counter to it.

The hordes of friendly aircraft in the sky at any one time posed real problems in air traffic control, and this was not made any easier by the need for in-flight refueling on all longer-range missions. Ground control naturally played a part, but most

LEFT: A Panavia
Tornado ADV of the
Royal Saudi Air
Force skims low
over the desert,
casting a hard black
shadow on the
sand. The "below
the radar" ultra-low
level attack profile
allows high speed
penetration of
defended areas
withminimal risk.

were marshaled out and back under the benevolent electronic eyes of E-3 Sentry AWACS and E-2C Hawkeye AEW aircraft.

AWACS and AEW also played a vital part in the few air combats that took place. Only rarely did the Iraqis come up to fight, and when they did they showed little stomach for the task. This was of course hardly surprising; they were heavily outnumbered, and with ground control either out of action or jammed, they had little idea of what was going on outside the confines of their cockpits. Furthermore, they were up against the world's best, and they knew it. Of the three dozen Iraqi airplanes lost in air combat, most fell to the F-15/Sparrow combination, and few made really aggressive moves. Coalition air-to-air losses were nil, although a slight element of doubt exists in just one case. However, in such a crowded sky, it reflects great credit on the controllers that the Coalition suffered no air combat losses to friendly fire, although on at least two occasions it was a near-run thing!

The angular black shape of the Lockheed F-117 Nighthawk had made its combat debut over Panama in December 1989. Now it flew for the first time against a modern air defense system, with great success, making precision attacks against targets in Baghdad. Virtually all its sensors were passive, while its nav/attack system enabled it to bomb on time almost to the second. Consequently the Iraqis were generally unaware of its presence until the bombs went down. A turkey in maneuver combat, the F-117 was restricted to the hours of darkness, but its stealthy qualities had one tremendous advantage. It needed no fighter escort, or backup by jamming and defense suppression airplanes, thus saving scarce resources.

BELOW: The Gulf War
of 1991 saw the
operational value of
stealth, in the
sinister shape of the
Lockheed F-117A,
fully proven.
Nighthawks
madeprecision
attacks on high
value targets in Iraq
without loss.

RIGHT: Precision
guided weapons
rendered even small
targets vulnerable in
the Gulf War. This
hardened aircraft
shelter has been
wrecked by a direct
hit, destroying any
aircraft inside it.

BELOW: The weird
shape of the
Northrop B-2A Spirit
is seen here with
bomb doors open
as it drops a
conventional 2,000
pounder on the
range. Stealth is
the shape of future
air warfare.

Airfield attacks were high on the agenda, but in Iraq this posed special problems. For a start there were no fewer than 66, of which over 30 were main operating bases. Some of these were huge, more than double the area of London Heathrow, and liberally sprinkled with hardened aircraft shelters (HAS).

The approved method of airfield attack was to cut the runways, making them unusable by fast jets, but the number of cuts needed to render two very long main runways and literally miles of taxiways and hardstandings inoperable was simply beyond the resources available. Instead, selective cuts were made at as many airfields as possible, with the object of isolating large HAS complexes from the main runway, thus severely restricting Iraqi air operations rather than halting them alto-

gether. This task fell mainly to RAF Tornado GR.1s, using JP233 weapons dispensers at very low level.

Whereas HAS provided a fair degree of protection in the days of "iron" bombs, the accuracy of the laser-guided variety meant that they could now be reliably hit from medium level. This gave rise to another problem. Prior to the attack, it was impossible to tell which were occupied and which were empty. Then often a bomb punched a neat hole through the roof and exploded inside, leaving the structure basically intact and reusable. The problem then became, did an apparently damaged HAS contain an operational aircraft, or was it empty? This was never satisfactorily solved.

Smart bombs are not infallible, and they are far more costly than the conventional variety. On the

other hand, it takes far less of them to destroy a given target, thus saving a heap of resources. Fewer attack aircraft are needed; less fighters, less ECM and defense suppression, and less tankers. This makes their use an economic proposition. To give one rather extreme example from the Gulf War, a large formation of F-16s dropped 80 "iron" bombs at an Iraqi runway.

The acceleration caused by diving attacks quickly made the F-16s supersonic, but unfortunately their weapons computers were only programmed to handle speeds up to Mach 0.9. Nineteen near misses were poor compensation. Smart bombs would have given hits with far less effort.

Coalition qualitative and tactical superiority soon proved decisive. Air supremacy was gained in a matter of days, and the Iraqi army was given such a pounding that when the ground war started, what Saddam Hussein called the Mother of All Battles quickly became the Mother of All Retreats, monitored by two E-8 Joint STARS reconnaissance aircraft. So effective was this that it was said that if Iraqi troops wore a radar reflector in their hats, all of them could have been tracked.

The future

Nothing ever stands still. Stealth will exert a decisive influence on future air warfare for those few countries able to afford it. The Northrop B-2 is its most advanced manifestation, while the Lockheed F-22 fighter and the proposed Joint Strike Fighter both have many stealth features, including internal weapons carriage. By reducing detection ranges, stealth may largely negate medium range combat. If this happens, priority will go to visual-range combat, which in turn will demand ever more capable short-range AAMs, and ever more agile fighters.

The latest missiles now have a high off-bore-

sight capability which in turn needs a helmet-mounted sight to cue them. A missile able to be launched at a rear aspect target is technically feasible, but poses intractable tactical problems.

The F-22 also features supercruise, the ability to maintain high supersonic speed without the use of afterburner. This crimps the engagement envelopes of hostile fighters and missiles, and gives a much smaller IR footprint at very high speeds.

Finally, there is thrust vectoring. First introduced on the Harrier to allow vertical takeoff and landing, it has now been adapted to provide greater maneuvrability. Whereas conventional machines relied on wing lift for maneuver, adding vectored thrust tied into the flight control computer allows full control at speeds below the stall, and previously impossible maneuvers to be flown. The current exponents of this are the Lockheed Martin F-16MATV, and the gigantic Sukhoi Su-37.

ABOVE: The Lockheed F-22 Raptor is the fighter of the future. Combining stealth with supercruise and thrust-vectoring, it is as good in beyond visual combat as it is in the dogfight.

LEFT: Even as the F-16 was added to the F-15 to give a hi-lo mix, so the Joint Strike Fighter is to add numbers to the quality of the F-22. Here is the JSF entry submitted by Northrop, McDonnell Douglas, BAe and Grumman.

CHAPTER FOUR
The Aviators

RIGHT: Otto Lilienthal airborne in his biplane hang-glider *No 13* of 1895; earlier essays had included the monoplane hang-gliders *Nos 11* and *16* of 1894. He was to be killed flying *No 11* in 1896.

IT IS QUITE POSSIBLE that, as Mankind approaches the end of the second Millennium AD, more of its adult members will have traveled in an aeroplane than have sailed in a sea-going vessel. One hundred years ago fewer than a dozen men had been carried aloft in a heavier-than-air craft: one of these men was the German Otto Lilienthal; another was probably the anonymous coachman's son, employed by Sir George Cayley half a century earlier to occupy his glider on the first manned flight by a heavier-than-air craft. The second half of the 19th Century was littered by would-be model-making aerodynamicists, few of whom recognized that Cayley's design represented, in essence, all the essentials of a successful glider, and that, given a suitable powerplant, it stood the best chance of attaining controllable free flight.

Sir George Cayley (1773-1857), whose fundamental research went unrecognized for more than a century, probably made more progress in understanding aerodynamics that any other man, for he was the first

a) to inaugurate the concept of a fixed-wing powered aeroplane,
b) to employ model gliders for aerodynamic research, (flying his first modern configuration glider model as early as 1804),
c) to build and to enable to be flown a man-carrying glider,
d) to investigate the movement of the center of pressure of an aeroplane,
e) to demonstrate in practice the control of flight using an adjustable tailplane and fin,
f) to advocate an internal combustion engine, driving a propeller, for aircraft propulsion, and
g) to realize the existence of a region of low pressure above the upper surface of a wing, and therefore its lifting potential,

among many other fundamental proposals which, had they been examined with careful logic, would have brought successful manned, powered flight much earlier than the epoch-making achievement of the Wright brothers in America. Alas, Cayley died only half a decade after the manned flight of

RIGHT: The American-born showman, Samuel Cody, at the controls of his *Army Aeroplane No 1* in 1908; it failed to complete a sustained, controlled flight.

LEFT: A Wright biplane in 1910; Orville is the figure on the right, wearing reversed cap, and Wilbur, holding a tail boom, wears Derby hat and jacket.

his glider, and some years before the creation of Britain's Aeronautical Society (later Royal) wherein the fruits of his labors might have been lodged and examined by would-be aerodynamicists.

Gradually progress was made, largely by trial and error. In July 1874 a Belgian shoemaker, Vincent de Groof, was killed when trying to fly his ornithopter in London; the Russian naval officer Alexander Mozhaiski built and flew a man-carrying aeroplane in about 1884, but this took off only after sliding down an inclined ramp and crashed from no more than a trajectory rather than a powered flightpath.

It was between 1891 and 1896 that Otto Lilienthal (1848-1896) undertook his famous piloted gliding flights in the Rhinower hills in Germany, his aircraft being what would today be termed hang-gliders; by twisting his legs and torso, he found that he could adjust the aircraft's center of gravity, as well as achieving a degree of control in pitch, roll and yaw. This most courageous "pilot-designer" was killed on August 9 1896 (when his No 11 Monoplane glider entered a deep stall which he could not counter because he possessed inadequate pitch control).

The Scotsman, Percy Pilcher (1866-1899), was also experimenting with a hang-glider at that time, and would undoubtedly have overtaken the German had he read and understood exactly what fundamental progress had been made by Cayley, particularly in the necessity for efficient tail controls. Nevertheless, Pilcher was slightly ahead of Lilienthal in the matter of a power plant and had patented a most promising design for a powered monoplane when he met his death in 1899. Also at that time the French-born American civil engineer, Octave Chanute (1832-1910) was using a truss-biplane hang-glider with tail-mounted aerofoils for pitch control.

Thus the search for practical, powered and manned aeroplanes, began in 1899, and the scramble began to exploit the advances made in harnessing the form of a box kite to a practical power plant. Indeed, the break-through achieved by the Wright brothers, Orville and Wilbur, in acquiring such an engine logically put them ahead of the field, for they also possessed experience in flying and controlling gliders, and in the absence of an existing engine they designed and built their own. The world's first sustained, powered and manned flight by a heavier-than-air craft, named *The Flyer*, was made by Orville Wright on December 171903 at Kill Devil Hills, North Carolina, lasting just 12 seconds and covering about 40 yards (36m). The fourth flight covered about 290 yards (265m).

The Wrights were astute businessmen and, during the next few years, did relatively little flying, confining their practical efforts to producing The Flyer II and III. Most of their efforts were spent in protecting their patents rather that sharing the profits of their research and achievement. The effect of that achievement on would-be aviators in Europe and elsewhere was nothing short of shattering. At a stroke, it seemed that attempts being made in France and elsewhere had been leapfrogged, although it was gradually being accepted that the ultimate flying machine would indeed take the form of a powered box-kite of some sort. It only remains to be said of the Wrights that when they resumed an intense program of flying in 1906 the Wright Flyer III achieved a flight of 24 miles (38km) in 33 minutes 17 seconds.

In Britain, the expatriate American-born Samuel Cody was engaged in the development of kites and some of his achievements in this field were quite remarkable although their practicality was noteworthy in other respects, such as weight-lifting and traction – by utilizing the power of the wind. Gradually, however, Europe began to catch up on America (largely owing to the intransigence of the Wrights in the matter of patents, this also stifled competition in their own country). The first official powered "hop-flight" in Europe was made by the Brazilian (French-domiciled) Alberto Santos-Dumont (1873-1932) on November 12 1906 with a flight which lasted just 21½ seconds and covered 720ft (220m). In England Cody, always handicapped by the lack of funds, managed in 1907 to achieve powered, unmanned flight by an engined kite which flew along a wire, while the same year the Dane, Jacob Ellehammer (1871-1946) tested a full-size powered triplane. By the spring of 1907 a Frenchman, Louis Blériot (1872-1936), was emerging as the leading protagonist of the monoplane. On November 10 1907 Henri Farman (1874-1958), the English-born, French-domiciled artist turned motor racing driver,

RIGHT: The first passenger to be killed in an aeroplane accident, Lieut Selfridge (left), in conversation with Alexander Graham Bell, shortly before his death in 1909.

government, progress remained very slow, most of the enthusiastic amateur constructor-pilots constantly battling against bankruptcy. The first flight in Britain by a British-born pilot was made by J. T. C. Moore-Brabazon who, having learned to fly in France in 1908, brought to England a French Voisin which he first flew at Shellbeach, Kent, in April 1909. He later bought a Wright, license-built by Short Bros, and won the *Daily Mail's* £1,000 prize for the first flight by a Briton in a British-built aircraft. The most famous British pilots of this time were, however, Claude Grahame-White (1879-1959), an outstanding sportsman pilot who narrowly missed winning the £10,000-prize *Daily Mail* London-Manchester air

RIGHT: The Frenchman, Louis Blériot, in his Blériot Type XI at Sandgatte shortly before his epoch-making cross-Channel flight on July 25 1909.

remained aloft for 1 min 9 sec in a Voisin, the first time the Wrights' first flight duration of 1903 had been bettered outside America. As Cody persevered with his powered kites, Farman and Blériot became Europe's leading aviators, culminating in the latter's momentous crossing of the English Channel on July 25 1909, a flight that must rank as one of the most courageous of all time – having regard to the frailty of the Blériot Type XI aircraft with its three-cylinder, 25hp Anzani engine and wing-warping controls. Competing for the feat of being the first to cross the Channel was the popular aviator, Hubert Latham (half-French, half-English, 1883-1912), who made two attempts in *Antoinettes* to cross the 22-mile (35km) stretch of water but on both occasions suffered engine failure and fell into the sea. The second attempt was made in an aircraft with a 100hp 16-cylinder Antoinette engine; the aircraft fell into the sea only a mile from the English coast.

The successes that began to attend the efforts of French and other European pilots – more often than not in French aeroplanes – brought numerous orders for their manufacturers, both Blériot and Farman becoming established as founder members of a growing French aircraft industry. In Britain efforts continued to catch up but, without the slightest interest in aviation being paid by the

race of 1910 in a French Farman (won by the Frenchman Louis Paulhan), the other being the Hon Charles Stewart Rolls who, though never foolhardy, gave superb displays of flying as well as being the first pilot to make an 'out-back' crossing of the Channel. Tragically, he was to become the first Englishman to be killed while flying when his French-built Wright suffered a structural failure at a Bournemouth flying meeting on July 12 1910.

By the end of 1910 France held all the major world flying records: for speed, Leblanc in a Blériot at 68.2mph (109.7km/h); for altitude, Legagneux also in a Blériot at 10,476ft (3,193m); and for distance in a closed circuit, Tabuteau in a Maurice Farman at 363 miles (584km).

Much was to change in 1911 and, although French pilots and aircraft still held all the world records, British pilots achieved world class with Cody, T. O. M. Sopwith, Grahame-White, Gustav Hamel, Graham Gilmour and Howard Pixton making distinguished contributions in feats of flying, and often in aircraft of British origin.

Most nations had recognized the potential of the aeroplane in the sphere of military aviation, although to most aviators such a thought was anathema. They saw the flying machine as an instrument of sport, or endeavor (both human and mechanical). However, following in the footsteps of lighter-than-air craft which had become accepted ever since captive balloons had made their appearance during the American Civil War and elsewhere, it was inevitable that the aeroplane could play its part for reconnaissance over the land battlefield. In America the first man to die in an aeroplane had been Lieutenant Thomas E. Selfridge when on September 17 1909, during military trials at Fort Meyer in Virginia, Orville Wright crashed; Wright survived with a broken leg, but his passenger (of the US Balloon Corps) was killed.

Several senior British Army officers had attended the great Reims air meeting in 1909 and had been deeply impressed by the sight of so many Frenchmen (not to mention Wilbur Wright from America) in complete mastery of their aeroplanes, and recommended that the Army should be adequately financed to pursue the development of military aeroplanes for reconnaissance purposes. The result was a miserly grant of £2,000 for the following year – and then the Army Council redirected this motley sum elsewhere, believing that to spend such a sum on an aeroplane would be construed as misappropriation! This did not discourage numerous Army and Royal Navy officers and NCOs from learning to fly at their own expense with the fast growing number of flying clubs appearing all over Britain.

Britain competes with France

By the end of 1912 British pilots and aircraft had still not entered the list of world records, but men like Howard Pixton, Geoffrey de Havilland, Fred Raynham, Harry Hawker and T. O. M. Sopwith had all returned world class performances, while aeroplanes built by A. V. Roe, Bristol and Blackburn were demonstrating reliability at least comparable with those of France. Perhaps the most remarkable of the above pilots was Harry Hawker, an accomplished practical mechanic who arrived in England from his native Australia almost destitute, but joined T. O. M. Sopwith who was working to produce adaptations of Wright biplanes at Brooklands, as well as flying them. Hawker was destined to become one of the most talented of all British pilots in the second decade of the century.

In the final year before the outbreak of the Great War, British aeroplanes and aviators at last matched those of France on a broad front, hitherto accepted as world leaders in aviation, for the United States had failed to sustain its early technical momentum. Harry Hawker, who had learned to fly at T. O. M. Sopwith's flying school, had immediately shown himself to be an instinctive pilot possessed of great determination and an analytical approach. By early spring of 1913 (referred to by French historians as 'La Glorieuse Année') Hawker had been appointed Sopwith's company test pilot, won a cross-country race and beaten most of the acknowledged experts to take national records. By the end of June he had established three national altitude records (solo, and with one

and two passengers) and the endurance record. He had not yet being flying a year. 1913 was the year in which the great pioneer Samuel Cody lost his life when, on August 7, his large new aircraft collapsed in the air over Farnborough.

One final landmark in sporting flying was established before the war. The Jacques Schneider Trophy for racing seaplanes had been inaugurated in 1913 and won by the Frenchman Prévost in a 160hp Gnôme-powered Deperdussin at a speed of 45mph (72km/h). Having failed to cross the finishing line properly he was required to take off again to re-cross the line – hence his very low official time. None of the opposing pilots finished the course! The 1914 contest was to be won by the Englishman Howard Pixton at 85.5mph (137.6km/h) in a float-equipped Sopwith Tabloid against entries from France, Germany, Switzerland and the USA – the French pilots being men of such stature as Roland Garros, Levasseur and Espanet. Pixton continued for two further laps so as to qualify for a world speed record for seaplanes, which he established at no less than 92mph (148km/h).

The United States took no steps to accelerate development of military aircraft at the beginning of the Great War. On the other hand, most European nations had at least made a start on producing aeroplanes for military purposes. The French had probably made most progress in this respect, followed by Germany, and both nations possessed fully established air forces, although the number of aircraft deemed to be fully operational was still relatively small. Britain formed the Royal Flying Corps (a Corps originally intended to support the Army in the field) and Royal Naval Air Service (supporting the Home Fleet and responsible for attacking enemy installations behind the Western Front). The two British air forces possessed a surprising number of airmen who had a knowledge of the rudiments of flying (having

BELOW: The British pioneer, T. O. M. Sopwith, at the controls of his 60hp Howard Wright at Eastchurch on November 21 1910; he was granted his RAeC Aviator's Certificate (No 31) the following day.

qualified for Royal Aero Club flying certificates mostly at their own expense), and a nucleus of more capable pilots and observers who had received formal Service training at the Central Flying School which had formed at Upavon in 1912. In the matter of war-ready squadrons, the RFC could field half a dozen and the RNAS about half this number, all of which moved to France at or soon after the outbreak of war. And it was in France that the air war was to continue with growing ferocity until the final Armistice in 1918.

Among the first British formations to move to France was the Naval Wing commanded by the larger-than-life Charles Rumney Samson (1883-1933), who had been the first British airman to take off in an aeroplane from a warship.

During the first nine months some desultory skirmishing occurred, when the opposing airmen, if they were armed at all, fired all manner of guns at each other, from Service revolvers and shotguns to the occasional machine gun, mounted in such a manner as to enable it to be fired with a reasonable chance of missing the pilot's own propeller. The first great exponents of air fighting were the Germans, Max Immelmann (1890-1916) and Oswald Boelcke (1891-1916), who, flying Fokker Eindekker (monoplanes) with a machine gun capable of firing its bullets between the whirling propeller blades, began to take a heavy toll of British and French aircraft as they flew their reconnaissance patrols over the front lines. Both these men, the first of the great air aces, were eventually to be killed in air combat as, slowly, Allied airmen came to terms with the nimble

Fokkers. Boelcke fought until 1916 and, when eventually shot down, his personal score of air victories stood at 40.

Heading the great fighting scout pilots of France was René Fonck (1894-1953), a deadly marksman who frequently destroyed his opponent using scarcely a dozen bullets. He survived the war with the highest score among Allied pilots, 75 enemy aircraft falling to his guns. Second to Foncke was Georges Guynemer (1894-1917), a frail-seeming youth with romantic good looks; he survived being shot down seven times himself but finally failed to return from a patrol on September 11 1917 by which time he had gained 54 confirmed victories. Charles Nungesser (1892-1927), a flamboyant figure who suffered numerous crashes and wounds, and often had to be carried to and from his machine, eventually destroyed 45 enemy aircraft.

The RFC fighter aces were no less feted and decorated for their gallantry, being led by Edward Mannock (1887-1918) honored with the VC, three DSOs and two MCs, who destroyed 74 enemy machines, the Canadian Lt-Col William Bishop (1894-1956), with a score of 72, and Lt-Col Raymond Collishaw, another Canadian who destroyed 60 enemy aircraft (of which 40 were shot down while he was serving with the RNAS; he went on to serve throughout the Second World War with great distinction as a senior officer in North Africa). Albert Ball, only 18 years old at the beginning of the war and first of the great Allied fighter pilots, had already shot down 44 enemy aircraft, won the VC and four DSOs, and been killed

ABOVE: Max Immelmann, the first fighter "ace", was killed in air combat with Lt G. R. McCubbin of No 25 Squadron of the RFC on June 18 1916.

RIGHT: Blind in one eye, Maj Edward Mannock was the highest-scoring British pilot of the First World War, with 73 combat victories. He was killed on July 26 1918.

in action, before Major Mannock had started scoring. No fewer than 61 other pilots of the RFC and RNAS each destroyed 20 or more enemy aircraft. Another great Allied fighter pilot on the Western Front was the Belgian Chevalier Willy Coppen de Houthulst, whose air victory tally of 37 included the destruction of 26 observation balloons – always heavily defended by massed anti-aircraft guns.

Ranged against the Allies was a veritable galaxy of superb pilots, led by Rittmeister Manfred von Richthofen (1882-1918) – the "Red Baron" – who amassed a total of 80 combat victims, some of whom were high-scoring Allied pilots. His victory tally was followed by those of Oblt. Ernst Udet (62), Oblt. Erich Loewenhardt (53), Ltn. Werner Voss (48) and Ltn. Fritz Rumey (45). The highest-scoring Austrian was Hptm. Godwin Brumowski (1889-1937) with 40 victories.

Being late to join in the war, the American fighter pilots figured much lower in the lists of victories, only Capt Edward Rickenbacker (26) and Lt. Frank Luke (21) achieving more than a score of successes. Both were awarded Congressional Medals of Honor. However, the remarkably large number of American pilots who gained scores of five or six victories in the very short time they were at the front is ample testimony to the great potential that existed in the American Expeditionary Force in France by the time the war ended.

As the world recoiled from the thought of another World War, the confirmed "air enthusiasts" sought to apply aviation to peaceful pursuits, to sporting flying and commercial aviation. America possessed only a relatively small aircraft

LEFT: Highest-scoring of all fighter pilots in the First World War was Rittmeister Manfred, Freiherr von Richthofen, with 80 victories; he was killed on April 21 1918.

industry, still building mainly British aircraft under license. The French economy was exhausted and could afford only to adapt wartime aircraft to the half-hearted demand for civil aircraft.

The pre-war pioneering spirit returned with peace, as did the first great prize (in fact offered before the war) to attract a number of pilots, particularly in Britain. This was to be the first non-stop crossing of the Atlantic by an aeroplane. The great Harry Hawker, with K. F. Mackenzie-Grieve, made the first attempt in May 1919, but were forced down (being extremely fortunate to be found and rescued alive). Success, however, attended Capt John Alcock, RN (1892-1919) and Lieut Arthur Whitten Brown, RN (1886-1948), flying a Vickers Vimy from St John's, Newfoundland, to Co. Galway, Ireland, on June 14/15 that

LEFT: The highest-scoring American fighter pilot was Capt Edward Rickenbacker with 26 victories, gained mainly in French Spads, one of which is shown here.

BELOW: The Vickers
Vimy of Capts
Alcock and Brown,
taking off from
Newfoundland on
June 14 1919 on
the first non-stop air
crossing of Atlantic.

year. Both were knighted for their achievement, but Sir John Alcock was killed flying the following December.

Another Vimy, this time flown by the Australian brothers, Capt Ross Smith and Lt Keith Smith, completed the first flight from Britain to Australia, flying from Hounslow, England, to Darwin, Australia, between November 12 and December 10 1919. The first flight from Britain to South Africa was made by Col Pierre van Ryneveld and Capt Christopher Quintin Brand between February 4 and March 20 1920.

to Connecticut, USA, in a DH Dragon in July 1933. She was to lose her life while flying with the Air Transport Auxiliary on January 5 1941.

Amelia Earhart (Mrs Putnam) was a contemporary of Amy Johnson. Her outstanding achievements included the first solo crossing of the Atlantic by a woman, flying from Newfoundland to Londonderry on May 20/21 1932 in a Lockheed Vega; the first non-stop crossing of the United States by a woman, flying from Los Angeles to New York on August 25 1932. She also made a remarkable solo flight from Honolulu to Oakland, California, on January 11/12 1935. Her

In the United States, Lieut William D. Coney of the US Air Service made the first solo coast-to-coast flight during February 1921. This was followed the next year by the first coast-to-coast flight in a single day when Lieut James H. Doolittle (later to serve his country with great distinction) flew from Pablo Beach, Florida, to San Diego, California, in 21hr 20min in a de Havilland DH 4B on September 2 1922.

The first great world round-the-world flight was made by two of four Douglas DWC biplanes flown by Maj Frederick Martin and Lieuts Lowell H. Smith, Leight Wade and Erik Nelson, between April 6 and September 28 1924, a journey that included numerous stops, but included the first trans-Pacific flight and the first west-bound Atlantic crossing. These flights by Americans were eclipsed when, on May 20/21 1927, the American Charles A Lindbergh flew the Atlantic solo in the single-engine *Spirit of St Louis* from Long Island, New York, to Paris for the first time.

French pilots snatched the headlines late in 1927 when Dieudonné Costes and Lebrix, flying a Bréguet, made the first non-stop air crossing of the South Atlantic, flying from Senegal to Brazil on October 14. Three months later a well-known British pilot, "Bert" Hinkler, in an Avro Avian light aircraft, completed the first solo flight from Britain to Australia.

Women pilots periodically seized the headlines with some remarkable long distance flights in the inter-war years. Probably the best known of these were the British pilot Amy Johnson, and the American Amelia Earhart. Amy Johnson made the first solo flight from Britain to Australia in a de Havilland Moth light aircraft in May 1930, a solo flight to South Africa (and return) in a DH Puss Moth in November and December 1932, and a flight with her husband, Jim Mollison, from Wales

BELOW: The American,
Charles A Lindbergh,
was first to cross
the Atlantic solo
non-stop, in a Ryan
monoplane *Spirit of
St Louis* from New
York, to Paris on
May 20/21 1927.

aircraft disappeared between Howland Island and New Guinea on July 2 1937 while attempting a round-the-world flight with Capt Fred Noonan.

All these extraordinary flights, often undertaken with very limited financial resources, served to demonstrate that airline travel could not be far distant; nor were the early airlines themselves idle. October 1927 brought Pan American Airways' first scheduled service between Key West, Florida, and Havanna, Cuba, while in Europe short-hop stages between almost every country had been a reality for more than three years.

In other respects, flying was also advancing rapidly. The test pilot, as epitomised by Harry Hawker during the war, had been employed by the Sopwith company, and also undertook to lend his services to other manufacturers when the need arose. He possessed no manual to guide him, but gave his opinion as to how satisfactorily an aircraft flew. The science of test flying grew up at the Royal Aircraft Establishment, Farnborough, partly as the result of men like Henry (later Sir Henry) Tizard, a pilot in his own right, but first and foremost a brilliant scientist. Working with him was Flt Lt P. W. S. ("George") Bulman, almost certainly the greatest test pilot of the inter-war period. Bulman joined Hawker Engineering Ltd in 1925 and flew all the fine aeroplanes designed by Sydney Camm before 1939. Other famous British test pilots of that period were Howard Saint, Hubert Broad, Philip Lucas, Cyril Uwins (of Bristols) and, of course Geoffrey de Havilland, whose company did more than any other in Britain to popularize private flying. The famous flying boat manufacturers, Short Bros Ltd, who were to become so important during the 1930s, employed John Lankester Parker as the company's senior pilot for over 20 years, culminating with the company's Empire flying boats which established a wide-ranging network of flying services between the dominions and colonies of the British Empire.

In peacetime, military pilots seldom have the opportunity to become famous, except in the realm of record-breaking, largely because what little finance is made available for military equipment is spent in advancing the performance of new military machines. This was particularly evident in the matter of the Schneider Trophy races, which were resurrected after the Great War. This contest was effectively dominated by Britain, although it was not won outright until 1931. The United States however won the contests held in 1923 and 1925 with Curtiss seaplanes whose very advanced biplane designs bore testimony to the huge technical advances in aerosciences that had been made in that country. For instance, Lt James Doolittle (already referred to) flew the winning Curtiss seaplane in the 1925 contest at an average speed of 232mph (373km/h) – which compared with maximum speeds of around 160mph (257km/h) for the best European fighters, and they were not encumbered with floats! The Italian pilot, Major Mario de Bernadi, won the 1926 race in a Macchi M.39 at a speed of 246mph (396km/h).

The Trophy was won by Britain in 1927 (when the contest became biennial), 1929 and 1931, all three by a remarkable family of Supermarine monoplanes equipped with floats; these returned winning speeds of 281, 328 and 340mph (452, 528 and 547km/h), the last race being a walk-over for Britain. Such was the national prestige attached to this international contest that Britain followed the custom of other nations in 1927 by forming a special RAF High Speed Flight, whose pilots underwent rigorous race training. On the day of the 1931 contest the winner, Flt Lt George Stainforth, went on to capture the World Absolute Air Speed Record at 379mph (610km/h) at a time when the fastest military fighters were only just achieving maximum speeds of about 250mph (402km/h)! By the use of specially prepared fuels Stainforth raised the World Record to 407.5mph (655.7km/h) in the Supermarine S.6B in September 1931, a speed that was not equaled by British and German fighters for another eleven years.

Meanwhile other world records were being established. A specially prepared aircraft, the Fairey Long-Range Monoplane – a single-engine, two-seat monster with a span of no less that 82ft (30m), was flown by Sqn Ldr O. R. Gayford and Flt Lt G. E. Nicholetts from Cranwell to Walvis Bay in southern Africa non-stop on February 6/8 1933, a Great Circle distance of 5,431 miles (8,738km). This record, however, only remained unbeaten until August that year when the Frenchmen, P. Codos and M. Rossi, flew the Blériot-Zappata 110 *Joseph le Brix* from New York to Rayak in Syria, a Great Circle distance of 5,657 miles (9,102km).

In the realm of altitude records, the German First World War fighter pilot, Wilhelm Neuenhofen, had established a World Altitude Record of 41,790ft (12,733m) on May 26 1929 in

a Junkers W.34, powered by a British Bristol Jupiter engine. This was beaten in turn by the American naval pilot Soucek in 1930, and on September 16 1932 by Cyril Uwins in a Vickers Vespa biplane which reached 43,976ft (13,404m). The research which enabled the latter record to be established also led to the preparation of the Wallace aircraft, flown by the Marquess of Clydesdale over the summit of Mount Everest in April 1933. The Bristol company produced one other high altitude machine, the Type 138A, which regained the World Altitude Record for aeroplanes piloted by Flt Lt M. J. Adam from Farnborough in 1937 to a height of 53,937ft (16,440m).

Finally, RAF pilots of the Long Range Development Flight, led by Sqn Ldr Richard Kellet, established a new World Long Distance record of 7,157 miles (11,516km) in Vickers Wellesleys with a flight from Ismailia, Egypt, to Ross Smith Airfield, Darwin, Australia, in November 1938 – an epic flight, fraught with difficulties of adverse winds and appalling weather. Kellett's aircraft landed with only 45 gallons (205 litres) of fuel remaining. This record was to remain unbeaten for eight years.

The inter-war period was dominated by British and British Commonwealth pilots, although competition was often fierce, while the unknown quantity was the potential of Germany's secret Luftwaffe which had come into being in the mid-thirties. And while the appearance of such superb civilian airliners as the Douglas DC-3 and Short Empire flying boats, had enabled the United States, Great Britain, Holland and other countries to inaugurate extensive passenger-carrying services throughout the world, Germany had been hard at work creating a highly efficient domestic and European passenger service throughout Europe.

Such was the rapidity with which the German forces overwhelmed Poland, Denmark, Norway, Holland, Belgium and France, that the outstanding qualities of many of their fighting men were obscured for many years. However, many such men escaped from their homelands to Britain

BOTTOM: Amy Johnson flew a de Havilland DH 60G Gipsy Moth *Jason*, from Croydon to Darwin in May 1930, thereby making the first England-Australia solo flight by a woman.

BELOW: The American woman pilot, Amelia Earhart, pictured just before her attempted round-the-world flight on which she was to lose her life in July 1937.

ABOVE: Archetypal fighter pilot of the RAF, Sqn Ldr R. R. S. Tuck, who commanded a Hurricane Squadron during the Battle of Britain; this photo was taken later after he had been shot down and made a POW by the Germans.

RIGHT: Douglas Bader, hero with artifical legs, who led a Canadian Hurricane squadron in the Battle of Britain; he was also shot down later and taken prisoner. He is shown climbing into a Spitfire after the war.

with whose forces they carried on their fight against the hated Nazis. Several of them who joined the RAF were posessed of outstanding ability and courage. An example may be cited in the Czech fighter pilot, Josef Frantisek, who in the space of one month, September 1940, destroyed 17 German aircraft, to become the highest-scoring RAF pilot in the Battle of Britain. Alas, he was killed in a flying accident on October 8.

The pilots of RAF Fighter Command were, at the beginning of the war, the élite products of the recent years of expansion and and training. They were equipped with two of the best types of fighter in the world, the Hurricane and Spitfire, and had the benefit of a highly efficient radar chain. Yet, owing to inadequate funding of Britain's armed forces for too long, their professionalism was too superficial, albeit bolstered by incomparable individuality. The early campaigns, namely the expeditions to Norway and the Battle of France, apart from inflicting heavy casualties, brought home with brutal experience the reality of modern air warfare. The Battle of Britain, a pivotal struggle to ensure the survival of Fighter Command, came within an ace of destroying the vital air defense of the nation. At one point the Command was losing the equivalent in pilots and aircraft of two squadrons each day.

Many individual pilots gained immortal fame during that summer of 1940: the young "Ginger" Lacey (the highest-scoring pilot of the Auxiliary Air Force), Bob Stanford Tuck (the debonair Regular who commanded a Hurricane squadron and had destroyed 23 enemy aircraft by the end of 1940), Douglas Bader (the pilot with artificial legs who also commanded a Hurricane squadron and proved to possess an astonishing gift for leader-

ship), "Sailor" Malan (the South African ex-merchant seaman who brilliantly led a Spitfire squadron), "Al" Deere (the New Zealander who, during his eventful career as a fighter pilot, survived nine bale-outs and accidents), Johnnie Kent (the former RAF test pilot from Canada), Don Kingaby, Brian Kingcombe, "Cocky" Dundas, and a score of others, all of whom became household names for their courage and skill during that memorable battle.

In the German Luftwaffe, there were also many great pilots, of whom the most illustrious were: Adolf Galland (who later became the youngest general of the German Air Force at the age of 30 and gained 104 air combat victories) and Werner Mölders, who shot down 115 Allied aircraft before being killed in a flying accident on November 22 1941. Gordon Gollob, an Austrian, later amassed a total of 150 victories and also survived the war (all these pilots later held the Knight's Cross with Diamonds, Swords and Oakleaves – the highest award for gallantry in the German armed forces); and the extraordinary Swiss pilot, Walter Rubensdörffer, who led some of the most hazardous low-level attacks during the Battle of Britain before his death in action in the very heavy fighting of August 15 1940.

The night Blitz, the German all-out night assault on British cities and ports, which raged from mid-September 1940 until the following May, brought prominence to night fighting as a vital element in air warfare. Although it was Germany that was first to exploit this manifestation of "total war" against the civilian population, it was also Germany that suffered the systematic destruction of her towns and cities in the massive retribution wrought by RAF Bomber Command and, later, the American

Eighth Air Force. An early RAF exponent of night fighting was Wg Cdr John Cunningham who proved not only his great skill in partnership with his radar operator but all the instincts of a night hunter in achieving a veritable harvest of enemy night bomber victims. Once again, the Germans – who later were faced by far larger numbers of targets – provided some extraordinary exponents of night fighting skills, notably Major Heinz-Wolfgang Schnaufer, who destroyed 121 Allied bombers at night (on one occasion shooting down no fewer than seven RAF Lancasters in the space of 17 minutes over Germany).

In this matter of combat achievements, the German fighter pilots certainly amassed much higher totals of victories, largely owing to the inferior quality of Russian pilots and aircraft that opposed the Luftwaffe in the early stages of the war on the Eastern Front. The two highest scoring German fighter pilots were Erich Hartmann with 352 victories (including only seven aircraft of the Western Allies) and Gerhard Barkhorn with 301 (all gained on the Eastern Front). No fewer then 105 Luftwaffe fighter pilots gained scores of over 100 air victories in the Second World War. There were other contributory reasons for these enormous scores, not least of which was the continuity of operational service in the German forces; unlike Western air forces, the German airmen remained on operational duties for much longer periods between rests, and served for rather longer on a single unit, thereby becoming highly experienced in flying any particular fighter. However, there is little reason to doubt the validity of the Luftwaffe claims – one only has to examine the very high casualties suffered by the Allied bomber forces during the last three years of the war.

Apart from the high profile fighter pilots of the war, other areas of air operations brought forth airmen of outstanding ability. In the RAF there were numerous instances of great valor, so many of the men thus distinguished being killed within days of their feats. Not all the Victoria Crosses awarded to bomber airmen were won by pilots, as witness the two Sergeants, James Ward, a navigator, and Norman Jackson, a flight engineer. Both these men were in bombers that had been severely damaged and set on fire during bombing sorties, and both climbed out of their cabins on to the wing of their aircraft in attempts to extinguish fires. Ward, a New Zealander flying in a Wellington, extinguished the fire so that the aircraft returned safely (he was to be killed shortly afterwards on another raid). Jackson, in a Lancaster, had already been severely wounded when his aircraft was attacked and set on fire; he failed in his attempt to save the aircraft and was swept off the wing before the Lancaster's captain ordered the crew to bale out. Miraculously, Jackson survived to be taken prisoner and returned home after the war.

Perhaps the best known of the great bomber personalities was Guy Gibson who led the famous No 617 Squadron (the "Dambusters") on its epic attack on the German dams in 1943, but without question the most illustrious airman in Bomber Command, indeed possibly in the whole of the Royal Air Force, was Gp Capt Leonard Cheshire (later Lord Cheshire, VC, OM, DSO**, DFC*). His Victoria Cross citation made it clear that his gallantry on operations was unique; not awarded in his instance for a single or a few acts of great bravery, Cheshire's Cross was cited for four long years of outstanding leadership, skill and exceptional valor on numerous occasions.

When the Americans entered the war, following the débâcle of Pearl Harbor in December 1941, they were relatively slow to find their feet in the environment of total war, suffering a string of setbacks in the Pacific. In agreement with Chuchill, the Americans decided to concentrate on finishing the war against Germany before

ABOVE: The highest-scoring fighter pilot ever, Erich Hartmann, who destroyed 352 aircraft. He is shown wearing the Oakleaves, Swords and Diamonds of the Knight's Cross.

TOP: Maj Gerhard Barkhorn, second highest-scoring pilot of the Luftwaffe in the war with 301 victories. He survived and later rose to senior rank in the post-war Luftwaffe.

LEFT: Adolf Galland, seen here disembarking from a Messerschmitt Bf.109 early in the war. With over 100 victories, he was to become Germany's youngest general.

RIGHT: Maj Richard Bong, highest-scoring American fighter pilot in the Pacific War (right) and Gen Hap Arnold, commanding the USAAF.

taking the lead among the Allies in defeating Japan. By the end of 1942 the flow of aircraft to Britain was assuming impressive proportions as the great Eighth Air Force (mainly B-17 and B-24 heavy bombers, with P-38, P-47 and P-51 fighters) moved into dozens of airfields made available for them by the British. Unlike the RAF heavy bomber force, which flew the great majority of its great raids by night, the Americans – with their

The eventual introduction into service (with the RAF) of the first Allied jet fighter, the Gloster Meteor, was the culmination of considerable pioneering test flying by such pilots as P. E. G. Sayer (who flew Britain's first experimental jet aircraft, the E.28/39 on May 15 1941), "Michael" Daunt who flew the first Meteor on March 5 1943, John Grierson, John Crosby-Warren, Llewellyn Moss and Digby Cotes-Preedy. The de Havilland company pioneered the single-engine jet fighter with its small Vampire single-seat aircraft; this was flown by that famous test pilot Geoffrey de Havilland Jnr on September 20 1943, but this just failed to enter RAF service before the end of the war. Philip Lucas of Hawkers had been awarded the George Medal in 1940 when he opted to land the prototype Typhoon fighter after it had suffered a critical structural failure, rather than abandon the important aircraft.

The Russians had paid the highest price of all the Allies, huge areas of their territory having been overrun by the Germans. The air fighting over the Eastern Front had been proportionately bitter. After the early stages of the German campaign, when Russian aircraft were swatted down like flies

ABOVE: Britain was first after the war to establish a new World Speed Record. Gp Capt H. J. Wilson gained the record at 606mph (970km/h) in 1945 flying this Meteor, named *Britannia*.

very heavily armed bombers – preferred to operate by day, frequently suffering very heavy casualties from ground flak and the guns of very experienced Luftwaffe pilots, who sold their lives dearly in defense of their country. Among the great American airmen were many who displayed unsurpassed courage and skill. Col Leon Johnson led the famous B-24 low-level raid on the Ploesti oil installations at the head of the 44th Bomb Group. Finding the defenses fully alert, Johnson persevered and thereby drew the fire away from the other Groups, attacking immediately behind him.

Among the famous American fighter pilots were men like Maj Richard I Bong, a P-38 pilot in the Pacific theater, who was the highest-scoring American of the Second World War with 40 victories; the highest-scoring American pilot in the European theater was Col Francis Gabreski who destroyed 31 enemy aircraft (this pilot also served with the United Nations forces in Korea, shooting down six Communist aircraft). The highest-scoring American naval pilot was Capt D. McCampbell with a tally of 34 enemy aircraft destroyed.

by the much superior men and machines of the Luftwaffe, the Red Air Force gradually gained the upper hand, not so much by better aircraft but by growing numerical superiority and improved training. The highest-scoring fighter pilot of the Red Air Force was Guards Colonel Ivan Kozhedub with a victory score of 62.

In the Pacific, the American air forces, after have been ill-prepared to meet the well-equipped and organized land- and carrier-based air forces of Japan, gradually gained the initiative as much improved aircraft began to enter service. Unlike the RAF's fighters and bombers fighting in Europe, the emphasis on long range was paramount in American aircraft, such were the huge distances involved in operations. Nevertheless, the highest-scoring Japanese fighter pilot was Sub-Officer Hiroyoshi Nishizawa with a score of 103 British and American aircraft shot down – more than twice that of Major Richard Bong (see above).

With the descent of the Iron Curtain as the predictable outcome of Stalin's determination to impose Communism on those nations "liberated" during the Red Army's spectacular advance westwards in the last year of the war, it was inevitable that America – determined never to be caught unprepared for war again – should assume the leading rôle in worldwide defense against the Soviet Union. The manifestation of this stance was the creation of NATO.

The British emerged from the war economically exhausted and rapidly and drastically reduced the size of their armed forces, paring to the bone any financial support for research and development in aviation. The Americans, however, continued with the development and production of the aircraft which were about to enter service at the end of the war, and supported a very strong export of these aircraft to numerous other countries in the West.

This growing technical superiority was demonstrated by the appearance in 1947 of the P-86 Saber jet fighter which was transonic in a dive. From being at least two years behind Britain in jet engine technology in 1944, America at a stroke leapt ahead to take a six-year lead in 1947. In 1945 the RAF High Speed Flight was re-formed under Gp Capt H. J. Wilson for an attack on the World Speed Record, and this was duly established at 606mph (975km/h) in a Gloster Meteor, and the following year Gp Capt E. M. Donaldson, also of the High Speed Flight, increased this to 616mph (991km/h) in an improved Meteor. These achievements were two-edged swords for, should anyone suggest that the British government was being parsimonious with its financing of research, the Treasury could point to the apparent world leadership demonstrated by these records.

The Americans introduced the F-86 Saber into service without delay, prompted no doubt by the Soviet brinkmanship during the Berlin Airlift. Designed under the leadership of A. F. Weissenberger and A. C. Patch, the prototype XP-86 was first flown by George Welch on October 1 1947, and exceeded Mach 1 for the first time in a shallow dive, again flown by Welch. The American Bell X-1, a research aircraft flown by Capt Charles Yeager, had already exceeded the

speed of sound on October 1947 14. ("Chuck" Yeager was possibly the greatest high speed test pilot of all; in due course, he logged more than 10,000 flying hours on no fewer than 180 different types of aircraft.)

ABOVE: Highest-scoring Allied pilot of the war, Ivan Kozhedub shot down 62 German aircraft, mostly flying Lavochkins in the Ukraine, and ended the war as a Guards Colonel with three awards of Hero of the Soviet Union.

LEFT: Sub-Officer Hiroyoshi Nishizawa was the highest-scoring Japanese fighter pilot of the Second World War with a victory tally of 103 victories.

BELOW: George Welch, first pilot to fly the famous XP-86 Saber in 1947, went on to test fly the supersonic F-100 Super Saber in which he is seen here, but was killed on October 12 1954.

RIGHT: One of the true pioneers of supersonic flight, Capt Charles Yeager first flew the Bell X-1 research aircraft in supersonic level flight at 42,000ft (12,800m) on October 14 1947 having been air-launched from a B-29 bomber.

The British Meteor's speed record of 616mph (991km/h) had long been surpassed, first by a specially-prepared Lockheed P-80R at 623mph (1,002km/h), and then by a naval Douglas Skystreak at 650mph (1,046km/h) on August 25 1947. It was the Saber's turn to take the record when on September 15 1948 Maj Robert L. Johnson of the USAF flew an early production aircraft to take the record at 669mph (1,076km/h).

The onset of the Korean War in 1950 brought the USAF into combat with aircraft of the Communist bloc, at first both sides being equipped with piston-engine fighters. It was not long before MiG-15 jets arrived in North Korea, to which the Americans replied by despatching a Wing of Sabers. At first it was found that there was little to choose between the MiG and the F-86, although superior skill favored the American pilots, many of whom had fought in the Second World War and were accordingly more experienced.

The RAF, equipped wholly with subsonic, first generation Meteors and Vampires, was not involved in the land fighter operations, and at sea the carrier-borne propeller-driven Sea Furies, Seafires and Fulmars were employed in the ground attack rôle. The first Sea Fury pilot of the

RIGHT: Peter Twiss, chief test pilot of Fairey Aviation Ltd, was the first to establish a World Speed Record at over 1,000mph, (16,000km/h) flying the Fairey Delta II.

Royal Navy to shoot down a Communist MiG-15 was Lieut P. Carmichael of No 802 Squadron. A number of RAF pilots were sent to the United States to be trained on the F-86 Saber, and subsequently served and fought with USAF squadrons in Korea.

With the introduction of the F-86E, with its "all-flying" tailplane, the USAF pilots quickly achieved superiority over the MiG-15 and individual pilots' scores increased fairly rapidly, the highest-scoring pilot being Capt Joseph McConnell with 16 victories. Thirty-eight other pilots of the USAF, US Navy and the Marine Corps gained five or more victories before the war ended in 1953.

It was the mutual suspicions aroused by the descent of the Iron Curtain that brought about an entirely new exploitation of air power – that of aerial espionage. Yet, although the USAF was equipped to undertake long-range reconnaissance of Soviet territory, the American government was unwilling to risk provoking the Russians by flagrant violation of their airspace. However, the return of Winston Churchill as Britain's prime minister, who had no such inhibitions, resulted in the RAF undertaking a number of desperately hazardous reconnaissance flights over the Soviet hinterland. A number of USAF RB-45Cs were flown by British pilots, notably Sqn Ldr John Crampton (later awarded the AFC), from Sculthorpe in England in April 1952 to make wide circuits of Moscow to photograph the Russian capital's military installations. Penetrating about 1,000 miles (1,600km) into Soviet airspace, the aircraft were air-refueled over Germany on the outward and return stages. Later, as Soviet ground defenses improved, the British Canberra high altitude photo reconnaissance aircraft was employed on deep penetration flights in daylight, on at least one occasion narrowly escaping being shot down by Soviet interceptor fighters.

These clandestine operations were later joined by the American CIA during the late 1950s, using the radical U-2 high altitude reconnaissance aircraft, often flying diagonally across the Soviet Union between Norway and Iran from USAF airfields in Britain. On May 1 1960, however, one of these aircraft, flown by Francis Gary Powers was shot down at a height of over 70,000 feet (21,335m) by a Soviet surface-to-air missile. Only many years later did it emerge that the Western powers had been engaged in constant reconnaissance and ELINT operations over Communist bloc territories between the end of the war and about 1970, losing more than a score of "spy planes".

The introduction into service of the supersonic F-100 Super Saber, and the other "Century Series" of American fighters during the 1950s represented a significant advance in aviation technology. Meanwhile the arrival of the RAF's Lightning in 1960 demonstrated Britain's belated efforts to achieve some degree of "respectability" among the West's arsenal, although it represented little more than lip service to the defense structure of NATO. Not even the British achievement on March 10 1956 in recapturing the World Speed Record with the experimental Fairey Delta 2 had much relevance in the development of military aircraft at the time, although the "machinery" of record breaking, the precision of flight control and measurement gave an indication of British determination to keep abreast of American technology. The record flights were made by Peter Twiss, chief test pilot of the Fairey Aviation Company, and returned an average speed of 1,132mph (1,821km/h) (or a mean Mach number of 1.731). The record stood until December 12 1957 when an almost standard McDonnell F-101A Voodoo fighter was flown at a speed of 1,208mph (1,944km/h).

By the mid-1960s Mach 2 flight was commonplace among military aircraft of the world's air forces, and the appearance of the McDonnell Douglas F-4 Phantom (originally designed for the US Navy) represented the pinnacle of aviation technology at the beginning of that decade. First flown on May 27 1958 by McDonnell test pilot Robert C. Little, the prototype F4H-1 incorporated for the first time in a military aircraft such innovations as extensive integrated structure, chemical milling of structural components and the use of titanium in areas subjected to high temperatures. The following year early Phantoms were flown to recapture records then currently held by Soviet research aircraft, and the first of these, the World Absolute Altitude Record (employing an energy or "zoom" climb, which stood at 94,658 ft/28,852m), fell to a Phantom flown by Cdr Lawrence E. Flint USN on December 6 1959 reaching an altitude of 98,557ft (30,040m). Much more demanding – for pilot and aircraft – was the 100km (62-mile) Closed Circuit speed record which, in theory required the aircraft to fly a 12-sided figure, each side being approximately 9km (5.6 miles) in length; in practice it involved flying the Phantom in a constant circular turn around the imaginary figure. On September 25 1960 Cdr J. F. Davis flew a Phantom in a sustained circle at 46,000ft (14,020m) with 70 degrees of bank with full afterburners selected through 360 degrees, completing the maneuver in 2 min 40.9 secs, representing a speed of 1,390mph (2,236km/h) over the statutory 100km, and this was the speed entered for record purposes. In fact, as Davis had flown marginally outside the theoretical 12-sided figure, the actual distance covered was almost 105km (65 miles), representing an actual mean speed of 1,459mph (2,347km/h), an extraordinary flying achievement for an aircraft pulling a constant 3g. Numerous other performance record breaking flights were made by the Phantom, the majority of which have since been broken. The significance was that the Phantom alone established so many records for speed, altitude and climb times. The Phantom's ultimate achievement was the World Absolute Speed Record of 1,606mph (2,584km/h) (Mach 2.43)

attained by Lt Col Robert B. Robinson on November 22 1961.

At about this time, however, America had begun experimental flights with the North American X-15A, powered by a 57,000lb (25,855kg) thrust throttleable Thiokol liquid-fuel rocket engine. Three such vehicles were built and they were carried aloft by Boeing B-52 aircraft prior to launching for flight in the upper stratosphere. Flown between May 1960 and October 1967 by four USAF pilots, J. A. Walker, R. M. White, F. S. Petersen and W. J. Knight, the X-15 reached a maximum height of 354,200feet/67.08 miles (107,960m/107.9km) and ultimately recorded a maximum speed of 4,534mph (7,295km/h) (Mach 6.72) on October 3 1967, this flight being made by W. J. Knight. With speeds and altitudes such as these (attained by use of the air-launching procedure) the traditional World Records became, effectively, superfluous.

Before the end of the 1960s, America had become heavily involved in the Vietnam War, and once again her armed Services were called upon to fight a tenacious and well equipped enemy. Among the tactical fighter and fighter-bomber squadrons of the USAF, the US Navy and the US Marine Corps, the standard aircraft was the F-4 Phantom, and their principal opponents were MiG-17s and MiG-21s. Both sides suffered heavily, not only in air combat – in which the Americans were usually superior – but the Americans also from enemy surface-to-air missiles, with which the communists were well supplied. Most of the air combat was fought using air-to-air missiles and in this respect the Americans were slightly better armed. Only one American jet pilot reached a score of five enemy aircraft destroyed, namely Lieut Randy Cunningham, USN (with his radar operator Lieut Willy Driscoll in the rear cockpit) of Navy Fighter Squadron VF-96, embarked in USS *Constellation* (CVA-64). His last three victories were all gained in the course of one action-packed sortie, and his final victim (a

OVERALL PIC: First pilot to fly the very advanced McDonnell F4H-1 (later to become the F-4 Phantom) was Robert C. Little on May 27 1958, shown here on early tests.

BELOW: Lt-Cdr Randy Cunningham of the US Navy who, flying an F-4 Phantom, was the only American pilot to destroy four enemy jet fighters in a single sortie over Vietnam.

ABOVE: Brian Trubshaw, more familiar in the cockpit of a Concorde supersonic airliner, seen here in that of a propjet Viscount.

ABOVE RIGHT: The late Bill Bedford, Hawker Chief Test Pilot, after making the first landing by a V/STOL jet aircraft on a carrier (HMS *Ark Royal*) in a Hawker P1127 on February 8 1963.

BELOW: One of the most experienced Soviet test pilots is Eugeny Frolov, here shown in a Sukhoi Su-27; he was also responsible for testing the Su-29, Su-31, Su-35 and Su-37. His displays at Farnborough and Paris astonished Western observers.

MiG-21) by extraordinary coincidence was the highest-scoring North Vietnamese pilot, Colonel Toon. Both Cunningham and Driscoll were forced to eject from their Phantom following this combat, but were rescued unhurt from the sea by a US Marine helicopter.

Pursuing more peaceful activities in the air, American pilots returned to air racing in the USA, the annual Reno meeting attracting a breed of enthusiasts who acquired numerous examples of ex-military aircraft, notably P-51 Mustangs, British Sea Furies and Grumman Bearcats, and set about increasing their speed performance. Often modifying their airframes in the interests of reducing drag (but much to the detriment of their handling qualities) these owner-pilots went to considerable personal expense to acquire up-rated engines which were adapted to run on special high-volatile fuels. The most respected of these pilots was probably the 55-year-old (in 1988) Lyle Shelton who, between the 1960s and 1980s, won more Reno Gold Races in his much-modified Bearcat *Rare Bear*, taking the 1988 trophy at 456mph (734km/h), beating Bill Destefani's P-51 victory of the previous year at a speed of 452mph (727km/h).

By the end of the 1960s, Britain and France worked in partnership to develop the world's first supersonic airliner, Concorde – largely in the face

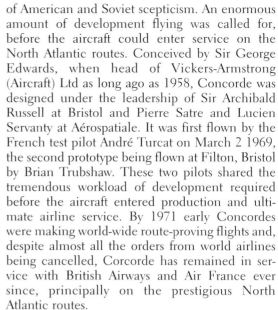

of American and Soviet scepticism. An enormous amount of development flying was called for, before the aircraft could enter service on the North Atlantic routes. Conceived by Sir George Edwards, when head of Vickers-Armstrong (Aircraft) Ltd as long ago as 1958, Concorde was designed under the leadership of Sir Archibald Russell at Bristol and Pierre Satre and Lucien Servanty at Aérospatiale. It was first flown by the French test pilot André Turcat on March 2 1969, the second prototype being flown at Filton, Bristol by Brian Trubshaw. These two pilots shared the tremendous workload of development required before the aircraft entered production and ultimate airline service. By 1971 early Concordes were making world-wide route-proving flights and, despite almost all the orders from world airlines being cancelled, Corcorde has remained in service with British Airways and Air France ever since, principally on the prestigious North Atlantic routes.

Another example of international collaboration in aviation was the Panavia Tornado tactical reconnaissance fighter bomber, which was originally intended as an F-104 Starfighter replacement. Belgium and Holland opted out of the partnership early in the project, leaving Britain (who had joined late), Germany and Italy to develop the project. Production was shared between the three countries, with test flying being undertaken in each. In overall charge of the flight program was Roland Beamont (formerly chief test pilot of English Electric and who had first flown the Canberra bomber and the Lightning Mach 2 fighter, as well as the ill-fated TSR-2), although he took no active flying rôle on the Tornado. First pilot to fly the Tornado was Paul Millett – a highly experienced pilot who had flown numerous very advanced aircraft, including the SEPECAT Jaguar, the Handley Page HP 115 slender delta, and the Bristol Type 188 stainless-steel research aircraft – and Nils Meister, the German Tornado project pilot. Other leading test pilots involved in the Tornado's early development included David Eagles, Tim Ferguson, Peter Gordon-Johnson, and Don Thomas, all of British Aircraft Corporation; A. Krauthann, Hans-Friedrich Rammensee and Fritz Soos of Messerschmitt-Bölkow-Blohm; and Edigio Nappi, Manlio Quarantelli and Pietro Trevisan of Aeritalia SpA.

Prehaps the most radical, yet wholly successful British military project is the Harrier, developed from P1127 prototypes (first flown by Bill Bedford in 1960) and thence by way of a tri-national evaluation squadron. Originally designed under the direction of Hawkers' eminent chief designer, Sir Sydney Camm, the Harrier was first flown by Bill Bedford on August 31 1966, later aircraft being flown by the other Hawker test pilots, Hugh Merewether, Duncan Simpson, John Farley, Tony Hawkes, Don Riches, Barry Tonkinson and Mike Snelling during the first ten years of production. This was a more-than-usually hazardous task of development flying, for all manner of new flying conditions could exist, such as ground debris ingestion during take-off and landing, bird strikes close to the ground and the critical difference between aircraft weight and engine thrust. Quick appreciation of these conditions allowed the Harrier to enter service relatively smoothly, and both it and the related Sea Harrier remain in service at the time of writing, not only with the RAF and Fleet Air Arm, but also the US Marine Corps, and the air forces of Spain and India.

Easing of tension between East and West during the late 1980s brought about an increased awareness of Russian technological progress during the previous Cold War as some of the latest Soviet military aircraft were shown to the Western powers. The leading Design Bureau, that of Mikoyan, displayed its excellent MiG-29 in the hands of Valery Menitsky, while at the Paris Air Show of 1989 another MiG-29 suffered a bird ingestion at very low level, causing one engine to fail; the pilot ejected at only 300 feet (91m) and survived with little injury. Such equality of technical advances by the Soviet Union had not been fully appreciated in the West, although in some respects the quality of manufacture was perhaps less sophisticated.

With the advent of in-flight refueling among all types of aircraft during the past 50 years, the pursuit of long-distance flight records has, perhaps, lost much of its significance. However, one such enterprise had never been attempted – that of an un-refueled non-stop round-the-world flight. Such a flight was at last successfully undertaken in a radical twin-engine aeroplane, named *Voyager*, designed and built by an American company at Mojave, California, led by Elbert L Rutan. Constructed largely of composite materials, the aircraft, with twin fuselage booms, canard foreplane and a central nacelle incorporating a small cabin as well as tractor and pusher engines, carried about six times its own weight in fuel. The flight, supported and organized by the Mobil Oil Company towards the end of 1986, was accomplished by Rutan's brother Dick and a female copilot Jeana Yeager, taking off and landing at Mojave after a nine-day non-stop flight of 25,012 miles (40,244km) at an average speed of 115.6mph (186km/h).

Looking back over the 20th Century, one may perhaps be forgiven for highlighting one of the most bizarre areas of aeronautical research – that of "invisibility", that is to say producing military aeroplanes that are virtually undetectable by radar. Such research originated in Operation *Have Blue* in America during the 1970s, a requirement issued to Lockheed Advanced Development Projects, Burbank, California (known as the "Skunk Works"). Termed the Lockheed XST (Experimental Stealth Tactical) aircraft, the first prototype was flown in great secrecy by Chief Test Pilot Bill Park early in 1978 – he was later to eject from a Stealth prototype and was seriously injured – and later entered service with the USAF as the F-117, an aircraft which played an unexpected though possibly vital part in ending the Gulf War in 1991. Undetected in advance, the arrival of most accurately aimed bombs on strategic targets was the first indication to the Iraqis that American bombers were somewhere overhead.

BELOW LEFT INSET: The first unrefueled flight around the world in the atmosphere was not by a multi-million dollar military bomber but by Burt Rutan's radical *Voyager* which provided its own interpretaion of "state-of-the-art".

BELOW: The two General Dynamics F-16 Fighting Falcon prototypes being flown by test pilots Barter and Anderson in the mid-1970s; both aircraft exceeded Mach 2 on their first flights.

CHAPTER FIVE
Spaceflight

RIGHT: Orbiter *Columbia* blasts off the launch pad on shuttle mission STS-65 in July 1994. It carries the European-designed Spacelab, in which seven astronauts will spend over two weeks performing experiments in the life sciences and materials research.

CENTER: Kathryn Thornton helps repair the *Hubble Space Telescope* on shuttle mission STS-61 in December 1993 on one of the five spacewalks carried out on the mission. She and her spacewalking colleagues demonstrate once again how necessary is the human presence in space.

The Space Age

Every month, a launch vehicle with the combined thrust of a fleet of jet airliners thunders off a launch pad somewhere in the world to deploy satellites into orbit, ferry astronauts to space stations or boost space probes toward a rendezvous with distant planets. Up in space the satellites may monitor the weather, relay communications across the globe or spy stars being born in distant galaxies, while space-suited astronauts recover and repair ailing spacecraft or assemble new structures. Some four decades after the beginning of the Space Age on October 4 1957, spaceflight has become almost routine.

Early days

People began traveling in space – in their imagination – long, long ago. The Moon was a favorite destination. Methods of propulsion into space chosen by writers included waterspouts, evaporating dew, flying swans and space cannons. The space cannon was the modus operandi of the French writer Jules Verne, in his 1865 story "From the Earth to the Moon". Uncannily, he sited the cannon in Florida, close to where the Apollo astronauts would set out for the Moon a century later.

Space cannons, like the other weird and wonderful methods of propulsion suggested, could not work in the real world. There is only one method of space propulsion we know that can work – the rocket. Only rocket motors can develop sufficient power to accelerate objects to the speed they require to overcome the Earth's gravity and get into space – at least 17,500mph (28,000km/h). And only rocket motors can work in space. This is because they do not, like jet engines, rely on the oxygen of the atmosphere to burn their fuel. Rockets carry their own oxygen supply and so can work in airless space.

It is perhaps strange that Verne and his fellow writers never considered the rocket as a potential power source. It had been around for centuries since its invention by the Chinese in about 1200 AD. And by the mid-1800s most European armies boasted a rocket squadron, as did Russia. Avidly following the exploits of the Russian rocket squadron was one Konstantin Eduardovich Tsiolkovsky, born in 1857. While still in his twenties, he began to wonder if rockets could be used for space travel. He became convinced that they could, and spent the next quarter century working out the principles of space rocket flight.

In 1903 he set down his ideas in a paper, entitled "Exploring Space with Reactive Devices", he wrote for a scientific journal. ("Reactive Devices" mean rockets, which work on the principle of reaction.) Among other things in his paper, he pointed out that much more powerful rocket propellants than gunpowder, used in the rockets of the day, would be needed for spaceflight. He suggested the use of high-energy liquid propellants such as liquid hydrogen and oxygen. He was spot on – these propellants are used in the space shuttle, for example.

Tsiolkovsky also realized that no single rocket would be able to achieve the speed necessary to travel into space. They could never have a high enough power to weight ratio. A space rocket would need to consist of a number of rocket units, or stages, joined together, which would fire and separate in turn. In this way, losing weight at each stage, the final unit could achieve the necessary speed. This is the concept of the multistage, or step rocket, which is used in all space launch vehicles.

It is interesting to note that here was Tsiolkovsky setting down ways of traveling into space before anyone had even flown in an airplane! The Wright brothers did not make the first airplane flight until several months later, in the USA.

LEFT: The beautiful ringed planet Saturn, snapped by a *Voyager* space probe. Probes like this have revolutionized the science of planetary astronomy, providing images and data impossible to obtain from Earth observations.

ABOVE: Robert Hutchings Goddard (second from right) and colleagues pose in April 1932 with their latest rocket at a launch site in New Mexico. Its advanced features include gyroscopes to help stabilize flight.

RIGHT: A model of *Sputnik 1*, the first artificial satellite which orbits the Earth on October 4, 1957. A 23inch (58cm) diameter sphere of aluminum, it remains in space for 90 days.

Rocketing into space

It was in the USA that the next stage of rocket development occurred. In March 1926 Robert Hutchings Goddard, a lecturer at Clark University in Worcester, Massachusetts, built and fired the first rocket using liquid propellants. Although his rocket, burning gasoline and liquid oxygen, fired for only a few seconds and rose just 185 feet (86m), it paved the way for the future. Goddard continued his work and by 1937 his rockets were reaching speeds of 700mph (1,100km/h) and heights of 1.7 miles (2.7km).

Unbeknown to him, and indeed to most of the world, Goddard's work was being eclipsed in Germany. On the Baltic island of Peenemunde, a team under the direction of the brilliant Wernher von Braun was developing a series of advanced liquid-propellant rockets. By the time the Second World War broke out in 1939, von Braun's team were working toward a practical ballistic missile capable of delivering a high-explosive warhead over a distance of several hundred miles. The first successful firing of this weapon, designated A4, took place in October 1942. Two years later it was in full production and being fired against targets in England as Hitler's second Vergeltungswaffe ("revenge weapon"), or V-2.

Launched from mainland Europe, the V-2 was a terrifying, unstoppable weapon, dropping without warning out of the sky and exploding on impact at some 2,500mph (4,000km/h). V-2s claimed the lives of over 2,500 men, women and children by the war's end in 1945.

After the war's end, as part of their booty, the

Americans and Russians shipped unused V-2s to their respective countries, taking with them members of the German rocket development team. Team leader von Braun went to the USA and directed further rocket research at the Army's White Sands Proving Ground in New Mexico. In 1949, his team fired the world's first multistage rocket, Bumper, which used a V-2 first stage and a WAC Corporal sounding rocket as second stage. The last two flights in the series took place at a new launch site at Cape Canaveral in Florida, a

V-2

The V-2, developed as the A-4 by Wernher von Braun's team on the Baltic island of Peenemunde, can be seen as the immediate ancestor of the space rocket. It was by far the most advanced rocket of its day, with ethanol (alcohol) and liquid oxygen as propellants, turbo-pumps to pump the propellants into the combustion chamber, which was regeneratively cooled. This meant that cold liquid fuel was circulated through its walls to prevent the chamber burning through. Guidance and control were via a gyro platform, which acted through steerable rudders on the four rear stabilizing fins and through movable vanes in the exhaust. The maiden flight of the A-4 took place on October 3, 1942, after two earlier launch failures. The rocket reached a height of 53 miles (85km) and traveled some 120 miles (190km). Exclaimed von Braun's superior, General Walter Dornberger, afterwards: "Do you realize what we accomplished today? Today, the spaceship was born!"

Length: 46 feet (14m)
Max. body diameter: 5.5 feet (1.7m)
Width across fins: 12 feet (3.6m)
Weight: 4 tons (empty), 13 tons (at launch)
Lift-off thrust: 25 tons
Payload: 1 ton high explosive
Maximum altitude: 60 miles (100km)
Maximum range: 200 miles (300km)

LEFT: A Bumper rocket lifts off the pad at the White Sands Proving Ground in 1949. Bumper is the world's first two-stage rocket, comprising a solid-propellant WAC Corporal rocket atop a V-2.

site that would develop into the famous Kennedy Space Center. Over in Russia, at a site at Kapustin Yar near Volvograd, similar developments were taking place under the direction of Sergei Korolev.

It was now the early 1950s, and the Cold War between the West and the East was intensifying. Both the USA and Russia possessed atomic weapons and were developing methods of delivering them over great distances. This led to the development of rocket-engined intercontinental ballistic missiles (ICBMs). The Russians fired the first ICBM, the SS-6, codenamed Sapwood, in August 1957. With a thrust exceeding 500 tons, it could carry a warhead for up to 5,000 miles (8,000km).

On October 4, 1957, however, slightly modified, it assumed a quite different role by carrying a small sphere of aluminum into orbit around the Earth. Named *Sputnik 1*, this was the world's first artificial satellite. As if to prove that this launch was no fluke, the Russians launched a second satellite, *Sputnik 2*, a month later. This carried the world's first space traveler, a dog named Laika, and weighed half a ton.

US space scientists were astounded. Two years earlier they had announced that they planned to launch satellites for the International Geophysical Year of 1957/58. Now they had been beaten to the post. And the satellites they were intending to launch weighed only 20 pounds (9kg) or so. After

RIGHT: The "Original 7" astronauts chosen to spearhead NASA's man-in-space program. From the left they are: (top row) Alan Shepard, Virgil Grissom, and Gordon Cooper; (front row) Walter Schirra, Donald Slayton, John Glenn, and Scott Carpenter.

FAR RIGHT: John Glenn is winched aboard a helicopter from the recovery ship *Noa* on February 20, 1962. He has just splashed down in his Mercury spacecraft *Friendship 7* after spending nearly five hours in space.

several abortive attempts, they eventually launched their first satellite, *Explorer 1*, on January 31 1958. Predictably, the army launch team was led by von Braun.

SPACE COUNTRIES

Country	First satellite	Date
USSR	Sputnik 1	October 4 1957
USA	Explorer	January 31 1958
France	Sterix 1	November 26 1965
Japan	Ohsumi	February 11 1965
China	China 1	April 24 1970
UK	Prospero	October 28 1971
India	Rohini 1	July 18 1980
Israel	Offeq 1	September 19 1988

The pioneering astronauts

Transparently, a race into space was developing between the world's two greatest powers. The Russians had won the first heat. And with their powerful launch vehicle, they were obviously favorites to win the next – the launch of a human

being into space. The Americans had other ideas. On October 1 1958, a new civilian space agency was created, the National Aeronautics and Space Administration (NASA) to coordinate the nation's space activities. Within the week, administrator Keith Glennan announced a US man-in-space program, later named Mercury.

The next year, the first seven astronauts were selected, experienced test pilots drawn from the Air Force, Navy and Marines. They were Scott Carpenter, Gordon Cooper, John Glenn, Virgil Grissom, Walter Schirra, Alan Shepard and Donald Slayton.

By February 1961 NASA announced the intention of attempting the first manned flight, in a Mercury capsule, following a successful flight the previous month by a chimpanzee. It would be a suborbital flight, with the capsule following a ballistic trajectory into space and back without going into orbit. Originally scheduled for March, it was postponed, with unfortunate consequences – for on April 12 Russians pilot Yuri Gagarin sped into orbit to become the first astronaut, or cosmonaut as Russians call their space travelers. He circled the Earth once in the capsule *Vostok 1* on a flight lasting 108 minutes. He returned to Earth to a hero's welcome apparently none the worse for pushing back the space frontier.

The US regained some credulity when Alan Shepard made a fleeting (15-minute) suborbital flight in the Mercury capsule *Freedom 7* on May 5 1961. It was the start of something big, or so thought President Kennedy days later when he announced before Congress a remarkable space initiative: "I believe that this nation should commit itself to achieving the goal, before this decade is out, of landing a man on the Moon and returning him safely to Earth." In so saying he launched what became the Apollo Moon-landing project. This was some goal indeed for a nation that had not yet even launched a man into orbit.

The US had to wait until the next year for that to happen. On February 20 1962, John Glenn became the first US orbiting astronaut when he

circled the Earth three times in his Mercury capsule *Friendship 7*. Over the next 15 months three further successful Mercury flights took place. The last, by Gordon Cooper in May 1963, lasted for 22 orbits. In all during the Mercury project, astronauts notched up a total of two-and-a-half days in space. It was a good start, but did not stand comparison with the two weeks or so that Russian cosmonauts spent in orbit during their Vostok program, which included the first flight by a female cosmonaut, Valentina Tereshkova, in June 1963.

ABOVE: The pioneering Russian cosmonauts Yuri Gagarin (right), who orbits the Earth once on April 12 1961, and Gherman Titov, who makes 17 orbits on August 6/7 1961 and spends more than a day in space.

MERCURY MISSIONS

Flight	Astronaut	Launch date	Duration
Mercury 3	A. Shepard	May 5 1961	115 min
Mercury 4	V. Grissom	July 21 1961	15 min
Mercury 6	J. Glenn	Feb. 20 1962	4 hr 55 min
Mercury 7	M. Scott Carpenter	May 24 1962	24 hr 56 min
Mercury 8	W. Schirra	Oct. 3 1962	9 hr 13 min
Mercury 9	L. Gordon Cooper	May 15 1963	1 day 10 hr 20 min

VOSTOK & VOSKHOD MISSIONS

Flight	Astronaut	Launch date	Duration
Vostok 1	Y. Gagarin	Apr. 12 1961	1 hr 48 min
Vostok 2	G. Titov	Aug. 6 1961	1 day 1 hr 18 min
Vostok 3	A. Nikolayev	Aug. 11 1962	3 days 22 hr 22 min
Vostok 4	P. Popvich	Aug. 12 1962	2 days 22 hr 57 min
Vostok 5	V. Bykovsky	Jun. 14 1963	4 days 23 hr 6 min
Vostok 6	V. Tereshkova	Jun. 16 1963	2 days 22 hr 50 min
Voskhod 1	V. Komarov	Oct. 12 1964	1 day 17 min
	K. Feoktistov		
	B. Yegorov		
Voskhod 2	A. Leonov	Mar. 18 1965	1 day 2 hr 2 min
	P. Belyayev		

first Gemini flight on March 23 1965, came another *Voskhod* mission, on which cosmonaut Alexei Leonov made the first spacewalk, or EVA (extravehicular activity).

That first Gemini flight, *Gemini 3*, was however highly successful, and success was the keyword of virtually every Gemini flight to follow. On the second mission, *Gemini 4*, Edward White made a spectacular spacewalk; *Gemini 5* made a record-breaking eight-day mission; *Gemini 6* and *Gemini 7* made the first space rendezvous; *Gemini 8* carried out the first space docking; *Gemini 12* saw a five-and-a-half hour spacewalk by Edwin Aldrin. When next he spacewalked – it would be on the Moon.

The flight of *Gemini 12* in November 1966 completed the Gemini project. During the 10 missions, 16 astronauts logged more than 80 days in orbit. They proved that humans could cope with spaceflight, with the high g-forces of lift-off and re-entry, with the peculiar state of weightlessness in orbit, and with spacewalking. And they

ABOVE: Virgil Grissom and John Young ride *Gemini 3* into orbit on March 23, 1965. It is the first mission in the 12-flight Gemini program, which will ready the US for their ultimate goal – a trip to the Moon.

Voskhod and Gemini

NASA, aiming for an end-of-decade lunar landing, had realized that it would be impossible technologically to jump straight from the Mercury project to the Apollo project. And so they embarked on an intermediate project they named Gemini ("Twins"), in which astronauts would travel into space two by two. By the fall of 1964, the first manned Gemini flight was imminent. Then came another morale-sapping Russian mission, in which three cosmonauts flew into space in the *Voskhod 1* capsule. And only five days before the

honed the piloting skills and rendezvous and docking techniques that would be needed for the ultimate challenge – an assault on the Moon.

Apollo preparations

Plans for that assault were now well advanced. Possible landing sites on the Moon had been chosen and were being reconnoitered by the Lunar Orbiter probes. Surveyor probes were soft-landing to take a close look at the lunar surface. Parallel missions by Luna probes suggested that the Russians were planning a manned lunar landing themselves. That this never happened was perhaps surprising in view of their proven track record of upstaging the USA in the past.

Work on the Apollo spacecraft was nearing completion. It was a three-module design, dictated by the technique that had been chosen to achieve lunar landing – lunar orbit rendezvous. The crew of three were accommodated in a cone-shaped, pressurized command module. This was

GEMINI MISSIONS

Flight	Astronaut	Launch date	Duration
Gemini 3	V. Grissom J. Young	Mar. 23 1965	4 hr 53 min
Gemini 4	E. White J. McDivitt	Jun. 3 1965	4 days 1 hr 56 min
Gemini 5	L. Gordon Cooper C. Conrad	Aug. 21 1965	7 days 22 hr 55 min
Gemini 7	F. Borman J. Lovell	Dec. 4 1965	13 days 18 hr 35 min
Gemini 6A	W. Schirra T. Stafford	Dec. 15 1965	1 day 1 hr 52 min
Gemini 8	N. Armstrong D. Scott	Mar. 18 1966	10 hr 41 min
Gemini 9	T. Stafford E. Cernan	May 17 1966	3 days 21 min
Gemini 10	J. Young M. Collins	Jul. 18 1966	2 days 22 hr 47 min
Gemini 11	C. Conrad R. Gordon	Sep. 12 1966	2 days 23 hr 17 min
Gemini 12	J. Lovell E. Aldrin	Nov. 11 1966	3 days 22 hr 35 min

LEFT: *Gemini 6* is pictured through the hatch window of *Gemini 7* when the two craft rendezvous in orbit in December 1965. In this, the first space rendezvous, the two craft maneuver to within 1 foot (30cm) of each other.

connected with a cylindrical service module housing equipment, propellants and a powerful engine. The two sections together formed the Apollo mother ship, the CSM (command and service modules). The third section was the lunar module (LM), the vehicle that would take two of the astronauts down to the surface. It consisted of two parts, the upper of which would carry the astronauts off the Moon and then rendezvous in orbit with the CSM.

With the crew aboard, the CSM weighed close to 45 tons. To lift such a weight and accelerate it to the 25,000mph (40,000km/h) necessary to escape from the Earth's gravity, required a massive launch vehicle, the *Saturn V*. This leviathan of a rocket, which stood 36 stories high on the launch pad and weighed nearly 3,000 tons, was the last in the Saturn series of heavy launch vehicles developed by von Braun's team at the Marshall Flight Center in Alabama.

LEFT: Against a cloudy backdrop, *Gemini 4* astronaut Edward White makes a spectacular spacewalk on June 3 1965. In his right hand is the gas gun he uses to maneuver. A gold-covered umbilical tube feeds oxygen to his spacesuit.

RIGHT: Dave Scott
emerges from the
hatch of the
command module
during the *Apollo 9*
mission, which sees
the lunar module
tested in space for
the first time. Here
the two modules are
still mated. Later
they will separate
and practise
rendezvous and
docking.

BELOW: A *Saturn V*
launch vehicle
leaves the
mammoth Vehicle
Assembly Building
(VAB) at the
Kennedy Space
Center, mounted on
its mobile platform.
The VAB stands no
less than 526ft
(160m) high.

SATURN V/APOLLO

The *Saturn V* launch vehicle was the largest rocket there has ever been, a suitably gargantuan vehicle for a gargantuan task – speeding the Apollo astronauts to the Moon. Earlier members of the Saturn series of heavy launch vehicles (*Saturn I* and *IB*) served to pioneer the technologies the *Saturn V* demanded. It was a three-stage vehicle, with the five F-1 engines of the first stage and the five J-2 engines of the second all burning kerosene and liquid oxygen propellants. The third stage was a single more advanced engine burning liquid hydrogen and liquid oxygen. The Apollo spacecraft was located at the top of the launch vehicle, surmounted by a solid-rocket launch escape system.

SATURN V
Maiden flight: November 9 1967
Overall height: 365 feet (111 m)
Overall weight: 2,900 tons
Lift-off thrust: 7.5 million pounds (3.4 million kg)
First stage (S-1C): 150 feet (46m) long,
                33 feet (10m) in diameter
Second stage (S-II): 82 feet (25m) long,
                33 feet (13m) in diameter
Third stage (S-IVB): 59 feet (18m) long,
                21 feet (6.5m) in diameter

APOLLO CSM
Length: 34 feet (10.4m)
Max. diameter: 13 feet (3.9m)
Weight: 30 tons

APOLLO LUNAR MODULE
Length: 23 feet (7m)
Max diameter: 8 feet (2.4m)
Weight: 16 tons

Inland from the existing launch facilities at Cape Canaveral, a new launch site, Complex 39, had been built to handle the upcoming Apollo flights. Dominating the complex was the mammoth Vehicle Assembly Building (VAB), a 50-story building in which the *Saturn V* would be put together. The first flight on the new rocket, unmanned, took place in November 1967 and was wholly successful.

But not everything had been going so well. In January 1967, during training for the first Apollo test flight, a flash fire in an Apollo spacecraft had killed the three astronauts – Virgil Grissom, Edward White and Roger Chaffee. This triggered a redesign of the command module that put the first Apollo mission on hold until October 1968. The year 1967 was a bad one for the Russians too. In April, while testing a new modular spacecraft named *Soyuz*, pilot Vladimir Komarov was killed when his capsule smashed into the ground on landing after the braking parachutes became entangled.

The first manned Apollo mission of October 1968, designated *Apollo 7*, saw three astronauts test-fly the CSM, with huge success. Their 10-day mission paved the way for the next great leap into the unknown, a circumnavigation of the Moon by *Apollo 8*. This mission, launched by a *Saturn V*, carrying a crew for the first time, took place in December 1968. The world watched spellbound at live telecasts of the lunar surface when *Apollo 8* circled the Moon on Christmas Eve. The crew – Frank Borman, James Lovell and William Anders – read movingly from the Book of Genesis: "... And God saw that it was good."

The *Apollo 8* crew survived re-entry, perhaps the most hazardous part of a Moon flight, and their successful mission crystallized plans for a Moon landing the next summer. But two further flights were needed to insure success. First the lunar module had to be tested; this happened during a 10-day mission in Earth orbit by *Apollo 9* in March 1969. Next came a near dress rehearsal for landing, with *Apollo 10* performing separation, rendezvous and docking manouvers in lunar orbit

LEFT: Edwin Aldrin clambers down the ladder of *Apollo 11*'s lunar module *Eagle* to become the second astronaut to plant his footprints in the lunar soil. He joins the photographer, Neil Armstrong, for an EVA lasting over two hours.

in May. Both flights were flawless. The stage was set for the greatest adventure in the history of humankind that sought to plant human footprints in the lunar soil.

Apollo: the landings

That adventure began at the Kennedy Space Center on July 16 1969. At 9.32 am local time the Center reverberated to the thunderous roar of the first-stage rockets of the mighty *Saturn V* as they lifted the monster off the pad. *Apollo 11* was on its way, destination Moon, crewed by Neil Armstrong, Edwin Aldrin and Michael Collins. Eleven minutes later *Apollo 11*, with the third stage of the *Saturn V* still attached, was in Earth orbit. After final checks, the third stage fired again

to blast the spacecraft into a looping trajectory that would take it to the Moon.

On July 19, *Apollo 11* was close to its target and fired its engine as a brake to slow down so it could enter lunar orbit. Next day Armstrong and Aldrin transferred from the CSM (callsign "Columbia") to the lunar module (*Eagle*). They separated and swooped down to the surface of the lunar plain known as the Sea of Tranquillity, touching down with only 30 seconds of fuel for maneuvering remaining. Reported Armstrong to Mission Control: "Houston, Tranquillity Base here. The Eagle has landed."

Some six hours later, he was opening the hatch of the lunar module and stepping down on to the Moon. "That's one small step for a man," he said, "one giant leap for mankind." Aldrin soon joined

RIGHT: John Young test-drives the lunar roving vehicle, or Moon buggy, on the *Apollo 16* mission in April 1972. This collapsible battery-powered vehicle has a top speed of about 10mph (16km/h)

FAR RIGHT: The Apollo Moon missions are brought to a close as the *Apollo 17* command module descends to the ocean on December 19 1972. During thge six Moon landings, 12 astronauts have traveled over 60 miles (100km) of the surface during EVAs totalling 170 hours.

RIGHT: The experimental space station *Skylab*, pictured by the third team of astronauts as they leave the space station on February 8 1974. They have been in orbit for a record 84 days, during which time they have traveled a distance of 34 million miles (55 million km).

him and together they roamed the surface for some two-and-a-half hours, carrying out experiments and collecting rocks and soil. Next day they returned to orbit and prepared for their journey back to Earth. They splashed down in the Pacific on July 24. The world joined NASA and its astronauts in celebration. They had achieved the seemingly impossible task of landing men on another world and moreover had beaten Kennedy's deadline by nearly six months.

Over the next two-and-a-half years US astronauts embarked on five more successful landing missions. *Apollo 12* set down on the sprawling Ocean of Storms, *Apollo 14* near the ruined crater Fra Mauro, *Apollo 15* in the spectacular foothills of the Apennine Mountains, *Apollo 16* in the lunar highlands near the crater Descartes, and finally *Apollo 17* in the Taurus-Littrow region on the edge of the Sea of Serenity. Altogether the 12 astronauts who left their footprints in the lunar dust explored the surface for a total of 166 hours, roamed for nearly 60 miles (100km) and brought back 850 pounds (385kg) of Moon rocks and soil.

As will be noticed, *Apollo 13* does not appear among the landings. There was a mission 13, which set out in April 1970. But two days into the journey the spacecraft was crippled by an explosion in the service module. The landing had to be cancelled, and the crew was able to survive only by using the lunar module as a liferaft. NASA recorded the mission as "the most successful failure in the history of spaceflight".

Apollo: spin-off missions

Originally NASA had planned for three further landing missions and had constructed most of the hardware for them. But budget cutbacks and dwindling public interest forced their cancellation. NASA therefore came up with two further projects that would use the surplus hardware. The first was an experimental space station called Skylab. The second was an international space

APOLLO MISSIONS

Flight	Astronaut	Launch date	Duration
Apollo 7	W. Schirra	Oct. 11 1968	10 days 20 hr 9 min
	D. Eisele		
	W. Cunningham		
Apollo 8	F. Borman	Dec. 21 1968	6 days 3 hr 1 min
	J. Lovell		
	W. Anders		
Apollo 9	J. McDivitt	Mar. 3 1969	10 days 1 hr 1 min
	D. Scott		
	R. Schweickart		
Apollo 10	E. Cernan	May 18 1969	8 days 3 min
	J. Young		
	T. Stafford		
Apollo 11	N. Armstrong	Jul. 16 1969	8 days 3 hr 18 min
	E. Aldrin		
	M. Collins		
Apollo 12	C. Conrad	Nov. 14 1969	10 days 4 hr 36 min
	R. Gordon		
	A. Bean		
Apollo 13	J. Lovell	Apr. 11 1970	5 days 23 hr
	J. Swigert		
	F. Haise		
Apollo 14	A. Shepard	Jan. 31 1971	9 days 2 min
	S. Roosa		
	E. Mitchell		
Apollo 15	D. Scott	Jul. 26 1971	12 days 7 hr 12 min
	A. Worden		
	J. Irwin		
Apollo 16	J. Young	Apr. 16 1972	11 days 1 hr 51 min
	T. Mattingly		
	C. Duke		
Apollo 17	E. Cernan	Dec. 7 1972	12 days 13 hr 52 min
	R. Evans		
	H. Schmitt		

mission with the Russians, the Apollo-Soyuz Test Project (ASTP).

Skylab was built around the third rocket stage of a *Saturn V*, which formed the main habitation area for the station. Other sections included a telescope assembly and a docking module. The latter provided the interface for the Apollo CSMs that would ferry crew up to the station. Plans for *Skylab* were firmed up in 1970, with a launch planned for 1973. But hopes that it would become the first space station were dashed in April 1971, when the Russians launched a purpose-built space station called *Salyut*. A three-man crew in *Soyuz 11* took up residence in the station in June for nearly two weeks, breaking all space endurance records. But tragedy struck during re-entry, when their capsule depressurized and killed them. This halted Russia's space station plans for the time being.

NASA pressed ahead with *Skylab*, which was launched by a *Saturn V* in May 1973. But the apparently perfect launch was flawed. One of the main solar panels of the station was ripped off, others were jammed, and a section of insulation was missing. The station was crippled. The first manned mission to the station was delayed for 10 days until NASA had worked out ways of rescuing the station. Up in orbit, the first crew carried out the necessary repairs and *Skylab* became habitable. They remained in orbit for 28 days, and were followed over the next nine months by two further crews, who remained in orbit for periods of 59 and 84 days. Up in orbit the crews performed a series of experiments in the life sciences and materials technology, carried out Earth observations and made a concentrated study of the Sun. Thanks to

SKYLAB MISSIONS

Flight	Astronaut	Launch date	Duration
Skylab 2	C. Conrad	May 25 1973	28 days 50 min
	J. Kerwin		
	P. Weitz		
Skylab 3	A. Bean	Jul. 28 1973	59 day 11 hr 9 min
	O. Garriott		
	J. Lousma		
Skylab 4*Skylab 4*	E. Gibson	Nov. 16 1973	84 days 1 hr 16 min
	W. Pogue		

SPACE SHUTTLE

The space shuttle was the first re-usable launch vehicle, which made its maiden flight on April 12 1981. Of its three major components – orbiter, solid rocket boosters (SRBs) and external tank, only the latter is not re-used. The orbiter carries the crew in a pressurized cabin, while payloads (cargo) are carried in an unpressurized payload bay. A remote manipulator system (robot arm) is located in the bay to assist satellite launching and recovery operations. Lift-off propulsion is provided by three main engines, burning liquid hydrogen and liquid oxygen. Insertion into orbit and de-orbit burns are carried out by a pair of orbital maneuvering system (OMS) engines, which use hydrazine and nitrogen tetroxide propellants. Heat shielding of the aluminum alloy airframe is provided mainly by some 35,000 silica tiles. Fuel cells supply power to the orbiter and water for use by the crew.

ORBITER
Length: 122 feet (37.2m)
Wingspan: 78 feet (23.8m)
Height: 46 feet (14.1m)
Weight: 90 tons
Payload bay: 60 feet long and 15 feet wide
(18.3m and 4.6m)
Lift-off thrust (3 main engines): 1,124,000 pounds
(510,000kg)

SOLID ROCKET BOOSTERS (SRBs)
Length: 149 feet (45.5m)
Diameter: 12 feet (3.7m)
Weight: 570 tons
Thrust: 3,300,000 pounds (1,500,000kg)

EXTERNAL TANK
Length: 154 feet (47m)
Diameter: 27.5 feet (8.4m)
Weight: 760 tons
Capacity: liquid hydrogen 103 tons,
liquid oxygen 617 tons

ABOVE: Two minutes into the flight of the shuttle, the SRBs separate, before parachuting back to the ground. The main engines continue firing for another six-and-a-half minutes, before the external tank is jettisoned.

a regular exercise regime on board they suffered little from their lengthy stays in space. This augured well for the long-term future of human space exploration.

Apollo hardware was used for the last time on the ASTP mission, in July 1975. A three-man American crew in an Apollo CSM met up in orbit with a two-man Russian crew in a Soyuz spacecraft, linking together via a docking module carried by Apollo. Any "space race" was forgotten as astronauts and cosmonauts worked together in a spirit of camaraderie. This was the way to explore space: cooperation not competition. But it would be another two decades before astronauts and cosmonauts mingled again.

The Space Truck

The ASTP mission was for the Americans not only the end of the Apollo era but also the end of the expendable era in manned spacecraft. Henceforth US astronauts would ride into space in a new kind

of craft, which could be used again and again. It would be more like an airliner than a rocket ship, in which people could fly without experiencing the punishing g-forces of the launch rockets of the expendable era. This new launch vehicle, the space shuttle, in short would revolutionize space travel.

The final design chosen for the shuttle system comprised three main pieces of hardware. Crew and cargo would be housed in a delta-winged orbiter about the size of a medium-range airliner. It would take off like a rocket, but return to Earth as a glider.

The orbiter's rocket engines would be fed with liquid hydrogen and liquid oxygen propellants from an external tank. Extra thrust for lift-off would be provided by twin solid rocket boosters (SRBs) strapped to the sides of the tank. Shortly after lift-off the SRBs would separate and parachute back to Earth for re-use. When the external tank emptied, it would be jettisoned but not recovered.

Work on the shuttle started as the last Apollo landings were taking place. But it was not until 1977 that the first shuttle craft took to the air. This craft was the prototype orbiter, named *Enterprise* to the delight of "Star Trek" fans. Flights in the atmosphere proved its aerodynamic worth, and work forged ahead on the first operational orbiter, *Columbia*. Technological problems, particularly with the main engines and the insulating tiles that formed the heat shield of the orbiter, wreaked havoc with schedules. And it was not until April 12 1981, that *Columbia* blasted off from the Kennedy Space Center on the first shuttle mission, designated STS-1 (STS for "Space Transportation System"). Close to a million

people watched as veteran astronaut John Young and Robert Crippen rode the new "bird" into the heavens. After a flawless mission, *Columbia* touched down at the Edwards Air Force Base in California two days later.

Columbia was ferried back to Kennedy atop a modified Boeing 747 carriier aircraft and by November was back on the launch pad. On November 12 it was again punching its way into the heavens. It was the first time any craft had flown into space more than once. The re-usable era in space travel had begun. The next year it repeated the feat three more times. On the last flight (STS-5) it became officially operational, carrying two commercial satellites into orbit.

A second orbiter, *Challenger*, went into service in April 1983, making three trips into space in the year. On the second Sally Ride became the first US female astronaut, being one of a record crew

ABOVE: On the first shuttle flight, in April 1981, *Columbia*'s commander John Young is pictured seated in his cockpit. He is making a record fifth flight into space.

BELOW LEFT: The prototype shuttle orbiter *Enterprise* is carried aloft on a converted jumbo jet in a captive flight test for the shuttle design in February 1977. In tests the following August *Enterprise* will be released and glide down to a runway landing.

ABOVE: A solid rocket booster emerges from the fireball that has just engulfed *Challenger* just 73 seconds after lift-off on January 28 1986, on shuttle mission 51-L. The seven astronauts that perish are the first in-flight victims in the US space program.

of five. In the November *Columbia* was back in harness, this time carrying a science laboratory called *Spacelab*, built by the European Space Agency, in its payload bay. Its record crew of six included the first European to travel on a US spacecraft, Ulf Merbold.

It was in 1984 that the remarkable versatility of the shuttle became apparent. In April spacewalking astronauts working from *Challenger* captured an ailing satellite named *Solar Max* and repaired it in the payload bay before relaunching it. They did so using a jet-propelled backpack called the MMU (manned maneuvering unit) and with help from the orbiter's robot arm. In November on the second flight of a new orbiter, *Discovery*, shuttle astronauts captured not one, but two satellites that had become marooned in uselessly low orbits, and this time brought them back to Earth.

The shuttle fleet expanded to four in 1985 when *Atlantis* became operational in October. With a fleet of four, orbiters would soon be shuttling into orbit every few weeks, or so it seemed. But it was not to be. On January 28 1986, *Challenger* rose from the launch pad on its 10th and the shuttle's 25th mission, designated 51-L. It was dubbed the teacher's flight for it carried Christa McAuliffe, who would give the first lessons to the nation's children from orbit. But

only 73 seconds into the flight the shuttle assembly exploded in a fireball in the Florida skies. *Challenger* was blasted apart and in an instant her crew of seven met an untimely death. Richard Scobee, Michael Smith, Ronald McNair, Gregory Jarvis, Ellison Onizuka, Judith Resnik and Christa McAuliffe became the first in-flight casualties in the US space program.

The remaining shuttle fleet was grounded as President Reagan set up the Rogers commission to investigate the disaster. The immediate cause appeared to be a faulty joint in one of the SRBs, which allowed hot gases to escape and torch the supporting structure. The SRB swung round and ruptured the external tank, which immediately exploded. The Rogers Commission recommended extensive modifications to the shuttle to prevent such a thing happening again, as well as operational changes prior to launch.

The fleet remained grounded until September 1988, when *Discovery* blasted off from the launch pad on mission STS-26 and spearheaded America's "return to flight". Its 4-day mission was flawless, drawing collective sighs of relief from NASA establishments around the nation. Nine years on, the shuttle would be celebrating its 80th flight and preparing for its next major role in space – aiding the construction of the International

LEFT: On shuttle mission 51-A in November 1984 Joseph Allen captures the rogue communications satellite *Palapa B2*, using a device called *The Stinger*. It is the first of two satellites the astronauts recover during the mission.

FAR LEFT: The Russian space shuttle, ready for its maiden flight in November 1988. The orbiter *Buran* is mounted on the powerful booster *Energia*. *Buran* is a near-twin of the US shuttle orbiter, with a length of 120ft (36m) and a wingspan of 80ft (24m)

Space Station.

On *Discovery*'s launch day in 1988, the Russians as ever tried to steal some thunder, announcing that they were about to launch a shuttle craft of their own, called *Buran* ("Snowstorm"). It would be an unmanned, automated flight. A planned October launch slipped into November, and *Buran* finally made it into orbit on November 15, circling the Earth twice before landing near its launch site at the Baikonur Cosmodrome. Though outwardly a shuttle lookalike, *Buran* did not use its own engines for lift-off. It rode into space piggy-back on what had become the world's most powerful launch vehicle, *Energia*. Its own engines fired on the fringes of space to thrust it into orbit. *Buran*'s maiden flight, however, was also its last. Plans for manned missions in this and other *Buran* craft were eventually abandoned because of lack of funds following the break-up of the Soviet Union.

Russian Salyuts

But *Buran*'s maiden flight came at a time when Russian space achievements were in the ascendant. While the USA had been concentrating on developing the space shuttle, the Russians had been accumulating vast experience of long-dura-

RIGHT: Russian cosmonauts in a *Soyuz* ferry photograph shuttle orbiter *Atlantis* as it moves away from *Mir* after the first historic docking between the two craft in June/July 1995.

tion flights in a series of space stations, building up to a continuous presence in orbit. As mentioned earlier, the first Salyut mission was marred by tragedy. With four further Salyuts, launched between 1973 and 1976, the Russians began to build up useful operating experience. But it was not until *Salyut 6*, launched in September 1977, that they began to surge ahead.

Salyut 6 was of much the same design as its predecessors, comprising three cylinders of different diameters, and measuring about 47 feet (14.5m) long. It differed from them in having docking ports at each end. The purpose of this soon became evident. It allowed a replacement crew to dock their Soyuz ferry craft at one port while that of the resident crew was still docked at the other. This first happened in January 1978, when *Soyuz 27* docked with *Salyut 6/Soyuz 26*. Shortly after *Soyuz 26* had returned to Earth, its place was taken by an automatic supply craft called *Progress*, which delivered fresh supplies to the crew.

With the facility for delivering supplies auto-matically, the stage was set for long-duration flights. And so it proved. In November 1978 two astronauts completed a 139-day mission. Records in *Salyut 6* continued to tumble – 175 days (1979), 184 days (1980). They continued to fall when *Salyut 7* took over in 1982 – 211 days (1982), 237 days (1984).

Missions to Mir

Salyut 7 was aging rapidly when in February 1986 a new-generation space station called *Mir* ("Peace") was launched into orbit. This was not unlike the Salyuts in appearance, but had a multiple docking module at one end, with six docking ports, as well as a single port at the other. This construction hinted at the spacecraft's purpose, as the base unit for a more extensive space complex. It would house the living quarters of the crew, while the main experimental work would be carried out in the add-on units that were to follow. The first unit, *Kvant 1*, docked with the base unit in 1987, followed by *Kvant 2* (1989), *Kristall* (1990), Spektr (1995) and *Priroda* (1996). With *Priroda* added, the *Mir* space station was at last complete, though, now 10 years old, was beginning to show its age.

Mir has been continuously inhabited since its launch, with its cosmonauts continuing to smash space duration records. In December 1988 Musa Manarov and Vladimir Titov became the first space travelers to spend a year in orbit. This feat was bettered by Valeri Polyakov, returning to Earth in March 1995 after 437 days. Another feature of missions to *Mir* have been visits by "guest" cosmonauts of many different nationalities. They have included European Space Agency astronauts like Ulf Merbold (1994) and Thomas Reiter (1995) on the so-called EuroMir missions.

Of particular significance have been the flights on *Mir* of US astronauts, beginning with Norman Thagard in March 1995. His flight was the prelude to the first international space link-up since the ASTP mission two decades before. This happened in June 1995 when space shuttle *Atlantis* docked with the Russian space station. It was a suitable spectacular to celebrate the 100th US manned flight. The resulting complex was the most extensive assembly of space hardware ever assembled in orbit and saw 10 astronauts and cosmonauts coming together for the first time. The flight also saw an exchange of crews, with two Russian cosmonauts transferring from *Atlantis* to *Mir* and two others, along with Thagard, transfer-

ring from *Mir* to *Atlantis*.

This was just the first of several shuttle missions to *Mir* to accumulate experience in joint operations as a prelude to working together in the launch, assembly and operation of the upcoming international space station (ISS), also known as

LEFT: On the Euromir mission, European astronaut Thomas Reiter (right) is pictured inside *Mir* with Sergei Avdeyev, one of his Russian colleagues. He will return to Earth in February 1996 after spending 179 days in orbit.

BELOW: *Salyut 7*, last and most successful of the Salyut space stations, pictured in orbit docked with a *Soyuz* ferry in 1985. Notice the huge arrays of solar panels, which have been added over the years to provide extra power.

SHUTTLE LANDMARK MISSIONS

Flight	Launch date	Highlight
STS-1	Apr. 12 1981	First flight, with orbiter *Columbia*.
STS-6	Apr. 4 1983	Maiden flight of orbiter *Challenger*; first shuttle spacewalk.
STS-9	Nov. 28 1983	First Spacelab flight.
41B	Feb. 2 1984	Bruce McCandless makes the first untethered spacewalk, in the MMU.
41C	Apr. 6 1984	Astronauts capture and repair *Solar Max*.
41D	Aug. 30 1984	Maiden flight of *Discovery*.
51A	Nov. 8 1984	Capture and recovery of *Palapa* and *Westar* communications satellites.
51J	Oct. 3 1985	Maiden flight of orbiter *Atlantis*.
61A	Oct. 30 1985	Record crew of eight on this German Spacelab mission.
51L	Jan. 28 1986	*Challenger* explodes after launch; crew of seven killed; shuttle fleet grounded.
STS-26	Sep. 29 1988	*Discovery* spearheads return to flight.
STS-31	Apr. 24 1990	Launch of the Hubble Space Telescope.
STS-40	Jun. 5 1991	First Spacelab mission devoted entirely to life sciences.
STS-49	May 7 1992	Maiden flight of orbiter *Endeavour*, *Challenger*'s replacement; capture and repair of *Intelsat VI* communications satellite.
STS-50	Jun. 25 1992	Longest shuttle flight to date (13 day 19 hr) in modified *Columbia*.
STS-55	Apr. 26 1993	On this German Spacelab mission, *Columbia* clocks up its 100th day in space and shuttle operations exceed a year in total.
STS-61	Dec. 2 1993	Highly successful repair in orbit of the Hubble Space Telescope.
STS-60	Feb. 3 1994	First US flight with a Russian cosmonaut, Sergei Krikalev.
STS-63	Feb. 3 1995	*Discovery* rendezvous in orbit with Russian space station *Mir*.
STS-71	Jun. 27 1995	*Atlantis* docks with *Mir* and exchanges crews.
STS-79	Sep. 16 1996	On this fourth *Mir* docking mission, *Atlantis* picks up Shannon Lucid after her record 188 day stay in *Mir*; John Blaha replaces her.

Alpha. On later shuttle/*Mir* missions the shuttle ferried up astronauts for a long-term stay in *Mir*, beginning with Shannon Lucid in February 1996. She remained in orbit for 188 days, the longest any female astronaut or cosmonaut had remained in orbit. Indeed it was the longest spaceflight to date by anyone in the West.

In prospect

In the immediate future, the efforts of the major spacefaring nations in the sphere of manned space travel will be concentrated on the construction of the ISS, which is scheduled to become fully operational in the year 2003. Of course, the launching of satellites and probes for commercial use and scientific research will continue unabated.

The ISS is masterminded by NASA, which is organizing the construction and assembly, which should begin in late 1997 and take five years. When complete the ISS, orbiting between about 220 and 280 miles (350 and 450km), will have a mass of more than 400 tons and measure some 330 by 250 feet (100m by 75m) across. It will be operated by an international crew of six, with crews rotating every few months.

The shuttle will be the prime vehicle for assembly tasks. The USA is also providing a variety of other hardware, including laboratory and habitation modules and connecting nodes to link modules together. Other elements of the ISS are being provided by Russia, the European Space Agency (ESA), Japan and Canada. Russia is supplying a number of modules and Proton launch vehicles to launch them. They are providing the module to be launched first (scheduled for November 1997), known as the Functional Cargo

Block, or FGB. It is a self-contained orbital vehicle that will provide power and propulsion to support the early phases of construction. Russia is also supplying service and laboratory modules and Soyuz craft as crew rescue vehicles.

ESA's main contribution is a laboratory module known as the Columbus Orbital Facility. In addition it is providing two nodes and an automated transfer vehicle (ATV), a propulsion unit for moving payloads in orbit. Japan is supplying a laboratory unit called JEM (Japan Experimental Module), while Canada is building a remote manipulator system, the main handling device for the station. All these space station elements will be supported by truss structures carrying giant solar panels to provide power.

With the construction of the ISS consuming rather more money that the Apollo Moon-landing project ($25 billion), budgets for new space programs have become tight. But developments continue. For example, work is progressing on a new generation of reusable launch vehicles that should eventually provide cheaper and quicker workaday access to space. In prospect are single stage to orbit (SSTO) vehicles like Lockheed's X-33 design, which NASA chose for development in 1996. Rocket-boosted lifting-body vehicles like ESA's *Hermes* and Japan's *HOPE* could also come into their own early next century.

Future grand projects some time next century will certainly include a return to the Moon, prob-

LEFT: The European Space Agency's project for a shuttle craft called *Hermes*. It is of lifting-body design and would be launched into space by the *Ariane 5* launch vehicle to ferry astronauts and equipment to the space station.

FAR LEFT: The international space station, as it should appear in orbit in 2002. It is now complete, with the modules provided by the US, Russia, the European Space Agency (ESA) and Japan (NASDA) in place and fully operational.

ably with the establishment of a permanent base there. Later a round trip to Mars could follow, although the technology required for such a daring venture seems beyond reach in the foreseeable future, and the suggested permanent colonies on Mars a mere pipe dream. But if the history of spaceflight has taught us anything it is that dreams become reality – and sooner than expected.

LEFT: Regular servicing of the *Hubble Space Telescope* will be among the routine tasks that astronauts will carry out in space in the years ahead, although the main thrust of activity will be related to space station construction.

Index

Figures in **bold** type represent references in captions to illustrations

A
Ader, Clement, 12
Aeroflot, 48
Aeromarine Airways, 47
Aerospatiale Alliance SST, **63**
Agricultural aircraft, 66, 67
AI(R) ATR.42/ATR.72, 65
Aichi D3A Val, 93
Air France, 48
Air mail services, First, 33, **33**
Air stewardesses, Earliest, **48**
Airbus Industrie A.300 series, 65, 65
 A340 cockpit, **29**
Airco, 35
Airco D.H. 2, 73
Aircraft carriers, 84–
Aircraft Transport & Travel Co. Ltd., 35, **35**
Airports, Early, 42
Airports, Modern, 67,
Airships at war, 74-75
Airships, Comercial, 54-55
Albatros biplane, 72
 CIII, **72**
 D.III, 79
 D.V, 79
Alcock and Brown, 111
Alcock, John, 37, 38
Aldrin, Edwin, **131**
American Airlines, 48
Amundsen, Roald, 45
Apollo missions, 129–
Arab-Israeli wars, 98
Arlandes. Marquis d', 10, **11**
Armstrong, Neil, 131
Armstrong-Whitworth Argosy, 46, **46**
 AW.27 Ensign, 57
 Whitley, 87
Astronauts, see chapter Spaceflight
Atlantis, 139
Autogiros, 20-21
Aviatik, 71
Avro Anson, **82**
 Lancaster, 88, **88**
 Lancastrian, 58, **58**
 Type F, 34, **34**

B
BAC 1-11, 61
BAC/Aerospatiale Concorde, back cover, 25, 62, **62**, 63, 120
Bader, Gp Capt Douglas, 87, 114, **114**, 6
BAe 146, 65
BAe Harrier/Sea Harrier, **24**, 27, **101**, 101, 105, 121
Ball, Albert, 78, 110
Ball, Eric, **87**, 6
Balloons, 30–
 at war, 68-69
Barber, Horatio, 33
Barkhorn, Maj Gerhard, 115, **115**
Barnstormers and stunt flying, 44-45
Batten, Jean, 52
Battle of Britain, 85-87
Beamont, Roland, 120
Bedford, Bill, 120, **120**
Beech Starship, **66**
Bell AH-1, **102**
 X-1, 26, 27, 117
 X-15, 26, 27
Bell Boeing V-22 Osprey, **26**, 27
Bell Model 30 helicopter, 21
Benoist flying boat, 34, **34**
Bentley, Lt. Dick, 40
Berlin Airlift, 95
Berson, Herr, 30

Bishop, William, 78, 110
Blackburn monoplane, 34
 Skua, 85
Bleriot, Louis, **14**, 14, 32, 33, 107, **107**
Bleriot XI monoplane, 14, 33, 1
Blitz, The, 87
Blitzkrieg, 85
Boeing 307 Stratoliner, 56, **56**
 314 Clipper series, **49**
 314A flying boat, **19**
 367-80, 60
 377 Stratocruiser, 56, 57, 6
 707, 24, 25
 727, 60
 737, **60**
 747, 63, **64**
 757, 64
 767, 64
 777, 64, **64**
 2707 SST, 62
 B-17, 89, **89**
 B-29, 94, **95**, 97
 B-52 bomber, 27, **99**
 F3B-1 fighters, **15**
 Joint Strike Fighter, 27, **27**
 Model 247, 55, 6 Model 40, 50
 NB-52, **26**
Boeing, William E., 41
Boelcke, Oswald, 72, 73, 110
Bolshoi Balitskii, 34
Bong, Maj Richard I., 116, **116**
Borodino, Battle of, 68
Brabazon Committee, 57, 58
Brand, C.J. Quintin, **38**, 39
Braun, Werner von, 124
Breguet XIXGR, 51
Bristol 175 Britannia, 59
 Beaufighter, 87, 89
 Beaufort, 88, 1
 Blenheim bomber, 17
 F.2b, 79, 81, 6
Bristol Mercury engine, 17
Britain, Battle of 85-87
Britten-Norman Islander, 65
Brown, Arthur Whitten, 37, 38
Buran, 137
Byrd, Richard, 45, **45**

C
Camm, Sir Sydney, 120
Campi, Joe, 44
Canadair CL.28 Argus, 59
 Regional Jet, 65
Caproni Ca 33, 76
Carpenter, Scott, **126**
Catalina flying boats, 57
Cayley, Sir George, 11, 106
Cessna Citation, 66
Challenger, 135–
Chanute, Octave, 31, 107
Cheshire, Gp Capt Leonard, 115
Cierva C.4 autogiro, 20
Cierva, Juan de la, 20, **20**
Civil War, American, **68**, 69
Cobham, Sir Alan, 39, **39**
Cockpit instruments, 28
Cody, Samuel, **106**, 107
Collins, Michael, 131
Columbia Orbiter, **122**
Columbia, 135
Coney, William D., 112
Consolidated B-24 Liberator, **90**
Convair 240, 340, 440, 880, 61
 B-58 Hustler, 96, 97
 F-106 Delta Dart, 96
Cooper, Gordon, **126**
Coral Sea, Battle of, 93

Cornu, Paul, 69, **69**
Cosmonauts, see chapter Spaceflight
Cunningham,Lt Cdr Randy, 119, **119**
Curtiss CW-20, 56
 flying boats, **37**
 H-12 flying boat, **15**
 Jenny, 44, **44**
 T-32 Condor, 56

D
Daily Mail newspaper, 32
Dassault Mirage III, 98
de Havilland, Geoffrey, **70**, **108**
De Haviland DHC-3/DHC-4/DHC6/DHC-7/DHC-8, 65
De Havilland (Hawker Siddeley) HS.125, 66
De Havilland Comet, 25, 59, 60, **60**
 D.H. 4, 77
 D.H. 9, 35
 DH. 16, 35, 35
 DH. 17, 36
 DH. 18, 36
 DH. 34, 36
 DH. 50J, 39
 DH. 66 Hercules, 46, **46**
 DH. 60 Moth, 39, **43**
 DH. 82A Tiger Moth, 44
 DH. 84 Dragon, 56
 DH. 86 Express, 56
 DH. 91 Albatross, 57
 DH.121 Trident, 61
 Mosquito, 89,
De Havilland Canada DHC-3/DHC-4/DHC-6/DHC-7/DHC-8, 65
Degelow, Karl, 81,
DELAG (Deutsche Luftschiffart AG), 12, 33,
Delta wings, 25
Deutsche Luft Hansa, 47,
Deutsche Luft Reederei (DLR), 35
Discovery, 136
Dixmunde airship, 54
Doolittle, James H., 112, 113
Dornier Do 17, 56, 85
Dornier Wal flying boat, 45
Douglas DC-1, **16**
 DC-2, **16**, 55
 DC-3, **16**, 55, 56
 DC-4E, 56
 DC-8, 61
 DC-9/MD-90, 61
 Devastator, 85
 World Cruisers, 39, 53

E
Earhart, Amelia, 51, 52 , **52**, 112, **113**
Eastern Airlines, 48
Edwards, Sir George, 120
Ely, Eugene, **84**
England-Australia, First solo flight, 40
English Channel (first flight), 32, **33**
English Electric Lightning, 24, **24**
Enterprise, **135**
Esnault-Pelterie, Robert, 32
Euromir, **139**
European Space Agency, **141**
Explorer 1, 126

F
Fairey Long-Range Monoplane, 113
Falklands War, 101
Farman Goliath, **43**
Farman, Henri, 32, 107
Fighters, Early, 71–
First humans to fly, 10
First World War, 69–
 pilots, 110–
Fischer, Henri, 34
Flaps (plain, split, slotted, Fowler), 16-17

Fleurus, Battle of, 68
Flyer, The, 9, **13**, 32, 107
Flying boats, 15, 49
Focke Wulf FW 190A, 90
Fw 200, 57
Fokker, Anthony, 41, 72
Fokker D.VI, 79
   E.1 Eindecker, 72, **73**
   F II, F III, F IV, F V, F VII, F VIIA, F VIIA-3m, 41
   F.27 Friendship, 61, **61**
   F.28 Fellowship, 61
   F.VII, F.VIIB, 41, **41**
   T.2, 39
   Triplane, 80
Fonck, Rene, 51, 81, 110
Ford 4-AT/5-AT, **50**
Ford, Henry, 50
Franco-Prussian War, 69
Frantz, Josef, 71
Freight carried (table), 67
Freight services, First, 34
Friendship 7, 127
Frolov, Eugeny, **120**

G
Gagarin, Yuri 126, 127, **127**
Galland, Adolf, 114, **115**
Garros, Roland, 72
Gates Lear Jet, 66
Gemini missions, 128-129
General Aviation, 66
General Dynamics (Lockhed Martin) F-16
   Fighting Falcon, 101, **126**
   F-111, 25,
Gibson, Guy, 115
Giffard, Henri, 11, **11**
Glanville, John, 8, 9
Glenn, John, **126**
Gloster E.28/39, 116
   Meteor, 23, **24**, 116, **116**, 117
Goddard, Robert Hutchings, 124, **124**
Gotha G IV/G V, 76, **76**
Grahame-White, Claude, 8, 9, 108
Grissom, Virgil, **126**, **128**
Grumman A-6 Intruder, 100
   E-2C Hawkeye, 101
   F3-F3, 85
   F4F Wildcat, 93, **93**
   F6FHellcat, **94**
   F-14 Tomcat, 25, **25**
Gulf War, 102-103
Guns, Early aircraft, 70
Guynemer, Georges, 78, 110

H
Hamel, Gustav, 33
Handley Page, 20
   0/100, **77**
   0/400, 35, 77
   Halifax, 88
   Hampden, 87
   HP. 42, **47**
   HP. 45
   W.8 airliner, 36, **36**, 37
Harris, Air Marshal Bert, 88
Hartmann, Eric, 115, **115**
Have Blue, Lockheed, 121
Hawker, Harry, 37, 109
Hawker Hunter, 98,
   Hurricane, 86
   Sea Fury, 118
   Tempest, 91
Heinkel He 111 bomber, **18**, 85, 86
   He 111H, 86
   He 111K, **86**
   He 178 jet aircraft, 22, **22**
Helicopters, 21
Helicopters, First, 69
Hermes, 141
Hinckler, Bert, 40, **40**
Hiroshima, Atomic bombing of, 94
Hot-air balloons, 66
Hubbard, Eddie, 41
Hubble Space Telescope, **122**, 141
Hughes H-1 Racer, 53

Hughes H-4 Hercules (Spruce Goose), 58, **59**
Hughes, Howard, 53

I
Ilya Mourometz, 34, **35**, 76, **76**
Ilyushin Il-62, 6
   Il-96, 61
Immelman, Max, 72, **110**
Imperial Airways, 46
International Air Transport Association (IATA), 66, 67

J
Jet engines, 22-23
Johnson, Amy, 52, 112, **113**
Johnson, Capt Leon, 116
Joint Strike Fighter, 105, **105**
Jones, Ira, 79
Junkers F 13, 40, **41**
   F 32, 49
   G31, 49
   Ju 52, **82**
   Ju 52/3m, 50
   Ju-87 Stuka, 85
   Ju-88, 85
   W34, 49

K
Kelly Act, 42
Kelly, Oakley, 39
Kennedy Space Center, 125
Keystone B-6A bomber, 16
Kingsford Smith, Charles, 52, 52
KLM, 45
Korean War, 96–
Kozhedub, Col Ivan, 116, **117**

L
La France airship, 11 1
Langley, Samuel P., 12, 31,
Leefe-Robinson, William, 75, **75**
Lewis machine gun, 18
Lilienthal, Otto, 12, 31, **106**
Lindbergh, Charles A. **42**, 51, **51**, 112, **112**
Lockheed 1011 Tristar, 64
   Constellation, 57, **58**
   Constitution, 58
   Electra, 53
   F-104 Starfighter, 24
   F-117 Nighthawk, 103, **103**
   F-22 Raptor, 105, **105**
   Joint Strike Fighter, 27, **27**
   P-38 Lightning, 90
   SR-71 Blackbird, 26
   Vega, 16, 53
   X-33, 141
   XST, 121
Lympne Trials, 43

M
Mach numbers, 22
Mackenzie-Grieve, K, 37, 111
MacReady, John, 39
Mannock, Edward, 81, **110**
Martin 123/B-10B bomber, 16, **16**
Martin T4M-1 torpedo bombers, 15
McCudden, James, 72, 81
McDonnell Douglas "big screen" fighter cockpit, **29**, 1
   DC-10/MD-11, 64, **64**
   F-15 Eagle, 101
   F-4 Phantom, 28, 100, **100**, 119
McKnight, Willie, 87
Mercury missions, 127
Messerschmitt Me 109, 83, **83**, 86, 87
   Me 163, 92
   Me 262, 92
Microlights, 66
Midway, Battle of, 93
Mikoyan Gurevich MiG-15, 24
   MiG-15, 97, 118
   MiG-17, 100
   MiG-19, 100
   MiG-19, 24
   MiG-21, 99, **100**
   MiG-23, 10

MiG-25, 96
MiG-29, 12
Mil Mi-26 helicopter, 23
Millennium, Operation, 88
Mir, 138, **138**
Missiles, Air-to-air, 98
Mitsubishi A5M2, 85
   A6M2 Zero, 92
   G4M, 93
Molders, Werner, 114, 6
Montgolfier balloon, **10**
Montgolfier, Etienne and Joseph, 10
Moon landing, 131, **131**
Morane-Saulnier M, 70

N
Nagasaki, Atomic bombing of, 94
Nakajima B5N, 85, 93
   G5N1Shinzan, 56
NASA, 126–,
Nesterov, Piotr Nikolaevich, 70
New York-Paris competition, 51
Nichols, Ruth, 51
Nieuport 11, 72
   27, 79
Nishizawa, Sub-Officer Hiroyoshi, 116, **117**
North American B-25 Mitchell, 90
   F-86 Saber, 24, **24**, 97, **98**
   F-100 Super Saber, **117**, 118
   P-51 Mustang, 90, **91**
   X-15A, 119
   XP-86 Saber, **117**
Northrop B-2A Spirit, 26, **104**
   F-117, 121, 6
Northrop, John K., 25
Nuclear weapons, introduction, 94-95
Nungesser, Charles, 51, 78, 110

O
Ovington, Earle, 33

P
Pacific war (WWII), 93–
Pan American Airways (Pan Am), 47–
Panavia Tornado, 25, **103**, 104, 120
Parmalee, Philip, 34
Passengers carried (table), 67
Pathfinders, 88
Pearl Harbor, 93
Pfalz D.III, 79, **79**
Philippine Sea, Battle of, 94
Pilcher, Percy, 12, 31, 107
Pilot controls, 18
Piquet, Henri, 33
Polar flights, 45
Polikarpov I-16, **82**, 83
Post, Wiley, 51 53, **53**
Powers, Francis Gary, 118
Pratt & Whitney PW4000 engine, **23**
Pressurization, 18
Prevost, Maurice, 34
Propellers, Variable-pitch, 17

Q
QANTAS, 57
Q-system air traffic information system, 43
Quenault, Louis, 71
Quintin Brand, Christopher, 112

R
Radars, 28
Reconnaissance flights, 118
Records, Flight, see chapter The Aviators
Reno Gold Races, 120
Republic F-105 Thunderchief, 99, **99**
   P-47 Thunderbolt, 90
Richthofen, Manfred von, 80, **81**, 111, **111**
Rickenbacker, Edward, 111, **111**
Robertson Aircraft Corporation, 42
Rockwell B-70 Valkyrie, 26
Rodgers, Calbraith, 34
Roe, Alliott Verdon (A.V.), 32
Rolls Royce Merlin engine, **18**
Round-the-world flight, First, 31, 112
Royal Aircraft Factory BE. 2, 70, **70**
   F.E. 2, 77, **77**

SE5a, **14**, 77, **78**, **79**, 80
Rozier, Pilatre de, 10, 11
Ryneveldt, Pierre van, **38**, 39, 112

S
Saab 340/2000, 65
Salyut missions, 137–
Santos-Dumont, Alberto, 13, 13, 31, 32, 32, 107
Saratoga, USS, 15
Saturn V, 130–
Saturn, **123**
Scheduled services, First, 34
Schirra, Walter, 126
Schneider Trophy, 34, 109
Seaplanes, 15
Second World War pilots, 114–
Selfridge, Lt. Thomas E., **108**, 109
SEPECAT Jaguar, 120
Serrate, 89
Shenandoah airship, 54
Shepard, Alan, **126**
Short S.8 Calcutta, **48**
  Stirling, 88
Sikorsky, Igor, **20**, 21, 34
Sikorsky S-42, **49**
  S-56 helicopter, **21**, 23, 1
  VS-300/R-4 helicopter, **20**, 1
Skylab, **132**, 133
Slats, 20
Slayton, Donald, **126**
Smith, Keith, 38, 112
Smith, Ross, 38, 39, 112
Sopwith Camel, 77, 80, **80**
  Tabloid, **70**
Sopwith, T.O.M., **108**, **109**
Soyuz, 133–
Space Shuttle, 134–
Space Station, International, 136
Spacelab, 136–
SPAD XIII, 78
Spanish Civil War, 83
Speed of sound, 22, 1
Spirit of St. Louis, 51, **51**
Sputnik 1, **124**, 125
Sputnik 2, 125
Stalling, 19
Stealth aircraft, 105
Stout Metal Airline Co., 50
Stressed-skin construction, 15, **16**

Sud-Est SE.210 Caravelle, 61
Sukhoi Su-24, 25
  Su-27, **120**, 6
  Su-29, **120**
  Su-31, **120**
  Su-35, **120**
  Su-37, 105
  Su-37, **120**
Supermarine Spitfire, **17**, 86, 91
Swept wings, 24-25
SYring, Professor, 30

T
Taranto, Swordfish attack on, 93
Taylor, Charlie, 13
Test pilots, see chapter The Aviators
Thomas, George Holt, 35
Thornton, Kathryn, **122**
Tizard, Sir Henry, 112
Trans-Atlantic flights (first), 34, 37
Transcontinental and Western Air (TWA), 48
Transworld Airlines (TWA), **16**
Trubshaw, Brian, 120, **120**
Tsiolkovsky, Konstantin Eduardovich, 123
Tuck, Sqn Ldr R.R. Stanford, 114, **114**
Tupolev ANT-20, 56
  Tu-4, 96
  Tu-104, 61, **61**
  Tu-144, 63, **63**
  Tu-204, 61
Turbojet engines, 22
Turboprop engines, 23,
Turboshaft engines, 23
Turcat, Andre, 120
Twiss, Peter, **118**, 119

U
Udet, Ernst, 78, 81
Ulm, Charles, 52, **52**
US Army Air Corps, 16
Uwins, Cyril, 113, 6

V
V-2 rocket, 124, 125, **125**
Variable sweep wings, 25
Vaulx, Count Henri de La, 30
Vertical takeoff, 27,
Vickers machine gun, **18**
Vickers R.100, 54, **54**
  R.101, 54

VC-10, 61
Viking, 58
Vimy bomber, 37
Vimy Commercial, 36
Vimy, 111, 112, **112**
Viscount, 58, **59**
Wellington bomber, **18**
Wellington, 87
Vietnam War, 98, 119
Virgin Atlantic, **67**
Voisin, 71, 71
Voisin, Charles, 32
Voskhod missions, 127
Vostok missions, 127
Vought A-7 Corsair, 100
  F4U Corsair, 94, **94**
Vindicator, 8
Voyager round the world flight, 121, **121**

W
Welch, George, 117, **117**
White, Edward, 128, **129**
Whittle, Frank, 22, **22**
Wilkins, Hubert, 45
Wilson, Capt H.J., **116**
Wing loadings, 15
Wright brothers, 9, 13, **13**, 31, 32, 32, 69, 107, **107**
Wright, Orville, 9

Y
Yeager, Capt Charles (Chuck), 117, **118**
Young, John, **128**, **132**, **135**

Z
Zeppelin airships
  LZ. 1, **12**
  LZ.7 *Deutschland*, 33
  LZ.13 *Hansa*, 33
  LZ.21, 74
  LZ.31, 75
  LZ.32, 75
  LZ.33, 75
  LZ.37, 75
  LZ.38, 75
  LZ.39, 75
  LZ.127 *Graf Zeppelin*, 54, **54**
  LZ.129 *Hindenburg*, 54, **55**
Zeppelin, Count Ferdinand von, 11, 30, **31**

Picture Credits

Jacket: front, TWA via Philip Jarrett; back, Aviation Photographs International (API). Page 1, via API; 3, via API; 4-5, US Information Agency via MEL; 6-7, via Mike Spick; 8, US National Archives via MEL; 9, via API; 10-11, left The Science Museum via TRH Pictures (TRH), top right via TRH, bottom right via Bruce Robertson; 12, via Bruce Robertson; top via MEL, bottom US National Archives via MEL; 14, via Bruce Robertson; 15, top via Bruce Robertson, bottom US Navy via MEL; 16, top via Philip Jarrett, bottom via Bruce Robertson; 17, top Philip Jarrett, bottom via Bruce Robertson; 18-19, left Philip Jarrett, centre RAF Museum via MEL, top via Bruce Robertson, right via TRH; 20, top via Philip Jarrett, bottom via TRH; 21, top via MEL, bottom via Philip Jarrett; 22, via Philip Jarrett; 23, via API; 24-25, background pic Boeing via TRH, others via MEL; 26, via MEL; 27, top via API, bottom via Mike Spick; 28, via MEL; 29, top via Mike Spick, bottom Airbus Industrie via TRH; 30, via TRH; 31, top via MEL, bottom via Bruce Robertson; 32, top via Philip Jarrett, bottom via TRH; 33, top via TRH, bottom via Philip Jarrett; 34-35, via Philip Jarrett; 36-37, top, center and left via Philip Jarrett, right US Navy via TRH; 38-39, background pic via Bruce Robertson, left and right via Philip Jarrett; 40-41, left and right via Philip Jarrett, bottom via MEL; 42-43, via Philip Jarrett; 44, via Philip Jarrett; 45, top vua MEL, bottom via Philip Jarrett; 46, top via TRH, bottom via Philip Jarrett; 47, Crown Copyright via TRH; 48-49, top and bottom via TRH, other via Philip Jarrett; 50, top via Philip Jarrett via TRH; 51, top via Bruce Robertson, bottom via MEL; 52, top via Philip Jarrett, bottom Pratt & Whitney via TRH; 53, via Philip Jarrett; 54-55, top via Philip Jarrett, bottom left via MEL, center US Navy via TRH, bottom right via Philip Jarrett; 56, top Arthur Gibson via TRH, bottom via Philip Jarrett; 57, top via Philip Jarrett, bottom British Airways via TRH; 58, top via Philip Jarrett, bottom Lockheed via TRH; 59, top via TRH, bottom via Philip Jarrett; 60, top via TRH, bottom via Philip Jarrett; 61, via Philip Jarrett; 62-63, top left via TRH, center Arthur Gibson via TRH, top right via Philip Jarrett, bottom Aerospatiale via API; 66-67, top and left via Philip Jarrett, top right Rolls Royce via TRH, bottom right Bae via TRH; 66, via API; 67, top E. Partridge via TRH, others via API; 68-69, left, US National Archives via TRH, center Crown Copyright via TRH, right via TRH; 70-71, top left via MEL, others via Bruce Robertson; 72-73, left via TRH, others via MEL; 74-75, top left via TRH, bottom via MEL, others via Bruce Robertson; 76-77, top left via Philip Jarrett, others via Bruce Robertson; 78-79, right David McLellan via Popperfoto, others via Bruce Robertson; 80-81, left and bottom via Bruce Robertson, right via MEL; 82, via Bruce Robertson; 83, via Philip Jarrett; 84-85, bottom left US Navy via TRH, others via MEL; 86-87, top right via Philip Jarrett, others via MEL; 88-89, bottom left via TRH, others via MEL; 90-91, top and right via MEL, bottom via TRH; 92-93, via MEL; 94-95, top left and far right via MEL; top center via Bruce Robertson, bottom US Navy via TRH; 96-97, left US National Archives via TRH, center via MEL, right via Bruce Robertson; 98-99, left and center via MEL, right via Bruce Robertson; 100-101, via MEL; 102-103, via MEL; 104, via API; 105, via Mike Spick; 106, top Popperfoto, bottom via Bruce Robertson; 107, top via Bruce Robertson, bottom Popperfoto; 108, top US Army via TRH, bottom via Bruce Robertson; 109, Popperfoto; 110-111, via Bruce Robertson; 112, via Bruce Robertson; 113, top Popperfoto, bottom via MEL; 114, top via Bruce Robertson, bottom Popperfoto; 115, top ands right via Bruce Robertson, bottom via TRH; 118-119, top left US National Archives via TRH, others via Bruce Robertson; 118-119, top left via MEL, bottom left Popperfoto, bottom right via TRH, background pic via Bruce Robertson; 120, top left Popperfoto, top right via Bruce Robertson, bottom API; 121, top via TRH, bottom via Bruce Robertson; 122-141, via Spacecharts.